W9-ARH-357

Dear Reader:

The book you are about to read is the latest bestseller from the St. Martin's True Crime Library, the imprint *The New York Times* calls "the leader in true crime!" Each month, we offer you a fascinating account of the latest, most sensational crime that has captured the national attention: St. Martin's is the publisher of bestselling true crime author and crime journalist Kieran Crowley, who explores the dark, deadly links between a prominent Manhattan surgeon and the disappearance of his wife fifteen years earlier in THE SURGEON'S WIFE. Suzy Spencer's BREAKING POINT guides readers through the tortuous twists and turns in the case of Andrea Yates, the Houston mother who drowned her five young children in the family's bathtub. In Edgar Award-nominated DARK DREAMS, legendary FBI profiler Roy Hazelwood and bestselling crime author Stephen G. Michaud shine light on the inner workings of America's most violent and depraved murderers. In the book you now hold, DEADLY MISTRESS, veteran true crime author Michael Fleeman follows the story of a husband and mistress who allegedly planned to kill his wife. When both husband and wife ended up dead, the mistress was accused of their murders.

St. Martin's True Crime Library gives you the stories behind the headlines. Our authors take you right to the scene of the crime and into the minds of the most notorious murderers to show you what really makes them tick. St. Martin's True Crime Library paperbacks are better than the most terrifying thriller, because it's all true! The next time you want a crackling good read, make sure it's got the St. Martin's True Crime Library logo on the spine—you'll be up all night!

Charles E. Spicer, Jr.
Executive Editor, St. Martin's True Crime Library

St. Martin's True Crime Library Titles
by Michael Fleeman

Laci

"If I Die…"

The Stranger in My Bed

Over the Edge

Deadly Mistress

A True Story of Marriage, Betrayal, and Murder

MICHAEL FLEEMAN

St. Martin's Paperbacks

DEADLY MISTRESS

Copyright © 2005 by Michael Fleeman.

Cover photographs of Kenneth Stahl, Carolyn Oppy-Stahl and crime scene courtesy Orange County DA. Photograph of Adriana Vasco copyright © 2003 Los Angeles Times. Reprinted with permission.

ISBN: 0-312-93740-7
EAN: 9780312-93740-9

Printed in the United States of America

St. Martin's Paperbacks edition / December 2005

St. Martin's Paperbacks are published by St. Martin's Press, 175 Fifth Avenue, New York, NY 10010.

10 9 8 7 6 5 4 3 2 1

Deadly Mistress

Prologue

The Weasel fortified himself by smoking an 8-ball of crack cocaine and consuming a case of beer. He found a big knife and walked into the Holiday Food Store in Suffolk, Virginia, a few minutes after 2 o'clock in the morning. The store's lone employee was about to drop money into the safe. The Weasel jumped up on the counter and demanded the cash. The employee bolted for the parking lot.

The Weasel grabbed the cash and fled the convenience store for a black Ford Blazer out front. The woman at the wheel drove off on Route 460 northwest toward Windsor. The employee called the police.

Hearing the report on the radio, a lawman identified in reports as Officer Everett responded from his position at a nearby Wal-Mart. Ten minutes later, Everett radioed dispatch; he had spotted a vehicle matching the description of the getaway car.

He pulled over the Blazer onto a driveway on a section of Route 460 called Windsor Road, across the county line about ten miles from the store. Officer Everett ordered the passenger out of the vehicle. The man complied.

Everett wasn't surprised at who he saw. Robbing a convenience store in the middle of the night was just the sort of thing the Weasel would do.

The Weasel was handcuffed and placed in the back seat of Officer Everett's police car.

The getaway driver, Lisa Stone Snell, was ordered to get out of the vehicle and was handcuffed.

Deputies had arrived from all over the area and this warm Southern night, August 13, 1999, was lit by headlamps and emergency lights and punctuated by the staccato of police radios. Officers questioned Snell and rummaged through the Blazer, finding a butcher knife in the back seat, a box cutter on the dashboard and a big knife in the holder between the front seats.

Among those who responded was a lieutenant, who was in charge of supervising the deputies. As he spoke to them, an unsettling thought struck him.

"Who is with the prisoner?" he asked.

Nobody seemed to know. The lieutenant went to Everett's cruiser and shined his flashlight into the back seat.

It was empty.

The lieutenant walked around to the other side of the car and found the rear driver's-side door open.

The red-faced officers fanned out, searching a house and a culvert.

Before daybreak, the convenience store employee would identify the Blazer as the vehicle used as the getaway car, and the big knife found between the seats as the weapon wielded by the robber. Snell was transported to police headquarters, where she was searched; "the stolen currency," wrote the lieutenant in his report, "was located on her person."

The Weasel was nowhere to be found.

Chapter One

The silver car idled on the side of Ortega Highway next to a telephone pole and an emergency call box. The high beams cut into the black nothingness that is Saturday night in the last wild region of Orange County. Nobody much drove this straight section of the one-lane highway this late on a weekend in the cool of fall. There were no street lamps, no house lights, nothing on either side of the car but dead brush, dirt, straggly bushes, barbed wire, broken bottles, rusty cans and darkness. Somewhere off to the east loomed the Santa Ana Mountains, and over them Lake Elsinore. Behind the car, eight miles to the west, was San Juan Capistrano.

At about 10 p.m., Tony Castillo drove his security patrol cruiser east on Ortega Highway. Working a routine patrol shift, Castillo was headed for the Ortega Rock cement plant to check the entrance gate. At Mile Marker 9 his headlights illuminated the rear of the silver car. The passenger-side door was open and somebody's foot stuck outside.

Castillo gave it only a passing thought. Out here, where the Ortega Highway winds through sandstone canyons, rugged ravines and strands of native coastal live oak and California sycamores, it's not unusual to see the occasional car parked to the side at night: drivers sleeping off a drunk, kids making out. Castillo drove on to the cement plant, glancing at the car to his right as he passed. He couldn't see anything inside.

He got to the entrance gate and "secured the lock and chain," he later wrote in a report. Castillo worked for Rancho Mission Viejo—his title was ranch deputy—patrolling the holdings of the landowner with 23,000 acres, some of it left alone to nature, some of it bulldozed into stucco housing developments. At this late hour, Ranch Deputy Castillo was the closest thing to law enforcement the Ortega Highway would see; an hour or two could pass before a CHP unit or Orange County Sheriff's Deputy car passed by.

The loneliness draws the lawless. It's here that "Freeway Killer" William Bonin deposited three of his estimated twenty-one victims; where serial killer Randy Kraft allegedly dumped the first of at least forty-five bodies; where many other victims of less notorious crimes found their final resting places in shallow graves.

After inspecting the cement plant gate, Castillo turned around and drove west on Ortega Highway, approaching the silver car, now to his left. Its high beams hit him in the face. As he moved away from the glare, he could see that the passenger door was still open and that a foot was still sticking out. He saw no movement inside.

Now more wary, Castillo headed for his next security check: a small collection of homes for about twenty ranch hands on a small side road north of the highway. Castillo was already behind schedule on his security rounds for his 5 p.m.–to–1 a.m. shift.

But he couldn't shake the sight of that parked car. He decided against going to the ranch worker homes, pulled his patrol car into the entrance of Caspers Campground, made a U-turn, and drove back. He pulled over to the shoulder about fifteen yards behind the car.

Up close, he could see that the car was a four-door Dodge Stratus, license plate 4AIV-340.

Castillo got out of his patrol car and walked up to the driver's side. The engine was running, the gear in PARK. Broken glass littered the pavement beneath the door.

Castillo peered in through the open window.

He only looked briefly, and it was dark inside, but he could make out the figures of two people, a man, who was slumped over in the driver's seat, and a woman next to him, lying on her left side, her head near the man's legs. Neither moved nor made any noises. They didn't appear to be breathing.

He rushed back to his security patrol car and tried to contact the Orange County Sheriff's emergency communications center on his radio. It took a few attempts—radio and cell phone reception was spotty out here. A dispatcher finally answered. Castillo told her where he was and what he had found. The dispatcher said fire department paramedics and sheriff's deputies were on their way from San Juan Capistrano, nine miles away.

Castillo waited, doing nothing. He knew not to disturb a potential crime scene. In addition to working as a security guard, he was a reserve police officer for the city of Costa Mesa. He had been trained in basic police procedures. He also had enough common sense to worry about his own safety. Except for the lights from his patrol car and the silver car, it was total darkness. He had no idea what had happened to those two people—and no idea who could be lurking in the bushes only a few feet away.

The paramedics arrived in less than fifteen minutes. A

fireman got out of his truck and asked Castillo to escort him to the parked car. The fireman reached through the open driver's-side window and checked the pulse of the slumped-over man.

"He's gone," the fireman said.

From over the fireman's shoulder, Castillo got his first good look at what was inside. The man was still strapped in his seatbelt. He had a gaping wound in the back of his head behind his left ear, leaving a trickle of blood, and a major wound to his right eye.

On the outside of the driver's-side door about eighteen inches to the left of the handle, there appeared to be a bullet hole.

The firefighter went around to the other side of the car and checked the woman's pulse: also gone. She was covered in blood. Her body appeared to be riddled with bullets. Outside the car on the passenger side were blood drops. Near the back tire, a lady's shoe sat on the pavement.

About this time, an Orange County sheriff's deputy arrived. He walked up to the parked car, reached in and turned off the ignition, but didn't touch anything else, also wanting to protect the crime scene.

By midnight, the CHP had blocked off Ortega Highway in both directions, and the area buzzed with the business of a homicide investigation, as detectives, crime-scene technicians, coroner's investigators, CHP officers and sheriff's deputies descended.

The first to make a close inspection of the car was Laurie Crutchfield, a forensic scientist from the Orange County Crime Lab in Santa Ana. She arrived at Ortega Highway at 11:30 p.m. for what would be an all-nighter. After she was briefed about the circumstances of the bodies' discovery, Crutchfield looked inside the Stratus.

The bodies still sat in the front seat of the car, the man

slumped to his right, the woman spread out and twisted onto her left side, her head resting near the steering wheel, her legs sticking out the passenger door. Both appeared to be middle-aged, the man tall, with graying brown hair and a lean, muscular build; the woman with shoulder-length brown hair, and heavy, perhaps 200 pounds or more.

They seemed to be dressed for a casual weekend night out. The woman had on blue eye shadow, lipstick and fake nails painted red. She wore a gold-and-diamond earring in the right ear—the left ear was missing its earring—a gold necklace with a diamond pendant, a gold-and-diamond bracelet and a gold watch studded with diamonds. She had on a colorful silk shirt-jacket combination, black pants and tan pantyhose. Her right foot was shoeless and pressed against the pavement, the left foot had on a red and black pump and dangled from the bottom of the door jamb.

The woman had been shot in the head, arms and torso—at least five wounds that Crutchfield could make out—with blood spattering on the windshield and a bone fragment landing on the passenger-side dashboard.

Outside the car, Crutchfield found a blood smear across the rear passenger door and a small trail of blood drops on the ground below. At the back of the car, near the rear passenger tire, sat the other red pump on the asphalt. It looked like the woman—while bleeding—had gotten out of the car and gone as far as the back tire, losing her shoe and leaving a trail of blood.

On the front seat of the driver's side was the man in his seatbelt. He wore dark blue slacks, a black polo shirt with a long-sleeved green striped shirt over it, a black fleece jacket and black dress shoes.

He had gunshot wounds to his head, including one that appeared to have gone through the back of his head and exited his right eye. A broken pair of wire-rimmed eyeglasses hung from his head. There were also bullet wounds to his right arm and upper chest. There was blood on the dash and on the gearshift.

Outside the driver's-side door was a small amount of shattered glass. Much more broken glass rattled around inside the door, suggesting the window had been rolled down when a bullet struck the door, shattering most of the glass inside. It appeared the shot had come from the passenger side.

From the car, Crutchfield recovered three bullets, one from the front passenger seat, one in the rear driver's-side door and one that had fallen out of the woman's jacket when Crutchfield removed it. She couldn't find the bullet that had struck the driver's door and shattered the glass, but did find an impact mark in the pavement from where the bullet had hit the ground and ricocheted away.

At about 2:30 a.m., shortly after Crime-Scene Technician Laurie Crutchfield started processing the scene, another forensic scientist, Deputy Coroner Elizabeth Kinney, arrived. Kinney was in charge of inspecting the bodies. After getting briefed, she looked at the man first, to try to determine how long he had been dead. Death-time estimation is an inexact science and the best that coroners can do is narrow a time down to a window. In this case, Kinney looked first for signs of lividity—the pooling of blood in lower parts of the body after the heart stops. It takes about twelve hours for lividity to completely set in, longer if the body has been moved.

It appeared the man had been shot while still buckled into his seatbelt and therefore hadn't been moved. Kinney estimated he had been dead for four to six hours, meaning he was killed sometime between 8:30 p.m. and when the bodies were found shortly after 10 p.m.

She also examined the body for rigor mortis, the stiffening of the joints from lactic acid in the muscles. Rigor mortis starts in the smaller muscle groups of the fingers and jaw and works its way toward the larger muscles of the legs and arms. The more active a person is before death, the more lactic acid is generated and the greater the extent of the rigor mortis.

Again, since the man appeared to have been inactive when killed—rigor mortis was not as advanced. Kinney found stiffening in his fingers, wrists and jaw. These findings also were consistent with the man being dead for four to six hours.

After more than an hour spent on the man, Kinney turned to the body of the woman. By now it was 3:45 Sunday morning. Unlike the man, the woman was not in a seatbelt, but flailed across the seat with her feet out the door. From the blood smear on the door outside and the blood drops on the ground, it appeared she had been moving around after she had been shot. "She looked like she put up a little bit of struggle," Kinney later recalled. "It looked like she was outside of the car and kind of diving into the car."

This apparent activity seemed to account for the more advanced stage of rigor mortis, with stiffening found in her knees as well as the fingers, hands and jaw. Lividity was the same as with the man. Kinney concluded, then, that despite the differences in rigor mortis, the woman had died during the same time frame as the man.

It appeared that the woman had been shot, probably in the torso and arms, then somehow gotten out of the car and dove back in, before she was finished off with the wound to the head, which would have been instantly fatal. At some point during this, the man was shot in the body and head, never even getting out of his seat.

Deputies kept the highway closed until the following Sunday afternoon, searching the surrounding brush- and rock-covered fields past the barbed wire for more evidence. All they found were some faint footprints and old beer bottles that seemed to have nothing to do with the shootings. There were no other shoeprints, no tire marks, no fibers, and, later analysis would find, no fingerprints of any use—only those later identified as belonging to the victims and to the sheriff's deputy who turned off the ignition. There was no gun found in the car, ruling out a murder–suicide. This was clearly murder. But why? It didn't seem to be a robbery. Money and credit cards weren't taken; the car wasn't stolen; the woman was still wearing her diamond jewelry.

The best clue was actually a non-clue. Deputies found no bullet shell casings. That strongly suggested the murder weapon was a revolver, which doesn't eject casings but keeps them in the cylinder after firing.

The driver's license in the man's wallet showed that he was Kenneth Stahl, age 57, of Huntington Beach, just twenty miles to the north. The license in the woman's black purse identified her as Carolyn Oppy-Stahl, at the same address in Huntington Beach. Next of kin were notified. They said the Stahls were a married couple; he was a physician and anesthesiologist, and she was an optometrist.

The pair were found on Saturday, November 20, 1999—one day after the dead woman's 44th birthday.

Chapter Two

At 9 a.m. the day after the bodies were found, while investigators were still processing the crime scene, the Orange County Sheriff's Department issued a press release announcing a "Double Homicide on the Ortega Highway." It gave the basic details—that between 9 and 10 p.m. on Saturday night, an unknown suspect or suspects had murdered Dr. Kenneth Stahl and his wife, Carolyn Oppy-Stahl, in their vehicle.

"Dr. Stahl pulled over on the Ortega Highway about nine miles east of the I-5 freeway, when an unknown suspect(s) shot both occupants in their vehicle," it read. The release added that, "The Sheriff's Department is requesting any and all information relating to this homicide. Anyone driving in the area around this time is encouraged to call homicide investigators . . . any time of the day or night," and it gave daytime and off-hours phone numbers.

Local Los Angeles television news quickly picked up on the double murders of the physician–optometrist couple, emphasizing the mysterious elements of the crime: how there was no obvious motive.

As *The Orange County Register* noted in its brief story on Monday, November 22, nobody could understand why the respected pair would be killed. "Robbery doesn't appear to be the motive," sheriff's spokesman Jim Amormino was quoted as saying. He didn't elaborate—there was no mention of the diamond and gold jewelry still on Carolyn, or the cash and credit cards in their wallets. "It's very weird," said the Stahls' former landlord, Brenda Huss, who'd rented them a condo in a gated complex before they bought their own unit. "They were nice people. Obviously successful. She was very outgoing and ebullient. . . . He had an interesting sense of humor."

The next day, the *Register* ran a longer story, this one by police reporter Bill Rams. It was the first of numerous stories by Rams, who would be pulled deeper and deeper into the bizarre story. Rams tracked down family and friends of what he called the "well-respected, well-liked doctors" who were "beloved" by those who knew them. "We are absolutely stymied," he quoted Kenneth Stahl's mother, Bobbie C. Stahl-Polley, as saying. "Nobody can figure it out."

Rams listed the key biographical details. The couple were hard-working professionals, routinely putting in six-day weeks, he at a Huntington Beach hospital, she at an eye clinic. They had been married for fourteen years and had no children together, though Ken had a grown son from a previous marriage. Ken also had a history of serious health problems, having even undergone a quintuple bypass about four months before his murder. "Had he passed away with a heart attack, I could've accepted that," his mother told the *Register*. "But the violence of this. These were two innocent people."

• • •

The newspaper article only told some of the story.

Born on February 15, 1942, Ken had grown up in Pomona, in eastern Los Angeles County, the son of a prominent surgeon named William Stahl, who in addition to his osteopathic practice also owned a small hospital. Ken's mother, Bobbie, was a nurse. Family life revolved around home, community, church and medicine. They attended First Baptist Church of Pomona, where the minister, interviewed years later by Rams, remembered Ken as an intelligent, intense "straight arrow."

But it was Ken's natural athletic talents that paid his way with a football scholarship through the University of La Verne, near Pomona, where he received a bachelor of science degree. From there, it was medical school in the Midwest, at Kansas City College of Osteopathic Medicine, where Ken chose the same medical field as his father, only going on to specialize in anesthesiology. He practiced in Oklahoma for about five years in the late 1960s and early '70s before returning to Southern California, settling in the Orange County suburb of Huntington Beach. He worked as a freelance contract anesthesiologist and, for a couple of years, ran his own pain clinic. He also worked in a Fountain Valley trauma center and at a clinic in Huntington Beach. Although professionally successful, his personal life had had its share of problems, with two marriages ending in divorce. His first marriage had produced a son, Kent, who after the divorce moved to Texas and rarely saw his father.

Ken also obsessed about his health. His father had long suffered from health problems, particularly heart ailments, and died in 1980. Ken feared he would have a similar fate. He exercised, at times to the extreme, working out in the gym regularly, taking twenty-five-mile hikes, skiing cross-country, riding his bike all over Orange

County. "He really cared about his body," said his sister, Tamara Stahl Parham. "He worked out a lot at the gym. He was very cautious about what he ate. His body was very, very important to him, and his health was important to him."

In the end, it was futile. Ken's heart was as bad as his father's. At age 35, he had a coronary bypass operation, but it wasn't enough; two years later, at just 37, he suffered a heart attack. He recovered and resumed his physical fitness regime, but he was always an inch away from another heart attack. In July 1999, just four months before his murder, he underwent a quintuple bypass.

It was around the time of his heart attack that he first met Carolyn at the Rio Hondo Hospital where they both worked. Less is known about Carolyn's life before Ken—her family has been more reserved and the public record is not as extensive. But it is known that she was born on November 19, 1955, grew up in Michigan and obtained a degree in optometry. She was always close to her mother, Ophia Sokolowsi, and her sister, Linda Dubay, who would become a general surgeon.

Before meeting Ken, Carolyn had been married and divorced, according to press accounts, but the details of her first marriage are unknown. Although Ken and Carolyn had known each other since 1980, she didn't begin a relationship with him until years later—in 1986—when, at age 31, she moved in with him for a year. "Carolyn liked the fact that Ken liked sports activities," her sister Linda told the *Register*. "She obviously took a really strong liking. She stopped seeing two other guys."

They married just after midnight on New Year's Day 1988 in Las Vegas, and settled into the upper-crust life of a medical couple, filled with hospital parties and adventurous vacations, including Colorado rafting trips and backpacking treks in Montana where Ken had a cabin.

Carolyn grew close to Ken's relatives, calling them her "California family." Ken's mother adored her, which was extremely important to Ken, because he had a close relationship with his mother.

Carolyn often visited Ken's cousin, Chuck Downing, and his family. "Nearly every evening after Carolyn's long day at work, we would hear a soft tap-tap-tap at the patio door," said Jocelyn Downing, Chuck's wife. "We knew it was Carolyn, because my son's face would light the room up when he saw her beautiful smile. He knew he was in for a great time because Carolyn would always play with him for at least an hour before going home."

Her co-workers spoke of her in equally glowing terms. "She was like an angel, so nice that it was almost sickening," said Dr. Marc Mintz, a longtime friend of Ken's, according to a *Register* article. "She was just so sweet, everything from her voice to her demeanor to her actions."

The murders of Ken and Carolyn had their families reeling. Ken's mother would describe the "pain that pierced my chest" the morning she was notified of his brutal killing. "I could never imagine that I would have to plan my own son's memorial service, that I would have to write his obituary, or that I would have to explain to my great-grandchildren how their uncle faced such a tragic death at the hands of another," she said. "I never imagined that my son would not be around to take care of me. He was always available to me and always came to visit just to be sure that I was all right. He was my only son."

Carolyn's mother, Ophia, who used to speak to her daughter from Michigan at least twice a week, cried for two weeks and suffered such severe insomnia that she was taking sleeping pills for three months. "I could not talk to my friends and did not want to see anyone," Ophia said. Her sister, Linda Dubay, said that at the time of her death, Carolyn was looking forward to visiting family in Michigan and seeing her nieces and newborn nephew over the holidays. "We, as a family, are fearful that unless some eyewitness can help with the case, the murders may go unsolved," said Dubay, "leaving no closure for both families."

The shock and the loss were heightened by the sense-lessness of it all. The couple had been slaughtered for no apparent reason: nothing appeared to have been stolen, there was no sign of carjacking, not even a struggle. They had no enemies anybody knew of, not even a single malpractice lawsuit or complaint to medical authorities between them. No one could even figure out why they were out on that remote road in the middle of the night. Ortega Highway didn't lead anywhere the couple were known to go. Rather, it led directly away from their home in Huntington Beach—and yet they had no luggage, no travel plans that anybody knew of. They were both supposed to have been back at work the following Monday.

On Saturday, December 4, 1999, these questions only increased the grief at the double funeral service at St. Andrew's Presbyterian Church in Huntington Beach. "Our Kenneth and our Carolyn were cruelly wronged," the Reverend Edward B. Cole told mourners, according to a *Los Angeles Times* account. "It happened because of a very evil world." He said that good people shouldn't die "by a pistol, on the side of the road, with the motor running and the headlights on." One by one, mourners spoke of the goodness of the couple. "Things like this, they don't make sense," said longtime Stahl family friend Keith Korestjens. "The destruction of two lives . . . that were devoted only to helping people, it just seems so wrong." A former neighbor of the couple said the memorial service was difficult enough to bear, but, added Denise Lowery, "then you add the uncertainty, the not knowing who is responsible for this, and it becomes unbearable."

Chapter Three

To solve the Stahl murders, the Orange County Sheriff's Department turned to veteran homicide detectives Joe Homs and James McDonald. Both drove out to the crime scene in the middle of the night to gather what little information was there. They took a statement from security guard Tony Castillo. They reviewed the forensic work of Laurie Crutchfield and Elizabeth Kinney and others at the scene.

But what they were left with, in that first critical twenty-four hours after a crime—when many cases are made or broken—was virtually nothing. There were no eyewitnesses or physical evidence. Not a single shoeprint, tire impression or fingerprint would be recovered. All they knew was that the couple had probably been killed by bullets from one or more revolvers.

The first avenue of investigation would come at the sheriff's crime laboratories in Santa Ana. As is often the case in homicide, the most important evidence was the bodies themselves. The hope was that the autopsies, conducted by Dr. David Katsuyama the day after the shootings, would offer even slim leads for the detectives.

On the autopsy table, before Katsuyama lay a 6-foot-tall, 192-pound Caucasian male with gray-brown hair who had been 57 years old at death. The body was bloody and marked by bullet wounds to his chest and head. One bullet had struck his left arm above the elbow, punctured his tricep and traveled into his left upper chest, gone straight through his body and exited through his back, leaving a slit-like tear. Another bullet had hit him in the chest just below the left collarbone and broken apart inside the body, with a small fragment landing near the vertebra in the neck area and the other near the right shoulder bone.

That broken-apart bullet had caused the most internal damage, tearing into both lungs and the aorta, the large vessel that takes blood from the heart to the lower portions of the body. "This [vessel] was torn up at about midchest level," Katsuyama later explained. "And this tear in itself would result in a relatively rapid loss of blood into the chest and would result with him sort of running out of blood to pump to the rest of the body to maintain his life."

Death was fast but not instantaneous. "Basically he would bleed out to the point where there would be very little blood in circulation. That could occur in a matter of, say, fifteen, thirty seconds, maybe a minute," the coroner said. Eerily, while Ken was dying from blood loss, his heart likely continued to beat for several minutes longer until it ran out of oxygen.

The more grisly wound, the one to the eye that the first people on the scene had observed, had been caused by a bullet hitting Ken in the back of the head and exiting through his left eye socket, shattering the eye. Oddly, as awful as the wound was, it probably wouldn't have been fatal had the bleeding been stopped. "It did not significantly fracture the skull around the brain," Katsuyama said, "and it did not show any obvious damage to the brain itself, although that kind of an impact could have easily stunned him, rendered him unconscious."

Cause of death was easily determined. In medical terms it was exsanguination: bleeding to death, caused by tears in the lungs and that major blood vessel, the aorta. All three wounds appeared to have come in a short period of time.

The same cause of death was determined for Carolyn, who at the time of autopsy was 5-foot-8 and 220 pounds— 75 pounds over what was listed on her driver's license. But her wounds were more extensive—and death didn't come as quickly.

Carolyn had been shot so many times it was difficult to tell what were entry wounds and what were exit wounds. One bullet entered near her left breast, another just below that. There were four wounds on the right side of her body near the back, some apparently entry wounds, some exit. The coroner found inside her body two "relatively intact" bullets near her back. "Those bullets had torn into portions of her lung, to her liver and spleen and bowel, causing tears in those," Katsuyama said.

As ravaged as her organs were by the shots to the torso, she still could have moved around. "The backbone was not struck by any of the bullets," said Katsuyama. "The tears in her organs of her chest and abdomen are not such that they would immediately cause her to collapse. They are essentially irreparable surgically, but as far as her collapsing immediately after sustaining those wounds, not necessarily." Still, she would have "some pain" but "she could have easily moved in spite of all the injuries." He said she could have moved for ten, fifteen seconds or more before succumbing to the internal bleeding.

These findings presented a tragic picture of Carolyn,

her body struck by bullets, still finding the strength to get out of the car, leaving blood smudges on the outside of the vehicle and the drops on the ground, then somehow getting back in the car.

What had finished off Carolyn was another pair of gunshots to the back of her head, one behind the right ear that had travelled all the way through her head and out the top, the other from the back of the head that had exited above her left eye. Those shots, fracturing her skull and tearing into her brain, had killed her instantly, and therefore occurred after the other injuries.

There were so many wounds to her body that it would be "very difficult to ascertain" how many times she was shot, said Katsuyama. The best he could calculate was that he had found two bullets in her body, two bullet wounds to her head and at least two more bullets that went in and out of her body. There were other in-and-out bullet holes in her left arm between her wrist and elbow that could have been fragments from those other bullets or new shots. All told, she was shot six to ten times.

Combined with the number of times Ken was shot, the assailant or assailants had fired between eight and twelve bullets into the couple over a period that the coroner estimated to have been fifteen to thirty seconds.

The autopsies offered two other findings of note. Inside Ken's stomach were roughly 500 cubic centimeters—about a pint—of food, including thin short noodle strands and some sort of vegetable material. That was as specific as the food description got. The same kind of food was found in Carolyn's stomach—about 600 ccs. Based on the extent of digestion, it appeared they had eaten about an hour to an hour-and-a-half before they died.

The other finding supported what Ken's mother would tell *The Orange County Register* a couple of days later:

that Ken had had a history of serious medical problems. The heart showed the results of a bypass operation, the leg revealing scars from where a vessel was removed for the graft. What's more, Ken's health problems weren't only in the past. At the time of death, his aorta—the one punctured by the bullet—was "moderately severely" clogged. He was a second heart attack waiting to happen.

But although the autopsies provided a cause of death, it only offered a hint at how the shooting had transpired. To reconstruct the sequence of events and determine what kind of weapon was used, other forensic scientists examined the damage to the Stratus and the bullets that were found in the car and inside the bodies. Five of the six bullets recovered were in good enough shape for analysis; the sixth was merely a fragment and the seventh—the one that had torn through the driver's-side door and hit the pavement—was never found, despite an exhaustive search.

The bullets were copper-plated lead. Scientist Laurie Crutchfield placed them under a microscope to inspect the markings left on the soft lead when it passed through the barrel of the gun. As a gun ages, and the grooves of the barrel change shape, the markings on the bullets become as distinctive as fingerprints. She found that all six bullets had come from the same weapon.

Looking in a reference binder called General Rifling Characteristics—a database by the FBI—she compared the caliber, weight, widths and number of lands and grooves, and the direction of the twist on the bullet. She then generated a list of possible firearms that could have fired these bullets: a .38 Special, a Smith & Wesson .357 Magnum or a Taurus .357 revolver. Since no casings were found at the scene, she thought it much more likely that the bullets had come from one of the .357 revolvers rather than the .38 Special, which would have ejected the casings. The .357 carries six rounds; seven rounds minimum were fired.

The shooter had to have reloaded—or used two of the same kind of gun, six bullets from one, one or more from the other.

An examination of the car provided some details of how the shooting may have taken place. Forensic scientist Maria Golonski found that the driver's-side window had in fact been rolled down. That presented several intriguing questions. November 20 had been a cool night, so the window likely would not have been rolled down for ventilation. Had Kenneth opened it when he'd seen his killer approaching? Perhaps to talk to the assailant, thinking it was safe? Or did he know the shooter?

It appeared that Ken had been shot through that window. The bullet had hit him behind the left ear—the ear facing the window—and he was found slumped to his right. He was probably the first one shot, having never even unbuckled his seatbelt.

Carolyn may also have been shot at least once from that window, or been struck by the same bullet that had passed through Ken's head or arm. Whenever she was first struck, the wound didn't keep her from getting out of the car, leaving the blood smudges outside, the blood trail leading to the back tire, where her shoe had come off. She'd gotten back in the car and been shot again, probably from the direction of the open passenger door.

Much of the gunfire appeared to have come from somebody standing just outside that door. A bullet had gone through the car and hit the driver's-side door, pushing it outward. To determine the bullet's trajectory, Golonski inserted a red stick through the hole. From the angle of the probe, it appeared that the bullet had come from the open front passenger side door, passing through the driver's door and striking the highway where the impact mark had been found. She put another stick through a hole in the passenger door behind the driver, and it appeared that bullet had also come from the same direction.

Somewhere in all this the shooter had apparently reloaded, being careful enough not to leave the spent casings at the scene, and resumed the bloody work.

If nothing else, the crime lab work showed the detectives what they were up against: a killer who was efficient, well prepared, perhaps familiar with one or both of the Stahls, calm and astute enough amid the carnage to leave no evidence.

Who, everyone was asking, would do such a thing?

Chapter Four

The Weasel's mother didn't wait until his father got out of
prison; she divorced him while he was still behind bars.
The Weasel was 10 years old at the time. The mother
quickly remarried, and the new husband wasn't any better
than the first. According to a probation report filed years
later, the new husband had been abusive toward the
Weasel's mother and the mother "didn't deal with it too
long before she left him."

The Weasel's mother got a second divorce, and then
married another man. That marriage also ended, though
not because of abuse. Rather the Weasel's mother, at the
time, was running a flower shop in Virginia when what
she really wanted was to move back to North Carolina
where she was from. The third husband didn't want to
move, so the Weasel's mom got another divorce.

The result of all this was a life of turbulence for the
boy. During these years, from the first divorce on, the
Weasel mostly lived with his maternal grandparents.
Sometimes the mother lived next door, sometimes not.

The bulk of the Weasel's rearing was done by his grand-parents. His grandfather, an official report would later say, "was the only father figure he ever really knew." The Weasel wouldn't live with his real father until years later, when it was all too late.

It was around the time of his grandfather's death, when the Weasel was 17, that he started drinking regularly, first on weekends, then during the week. By adulthood, he was known to be able to drink an entire case of beer. He lived with his grandmother for two years after his grandfather died, then dropped out of high school in the eleventh grade and started getting in trouble with the law.

He first used psychedelic mushrooms when he was 19 or 20, started using cocaine at age 19—it became his favorite drug, particularly in crack form—started using LSD as much as twice a week when he was 23, smoked marijuana for as long as anyone could remember and frequently took methamphetamine, or speed. About the only drug he never used was heroin. The only drug treatment he ever got was Narcotics Anonymous meetings in prison.

Curiously, despite filling his body with a host of illegal chemicals, he remained in good physical shape, aside from the occasional injury. He suffered an accidental gunshot wound to his left foot when he was a teen-ager, another gunshot wound to the back of his right leg years later in a fight, and razor blade cuts across his back and hand during a prison scuffle. Otherwise, an official report would find, the Weasel's health was "excellent."

His mental health was another matter. According to official reports, he would be diagnosed in the late 1990s with a personality disorder, for which he was prescribed an anti-psychotic drug called Haldol, used for hyperactivity, agitation and mania. He also had a history of auditory hallucinations, frequent anxiety attacks and paranoia.

Through it all, between committing crimes and serving time in jail, the Weasel always seemed to have one low-paying job or another, usually doing maintenance work or painting. He also was never starved for female companionship, though by all accounts the relationships were as abusive as the ones he'd witnessed with his mother when he was a child.

His longest relationship was with a hometown girl from Greenville, North Carolina, named Kimberly Brady, whom he had known since the late 1970s, and with whom he started living in 1990. The couple had two children, both boys. When asked years later about the nature of their relationship, Kimberly would answer, "Yeah, it was healthy." Then she would recount a string of domestic violence complaints she had made against the Weasel over the next decade—and then just as promptly recanted.

In one complaint, she accused him of hitting her in the face and knocking her to the ground. She later said she'd made it up, explaining that the Weasel "has a problem with sleeping with a bunch of women, and that was the only way I felt to get even with him." In another complaint, she alleged he'd pushed her in the shoulder and sworn at their boys, calling one son a "motherfucking liar." The cursing was true, she said, but not the violence. She made that up, too, "because of the cheating," she would claim. In one interview she told police that over the years the Weasel had tried to kill her by putting a knife to her throat, once shot at her, knocked her down, cracked her vertebrae, blackened an eye and caused her to put an ice pack on her face. She told them that he'd beaten her and she'd had to go to a hospital for six months for a nervous breakdown.

All of it, she said, she made up. "I wanted to keep the vehicle at our home and get him out because I was mad over the cheating," she said. "He has a very bad habit of cheating."

Kimberly would discover something about herself. She was finally diagnosed with a bipolar disorder. "For some reason," she said, "I wasn't able to carry a job because of my bipolar I did not know I had."

After Kimberly came Lisa, the woman who'd been at the wheel of the Blazer when the Weasel was arrested in the convenience store robbery. When Lisa's cousin would visit her and the Weasel at their mobile home in Virginia Beach, the Weasel would demean Lisa. "I'm going to get your pussy later," he would say, right in front of the visitor. If Lisa ever wanted to go out with a friend or relative, she'd have to get permission from the Weasel.

Lisa's cousin used to notice something else when she visited the Weasel's trailer. Nobody could watch television. There was a bullet hole through the screen.

Chapter Five

The Stahl case was big news in Orange County. It received regular coverage in the *Register* and the *Los Angeles Times* and on local newscasts.

The Wednesday after the murders, *The Orange County Register*, in a story by Bill Rams, quoted one of Dr. Kenneth Stahl's colleagues, a Dr. Aquilino Tan, who had spoken to Ken around 8 p.m. the night of the murders. Tan had paged Ken to ask if he could handle the anesthesia for a tooth surgery the following morning at 6:30 a.m. Ken called back and said that he was out with his wife for her 44th birthday and couldn't make the surgery the next morning. Ken didn't say where he was, where he was going or why he couldn't work the next day. "I assumed he was going home late that night and didn't want to get up so early," Tan said. "I never heard from him after that."

If nothing else, Tan's statement corroborated the finding of the coroner that the couple had died within about an hour to an hour-and-a-half before their bodies were found at 10 p.m., two hours after Ken had spoken to Tan.

It also corroborated the statements of the Stahls' family and other co-workers that Ken was taking his wife out for a birthday dinner. It didn't explain, however, why they were driving on Ortega Highway.

Meanwhile, a witness materialized. On Tuesday, November 30, Detective McDonald spoke to a woman who, on the night of the murders, was driving west on Ortega Highway to her job at Quest Diagnostics, a medical testing lab. She saw an off-white or beige full-sized car parked with its lights off, facing east, next to a call box just west of the entrance to Quest. As she passed, she saw another car, silver or white, and smaller—she thought it might be a Saturn or an Eclipse—traveling west on the highway, coming toward her. The smaller car passed her, slowed down and made a U-turn, then appeared to head into the turnout near the call box and the parked car. The woman assumed the smaller car had gone back and stopped to help the parked car.

She'd seen nothing else, had no idea who was in the cars and didn't have license plate numbers or other more specific identifying information on them. But the timing and circumstances strongly suggested she'd seen the Stahls' car parked on the side of the road and perhaps the car driven by the assailant. The woman had arrived at work at 9 p.m.—an hour after Tan had spoken with Ken and an hour before the bodies were found.

Some of the most intriguing information in the days after the murders came from interviews with people who knew the Stahls. While the media image of them was one of a happy, successful, professional couple, Detective McDonald and investigators working with him found that the reality was much different.

Witnesses revealed the reason why Ken's first marriage had crumbled: he was having an affair. Ken had married the woman with whom he had the affair, but she left him and the marriage was annulled three months later. The annulment came when Ken's health deteriorated and he had to have his first coronary bypass surgery at age 35. "He became deeply depressed," said a probation report filed years later that summarized detectives' interviews, though the reporter added that he "eventually recovered."

Detectives would also find that the circumstances of Ken marrying Carolyn were far from romantic. "After they had been living together a year, Carolyn gave Kenneth an ultimatum: either marry her or she would end the relationship," a probation officer would write. "Although he did not want to marry again, he gave in, particularly because his mother liked Carolyn and considered her a 'perfect' wife for him."

Midway into their marriage—about 1993 or 1994—Carolyn came home early from a trip to Michigan and found a woman lounging in her living room eating fast food. The couple went to marriage counseling, but Ken didn't change. He would have at least three more affairs—and those were the ones Carolyn knew about.

Carolyn's sister, Linda Dubay, confronted Ken about his affairs. "He'd act like he was just indifferent to the whole thing, kind of 'you take me the way I am' attitude," Linda told investigators. Nearly all the names in his address book were women, she said.

Once Ken even became violent with Carolyn. Linda said it happened when he'd caught Carolyn going through his locked desk in their home. Carolyn had grown suspicious of his secretiveness.

Linda said Ken had hit Carolyn, bruising her arms and hips. Carolyn had cried to her sister but refused to leave her husband. Over the years, Ken grew distant but he, too, wouldn't consider a divorce. "It sounded like neither one of them knew how to get out of this marriage," Linda told police.

Indeed, Ken battled depression for years, his health problems only making it worse. "Kenneth was frequently depressed and suicidal," according to the probation report. "He became even more depressed following a second coronary bypass in the summer of 1999. He told people he was tired of 'putting up a front,' was going to 'blow his head off' and wanted to die outdoors."

The report said Ken also "was having financial problems." Around the time of the 1999 bypass, Ken couldn't work because of health problems and had to sell his $700,000 home and move into a condo in Huntington Beach. It was these health problems that explained why the childless couple lived in a relatively modest home and drove two modest cars.

Carolyn tried to put up appearances. Family members told police that over the holidays Carolyn would buy her own Christmas presents, wrap them and put tags on them saying they were from Ken. She responded to the heartache in her marriage by overeating—and shopping. When police searched the house, they found scores of expensive dresses, many still in their boxes with price tags on them. She had run up tens of thousands of dollars in credit card debt.

The more detectives dug, the more unsettling details emerged—until they came to the most shocking discovery to date.

In December 1999, a month after the murders, Ken's sister, Tamara, told investigators that she had found out, to her surprise, that she was the executrix of his estate, in charge of making sense out of his finances and overseeing the disbursement of money to the appropriate heirs, in this case his son Kent, who would get the bulk of what was left, mostly proceeds from the sale of the Stahls' condo.

In going through Ken's financial records, Tamara came across an unusual transaction. On his November statement from Union Bank of California, she found a withdrawal from his checking account.

The amount: $20,000.

Ken's sister researched it to make sure that he hadn't bought something that she should be aware of for liquidating his assets—a car or a boat, for instance. But she never found anything—and no trace of the money itself. She watched the mail to see if something would arrive. She contacted the bank to find out what kind of withdrawal it was.

The money was missing.

Then, another witness came forward with even more disturbing information. It was a woman named Denise who admitted to being one of the women with whom Ken had had affairs. Denise said she and Ken had had their affair long before the murders, back in the mid-1990s. Even then, Denise said, "Kenneth was depressed and spoke of his wife 'blackmailing' him," according to a search warrant affidavit which contained details of the early weeks of the investigation. But Denise's information didn't stop there. "On many occasions Kenneth Stahl spoke of committing suicide," according to Denise, "and of killing his wife with a gun."

Chapter Six

Denise wasn't the only one to speak about the darkest secrets of Dr. Kenneth Stahl. Another witness was a woman named Patricia, who said she was a longtime friend of Ken, but hadn't been romantically involved with him—though she knew all about those who were, including Denise. Patricia said that in the seven years she had known Ken, he was in a constant state of depression. He would jokingly call himself "Dr. Beyond" and "Dr. No Life." According to the investigators' report of the interview, Patricia "stated that she believed Kenneth Stahl set up the murders."

Then came a witness named Richard "Chris" Anaya, an electrician who'd done work for the Stahls and become something of a friend of Ken's. Chris read about the murders in the newspaper and was so rattled he contacted police and told them everything.

Detective McDonald interviewed Anaya on February 16, 2000, almost three months after the murders. His story was chilling.

Chris Anaya had known Kenneth Stahl for a year or two, had done a lot of electrical work for him, was something of a friend. He had met Ken through the doctor's niece and nephew; Chris had been doing work for them and had gotten a referral. Chris had been to Ken's townhouse in a gated development in Huntington Beach four or five times; sometimes, Carolyn was there.

On one call, Ken started talking to Chris while he installed ceiling fans. The doctor seemed intrigued by Chris's tattoos, which were left exposed by the tank top he wore. Ken had decorated the house with what Chris would later call "Native American stuff." Chris was making flutes at the time, and Ken asked him to make one for him. They hit it off so well that Ken mentioned that he had a cabin in Montana, and invited Chris to come some time.

Ken was also intrigued by other tattoos Chris had—gang tattoos. He looked at each one, asking what it meant, how he'd gotten it and when. Chris explained that some tattoos bore the name of his old neighborhood, which he had left about five years earlier. Chris had been in a gang from age 13 to 19. Ken couldn't believe it. Chris was a responsible, friendly, hard-working contractor, a Christian man.

Ken asked Chris how he'd gotten in the gang, what had gone on and how he'd gotten out of it. It was a bad life, Chris told him. He had seen close friends killed in drive-by shootings. Ken would keep asking. Chris didn't mind—he figured that Dr. Stahl, as an educated man, was just curious, that he liked to ask lots of questions. This was a world seated deeply in Chris's past before he'd found religion.

Every time that Chris came to do work, Ken asked him about his Indian heritage and gang life.

Chris told the detective about the night a year earlier

when he'd received a phone call at about 10 p.m. Ken Stahl needed Chris to look at his smoke detectors. They were making noise and lights were flashing and Ken didn't know what was going on. That would normally be late for Anaya to get a call about electrical work, but Dr. Stahl had been a good customer over the years and given Chris a lot of work. Chris had always told Ken that any time he had an emergency, he should feel free to call. It didn't matter what time it was.

On this late-night call, Chris arrived at the Stahl residence. Chris checked three of the smoke detectors, taking them off the ceiling, testing them and putting them back. Ken had taken a fourth smoke detector off the ceiling himself. Chris checked that one too.

There was nothing wrong with any of them.

Ken insisted the smoke detectors were acting strangely—the flashing lights, what he thought were noises. Ken said it was keeping him up at night. Chris explained that the lights were supposed to flash, to show that the battery still had juice.

"That's how they work," Chris said.

He couldn't explain the noises.

That was fine with Ken. He told Chris that he had something else for him while he was there. He asked Chris if he knew anything about home alarm systems.

"I cut the horn out," Ken said. "You know, the horn that blows when the alarm goes off? I had to cut it out because it was making noise."

"Sorry, Ken, I know nothing about it."

Ken asked if Chris could disconnect the entire system. It was professionally installed with a monthly maintenance agreement, and connected directly to the police department. Chris said that was far beyond his expertise as an electrical contractor. He suggested that Ken call somebody certified to work with alarm systems. Ken said that since Chris was an electrician, he thought he could do the work, but Chris said he couldn't.

With that, Chris said that he was going to head home.

"I'll walk you out," Ken said.

By the front door, Ken became serious. "Hey, can I talk to you?"

"No problem. What is it?" asked Chris.

"You know, I'm having a problem here," said Ken. "There's someone bringing me some problems, and it's just not working out. They're coming to my office and creating big problems with me and the people working there."

Ken was smiling as he said it—at first.

"What's up?" asked Chris, puzzled. "I don't know what you want, man. What's going on?"

"Well, I kind of need to take care of this person. You know, it's just, things aren't working out right now."

Chris still didn't know where Ken was going with this. He asked him who this person was, what was going on. Was this somebody he worked with? Ken was evasive. He would only say that there was this person who was bothering him.

"Making my life hell," Ken said.

Finally, Chris asked him, "Ken, I don't know what you're talking about, man. What do you want me to do? I mean, what kind of help do you need?"

"Well, there's just this person bugging me and, well, it's my wife," said Ken. "I need somebody to take care of my wife. She is making my life a living hell. I was just wondering if you knew anybody."

Chris was stunned. "Wait a minute, man, are you joking around?"

Ken was known to be a kidder. People would describe

his unusual sense of humor. Each time Chris went on a call, he and Ken would laugh and joke, and Chris thought that this time it was more of the same.

Ken said that if Chris could find somebody, there would be some money in it for him. He said Chris would be well taken care of.

Chris asked again: "Are you joking?"

Then he saw the look on Ken's face. Eyes downcast. Pure misery.

"Oh, Chris, you don't understand," Ken said

Chris recalled that during those times that Ken would ask about his tattoos and gang life, he once asked if Chris had ever associated with the kind of person who would kill at the drop of a dime. Chris had mentioned seeing death in the streets. But he didn't tell Ken the whole truth—that there were gangbangers who would do absolutely anything, no matter how violent. He didn't tell him that it was never a question of money. It was revenge: somebody's cousin would get killed, and that would be followed by a killing to avenge that murder, and on it went. Gangs didn't accept contract murder assignments. It didn't work that way.

"Stop right there. Stop," Chris told Ken. "You know what, man? Me and you are going to pray, man."

Chris was friendly with Ken, but he didn't know him that well. Maybe the man had been drinking. Maybe he was just blowing off some steam.

"I'll pray with you about it, man," said Chris. "Get a divorce. If things aren't going right, get a divorce."

"She'll try to take me for everything that I have," said Ken, "and I'll really have nothing."

Again, Chris said, "Let's pray." And that's what they did, both of them. Chris asked the Lord to change Ken's heart, to help work things out. Over and over again, Chris told Ken, "Ask the Lord into your heart if you really want to change." And Ken asked the Lord to come into his heart, to help him change.

They prayed for about thirty minutes.

It seemed to help.

"Guy, you're right," Ken said. "I should have never asked you that. Oh, Chris, I'm so sorry. You're a good friend of mine. I should have never done that to you."

It was the last time Chris Anaya ever saw Dr. Kenneth Stahl.

By February 2000, detectives had the makings of a remarkable case, one that would seem improbable to those who'd known Ken Stahl. The witness interviews suggested the possibility that the respected Dr. Stahl was really a deeply depressed philanderer who had hired a hitman to kill his wife.

It was only a theory, but it made more sense than anything else.

But how could the detectives explain Ken's murder?

Why would a hitman kill the person who'd hired him?

Or did Ken also hire the hitman to commit a second murder—his own?

Was Ken Stahl depressed enough to commit a murder–suicide via a hitman?

The theory had some basis in evidence, including the $20,000 in cash that Ken had withdrawn not long before his own violent death and his alleged history in seeking out a contract killer.

But if this were true, what detectives were ultimately left with was a good story but no case.

They may have discovered the motive for why the couple was killed—if the theory were correct—but they were no closer to finding the brutal killer.

Nobody in Ken's life—not his co-workers, his former

flame, certainly not any family members—appeared remotely capable of pulling off such a horrible crime. Even Chris Anaya was eliminated as a suspect, his whereabouts easily ascertained the night of the murders.

And yet, there was one person left whom detectives thought might provide some answers.

Another woman.

Chapter Seven

Detective James McDonald had actually spoken to her on the Tuesday after the killings. He had tracked her down while calling all the numbers left on Ken Stahl's pager. One of the numbers had a prefix for Anaheim, the central Orange County home to Disneyland and the L.A. Angels baseball team.

A woman identifying herself as Adriana Vasco answered.

In a five-minute phone conversation, McDonald had asked her the same questions he'd asked of Dr. Tan and others who'd paged Ken that day: Who were they? Why were they calling? Where was Ken at the time? What was his demeanor? Did they know anything about the murders?

Adriana described herself as a longtime "friend" of Ken's. She confirmed that she had in fact spoken with him the morning of his murder. Ken was doing her a favor, helping her get her computer repaired, and she was calling to see how that was going. She said she'd spoken to him in the morning and he'd told her that he was planning to take his wife out for her birthday.

McDonald ended the conversation by asking Adriana point-blank if she'd been having an affair with Kenneth Stahl.

She said she hadn't.

Nobody seemed to know who Adriana Vasco was or what she was doing in Ken's life, or why she'd just happened to page him on the day he was murdered. The story about the computer didn't add up, nor did the fact that this woman who sounded so unsophisticated over the phone would be a friend of Dr. Stahl's.

McDonald made arrangements to speak with Adriana again in detail, after detectives had done more work. By February 2000, more than two months after first speaking with her, he had learned a lot. He knew about Ken's depression, his marital problems and his conversation with Chris Anaya about hiring a killer.

McDonald had so much more to ask Adriana Vasco.

The interview was set for February 29, 2000.

Chapter Eight

"I didn't really pay attention to him in the beginning because I was busy with other doctors."

Adriana Vasco was sitting across from Detectives Joe Homs and James McDonald in a modest house in Westminster, in central Orange County, not far from the Anaheim address traced to the phone number on Ken's pager.

Adriana was a 33-year-old single mother of two children. She was petite—about 5 feet tall, probably no more than 100 pounds—with curly brown hair, big, expressive brown eyes and a warm smile.

In the interview, Adriana told the detectives she had met Dr. Kenneth Stahl when they both worked at the National Pain Institute, a clinic on Center Drive in Huntington Beach, where he was a part-time anesthesiologist alleviating patients' pain with a novel treatment called "trigger-point injections"—anesthesia injected into specific areas. Adriana was a medical assistant working the front office. Dr. Stahl worked in another part of the clinic, and they rarely came in contact.

Then one day, about two months after she started, he noticed her. She came into the office bruised and limping. "He started giving me trigger-point injections for the pains that I had in my back, and then my bruises," she said. "And that's how we started getting into a personal level, what's happening in my house."

They were, on the surface, a mismatched pair. Adriana gave only the barest of details of her life, but from what detectives heard, she lived in an entirely different world from Ken's.

She said she'd been born February 1, 1967, in Mexico. "My mom died in an auto accident close to four years ago," she said. She never knew her father. "My dad—uh— I was conceived as a rape." She had a sister named Norma Luna, to whom she was close.

Adriana had been married once, to a man named Victor, with whom she had a son, Mark. That marriage eventually ended because, according to Adriana, Victor beat her "so many times," leaving the bruises and causing the limp that Dr. Stahl had noticed seven years earlier.

Adriana would pour out her troubles and Dr. Stahl seemed to understand. He never judged her, never lectured. He once told her she reminded him of his ex-wife.

Soon, he was doing more than treating her pain and paying for lunch. When Victor's abuse got so bad at home that Adriana had to leave with her 3-year-old son, Dr. Stahl paid for a motel room.

As they became closer, Dr. Stahl—or Ken as she was calling him by then—would also open up. Although on the surface he seemed to be a successful professional, he never warmed to an Orange County doctor's life, he told her. "One thing he always mentioned to me was that people were so fake," Adriana told the detectives. "He didn't like to hang around with doctors because he hated all this being proper and [doing] things the right way. I don't know."

Her words spilling out, often without any prompting from the detectives, Adriana painted a sad and lonely picture of the man whom they had found slumped over in his car on Ortega Highway.

Kenneth Stahl had no friends besides Adriana; his life was built around work and working out; he was constantly concerned about his health; he exercised a lot; he didn't like to drive very far, even from Huntington Beach to her apartment in Anaheim ten miles away; he preferred to stay in Huntington Beach where he lived and worked; he had an adult son from a previous marriage who lived in Texas, and never seemed to be able to find the time to visit him.

But overriding everything, she said, were the ongoing problems with Carolyn.

Detective McDonald asked, "What did he tell you about his marriage at the time?"

"He always mentioned that she was overweight and that turned him off," said Adriana. "He tried to get her into doing some exercise. He wanted to go with her and she didn't care to. And at that time they were already living—I mean sleeping—in separate bedrooms."

The troubles dated back to when Adriana had first met Ken, in 1992 or early 1993, and flared in the six years leading up to the murders.

"He wanted to divorce her. He didn't like her. I mean, if you would know him, he was very gentle, very caring," she said, her voice cracking, then turning to sobs, the first of many times during the interview that Adriana cried. "The kind of person that you'd think that would not even hurt a fly. She was not very nice to him towards the end. He was suicidal. He talked a lot about suicide."

Adriana said she urged him to see a counselor, get a

divorce, anything to make his life better. "And he said, 'I already did, and I told her she can keep the house, she could keep everything, but she won't let it go,'" recalled Adriana. "He said he went to talk to a lawyer but because they've been married I guess for ten years, she's entitled to, I don't know, I guess his retirement, his pension. I have no idea, because his concern was the money, you know. . . . He said that she was out to get him for every cent that she could."

The situation never improved, and Ken's complaints about his wife intensified.

"He would work at three different places just not to be home," said Adriana.

Ken portrayed his wife as not just greedy, but prying and suspicious.

"I remember one time he called me. He was really upset. And I said 'What's wrong now?'" recalled Adriana. "He came home and he found all his private stuff everywhere." Adriana's voice began cracking. "She had searched through his room, through his private stuff, through his cell phone numbers, his address book and his van, everything. He said, 'Everything's just upside down and I'm just getting fed up with this.'"

"Do you know how long ago that was?" asked McDonald.

"Probably maybe about a year and a half ago," said Adriana. "I mean, that's when things—from what he was telling me—aren't working. Really bad."

That was the time of Ken's bypass surgery.

"He became very depressed after his surgery, because he had lost a lot of weight and for him that was very important," said Adriana.

She burst into tears.

"Did it really happen?" she cried. "I'm sorry, it's just my whole world has just collapsed. He was my hero. He was my father, my motivation, you know, my strive to keep going. He was the only person that really believed in me. He was the only person that was there for me that I could count on and be, you know, my family."

She said that when she read the newspaper articles about the couple, how people were saying Carolyn was so perfect, Adriana grew upset "because I got to see her, you know, the other side."

Adriana said she didn't just hear of Carolyn. She'd spoken to her on the phone. Carolyn had been calling around to Adriana's friends, giving a fake name and asking who this woman was.

But the time that Adriana actually talked to Carolyn came, oddly, in a phone call from Ken. The couple seemed to be arguing. "They both sounded very excited over the phone," Adriana recalled. "I said, 'Are you guys getting physical now?' And he said, 'Yeah.' And I said, 'Oh God.' "

Then Ken put Carolyn on the phone.

"I talked to her, and she said, 'I want you to leave my husband alone,' " said Adriana. "And I said, 'You know what I'm telling you: We're friends. And stop calling my friends' houses and stop harassing me.' And she goes, 'Well, leave him alone.' I said, 'OK, fine, I won't call him. . . . ' But he was always the one calling me. He was the one looking for me. And at one point, I remember telling him 'You know what? Don't call me anymore. Don't come over. This is causing a lot of problems on your side.' "

Just a friend?

Or a lover?

When McDonald first spoke to Adriana, she had denied having an affair with Ken. Clearly, they had something much more than a simple friendship. Was Carolyn Stahl right about Ken and Adriana?

The detectives had a host of questions, but they would wait. They had Adriana talking. They didn't want to interrupt her. The information would have to come out of order, the pieces to be fit together later.

In the months leading up to the murders, Adriana said, "I hadn't seen him in a while, but I had talked to him."

"What did you talk to him about that morning?" asked McDonald.

Adriana started crying again. "Oh, my computer," she sobbed.

She said she had taken it to a CompUSA store to be fixed and he'd agreed to pay for it. "I told him I was happy because I was going to go in and pick it up and I said, 'Thank you for getting it fixed.' "

"That was the computer you got fixed?" asked McDonald.

"Yeah, which broke again—my son did something to it," she said. "And I asked [Ken] what he was gonna do that weekend, because he had mentioned that it was her birthday. So he says, 'I'm taking her out to eat.' And I said, 'Well, where're you guys going?' He goes, 'Oh, here and there, I don't have a place yet.' "

Adriana talked through tears now. She said she'd asked Ken where they planned to go after dinner. "I was always nosy: 'What'd you buy her?' 'Did you buy her anything?' 'What was it?' " But Ken never answered those kinds of questions.

"So you didn't know where they were going?" asked McDonald.

"No, he just said, 'I'm taking her out to dinner,' and he just said, you know, 'just kind of like a surprise thing, because she doesn't know either.' "

"What kind of mood was he in that morning?"

"He was happy because, I guess, I was happy," she

said. "I would never think anything because he was in a good mood. I mean, it seemed like he was OK for that morning that I talked to him."

The detective asked her if Ken had spoken often about suicide.

"Not necessarily saying the words," she said, "but he would use certain phrases like, 'It would be nice to see what it's like in another world and not having to worry about work, about confrontations, about anything at all.' And then at other times it was like, 'I just don't want to be here anymore.'"

He'd often talk this way in phone conversations about his marriage. When he was at his worst, she would ask him if he wanted to get together with her and talk in person. He'd say no, he just wanted to go and work out at the gym.

"So basically all he did was work out and work, and work out and work, and that was his life," she said. "He said that he couldn't have any friends because of her. The last argument that I knew about was she got mad at him because he went to a conference and he didn't take her. And the reason why he didn't like to take her is because he was embarrassed of her. And I go, 'God, that's pretty mean.'"

"Do you know when that was?" asked McDonald.

"I believe it was like sometime in October."

"So it was a month or so before he was killed?"

"Yeah," she said, and the tears returned.

The detective changed the subject.

"Did he ever give you any money? Give you any loans?"

"He would buy things for me when he would see that I needed things," she said. "When my car broke down, he went and bought me this car. He goes, 'Here, I'll buy you a car.'"

She said Ken was constantly asking her if she needed

money. She said she always told him no, that she had child support, had a part-time job. When he came to her house, she wouldn't let him look in her refrigerator because it was empty. But he'd sneak a peek anyway, then slip a couple of hundred dollars in her purse on his way out. "I would get mad like, you know, 'Don't be putting money like that because it makes me feel like you're buying friendship,'" she said. "'I'm your friend because I like you, because you've been there.'"

"Has he ever given you any large sums of money, like ten thousand dollars or twenty thousand dollars, anything like that?" asked McDonald, a reference to Ken's last major cash withdrawal from Union Bank.

"No," she said. "The most he's ever given me was money to buy a ticket to go to Mexico for me and my son because my relative was sick."

"Do you know anybody recently that he's given any large sums of money to?"

The only place she could think the money would go was to other doctors for the heart surgery. "He said his insurance didn't pay like sixty grand or something like that," she said. "He was trying to pay it off, pay off the doctors' office, but he didn't say how much. That's when he said that's why he was working so many hours."

"But he didn't tell you, like right before he died, or a month or so, he didn't tell you about giving anybody any money or anything?"

"No, he just mentioned that he needed to get some, he needed to pay off his doctor."

McDonald then asked her point-blank: "Did he ever talk about having his wife killed?"

"He couldn't do something like that," she said. Still, she admitted, "I don't know what he was thinking. He had changes of moods towards the end. One day, you know, sometimes I would talk to him and he was fine. Sometimes he was sad and sometimes he was crying. Sometimes he would just call me, he wouldn't want to talk about anything.

"Sometimes he would refer to her as, you know—'I just had an argument with,' you know, 'with the bitch from hell.'"

But he clearly felt differently about Adriana, she said. About three weeks before his murder, he gave her a CD. One of the songs was called "Angel."

"He said, 'This song reminds me of you. You're a little angel,'" recalled Adriana, breaking into sobs.

After the murders, she opened the CD and saw it had a picture of an angel and the words: "Time to say goodbye."

McDonald asked her if Ken ever spoke of how he would want to kill himself.

"He was like kind of obsessed—maybe not obsessed—*fascinated* with talking about how he wanted to die," she said. "'I want to go in the mountains in Montana where I like to hike,'" she said. "I'm like, 'Oh, my God.' Sometimes I think that maybe if I had said something to someone, maybe this wouldn't have happened. But you never think. I wish you would have met him. He was so loving, so gentle, so caring."

Implicit in what Adriana was saying was that she, too, thought maybe Ken had had someone orchestrate the murders, as kind and loving as he was. The question was whether Adriana Vasco knew any details of how he may have set this plan in motion.

Although earlier in the interview she'd said Ken never spoke specifically of wanting to kill his wife, McDonald broached the subject again, asking, "He never talked about trying to find anybody to kill his wife or anything like that?"

"He didn't say anything about that, no. He was always

trying to get rid of the relationship that he had with her and didn't want to give her the money."

"When he talked about wanting out, did he talk like he wanted to get a divorce and just get away from her?"

"Yeah, that's how I felt. That's how I took it."

He asked her how Ken had tried to get out of the relationship.

"What he had said was that he had talked to a lawyer but then they told him, 'She's entitled to this . . . ' and he did say he had a prenuptial agreement, and I said, 'So what's the problem?' I really could not get the point what the problem was. Why it was so hard to get out. I don't know."

It was more than an hour into the interview when McDonald finally asked the same question he had asked just days after the murders.

"You'd said you were friends," said McDonald. "Did you ever have a romantic relationship with him? Did you ever have an affair with him?"

Through tears, Adriana said, "You know what, to be honest with you, we had a lot of love. He knew and I knew that it was just something that, uh," she said, becoming overwhelmed by sobs. "This is very painful. I started falling in love with him. And I know he did too. And I'm just dumb. I just can't see him terminating the—divorce— so I just— We did for a while. But then I stopped it because I didn't want to get hurt. I didn't want to get in too deep and get hurt."

"When did you end that part of your relationship?"

"My daughter's two-and-a-half—probably about three to three-and-a-half years ago." It was the first time she mentioned a second child.

"Is that his daughter?"

"No," she said. "After that I was seeing somebody

else. I started a relationship with my daughter's father. And we moved in together and everything. . . . I'm moving on."

Moving on with this other man—yet still keeping a deep friendship with Ken Stahl, talking to him about their personal problems, accepting money from him, calling him the day of his murder. There was now yet another player in this melodrama that was Adriana's life.

"Did that guy know Ken?" asked McDonald.

"Yeah."

"OK," said McDonald, "was there any problem between he and Ken?"

Sniffling, Adriana said, "No."

"No?" said McDonald. "What was his name?"

"Greg."

"What's Greg's last name?"

"Stewart."

The detectives glanced around the house. "OK," said McDonald, "so this is his parents' house?"

Adriana answered with a sniffle.

"Uh, you guys obviously split up?"

"Yeah," said Adriana, "unfortunately violence came back to my life again."

She didn't give any details.

"OK, is there anybody else that you know of that would want to do something like this to Ken?" asked McDonald.

"No, I keep thinking about it, and I just don't know."

"Has he ever talked about having any enemies or anybody upset with him?"

"Not that I know of. Not that he ever mentioned anything, no."

"How about his wife? Did he ever say anybody was upset with his wife?"

"She mentioned something about her hiring a private investigator on him. But that was a while back."

Adriana said Carolyn hired the PI before Ken's surgery, so that would have been about six months to a year before the murders.

The detectives were now faced with another scenario: Perhaps Carolyn had hired a hitman to kill her husband, only *she*'d ended up dead.

So far, nothing the detectives had revealed to date supported that theory. There were no mysterious $20,000 cash withdrawals that she had made. By all accounts she was frustrated, hurt and angry with Ken over his infidelities, but wasn't depressed enough—or connected enough in the world of hired hitmen—to pull something off.

It was yet another avenue to explore, but not the most likely.

This time it was Detective Homs who started asking the questions. He circled back to a nagging thought.

"How's the relationship between you and Greg now?" he asked.

"It's fine," Adriana said. "We try to, you know— We ended up in good terms because of our daughter."

"Had you told him about your relationship with Ken?"

"He knew."

"Was he jealous at all?"

"No."

"Was he angry at you or angry at him?"

"No."

"Had you spoken with anybody else about what was going on between you and Ken?"

"Nobody," she said. "You guys are the only persons that I've talked to"—besides Greg's mother, Nancy Stewart.

Homs got more specific.

"Had he ever asked you if you knew anybody that could kill his wife or kill him?"

"Uh-uh," she said, sniffling.

Homs asked Adriana if Ken ever inquired of her "how much it would cost to do something like that?"

"Why?"

"Did he ever talk about that?"

"Why are these questions like this? I mean why?"

"Maybe he talked about suicide."

"Yeah, he talked about that."

"OK, how was he going to accomplish that?"

"He didn't mention, never mentioned anything."

"That's what I'm asking is, had he ever mentioned about how he would do it?"

"Oh, no."

"Was he ever so mad at his wife that he would say, 'I want to kill her and I'm going to hire some guy to do it,' or anything like that?"

"There was a couple of times where he was really upset and he had to leave the house, but, no I don't remember him saying—He was always, it was always, 'I'm going to end it all.' "

Homs kept pressing.

"Did you ever know him to try to kill himself? You know, slice his wrist or anything like that?"

"No, he never mentioned that."

"Drive his car off the cliff or something? He never said, 'I'm going to do that and I did that to scare you?'"

"He said it—just said, 'Blow my head off' once. 'I'm just going to blow my head off, and just . . . ' you know."

"Did he say how he was going to do that?" asked Homs. "Did you know him to have any guns?"

"Yeah," she said. "He told me, I think, he did at home, because he mentioned about the ones that he used to go shooting with before."

"Do you know what kind of guns he had at home?"

"No," she said. "I'm lame when it comes to stuff like that. I remember having arguments about him killing Bambis."

"There's nobody in your life at this point in time that would have been jealous of your relationship with him?"

"Nobody knew, nobody except my daughter's dad and my son, of course, and the grandparents," she said. "That's basically it. I just kind of kept everything to myself and I know that he did, too."

"You said your sexual relationship ended about three-and-a-half years ago?"

"Yeah, and since then he was a perfect gentleman," she said. "I was straight with it. I said, 'That's it. We can be friends. I'm going to move on.' He never tried to do anything. He said, 'Well, regardless if you go back to your ex-husband or whatever, I'll always be around and be your friend.'" She said her ex-husband, the father of her son, had never met Ken.

The detectives returned to the days and weeks before the murders, asking her again about money—though being careful not to tell her they knew about the $20,000 withdrawal.

"If he spent a large sum of money in the last three or four weeks before he was killed, do you have any idea where he would have spent it?" asked McDonald. "Did he go anywhere? Did he do anything? Any idea what he might have done with some money like that?"

For the first time, one of their questions seemed to rattle Adriana.

"Is there money missing?" she asked. "Because you guys keep bringing that up."

"Well, I'm asking if you knew," said McDonald, not answering her.

"No," she said. "I know he was a spender, I know he

liked to go and buy things." But he would buy tennis shoes and sportswear—nothing major in the month before his murder that she knew of.

As the detectives talked about the money, they happened to glance around the living room and saw something on the shelf.

"Whose trophies are these back here?" asked Homs.

"The grandparents'," said Adriana. "They have a shooting range that they go to. They used to go every Sunday."

Homs asked, "Do they ever shoot handguns?"

The Stahls had been killed with a handgun, probably a .357 Magnum or .357 Taurus revolver.

"No, it's just— I don't know, I think there's shotguns," said Adriana.

The detectives wrapped up the interview by hearing Adriana again deny that either Greg or her first husband were upset about her relationship with Ken, and that other issues caused those breakups—domestic violence issues. Both Victor and Greg had beaten her, she claimed.

"I don't know," she said, "I guess I have a magnet for that."

She was asked if she could think of anything else that would help the investigation. She said she had nothing more.

Then Adriana had a question. It was about Ken and the murders.

"Did he suffer or not?" she asked. "It's like I want to know, then I don't want to know."

They didn't tell her.

At just before 5 p.m., the detectives turned off their tape-recorder. The last sounds on the recording were Adriana Vasco crying.

Chapter Nine

After talking to Adriana Vasco, detectives Homs and McDonald felt it was now entirely possible—perhaps probable—that Kenneth Stahl had hired a hitman to kill Carolyn because he couldn't stand her anymore. The irony was palpable: The man who had dedicated his life to stopping pain had inflicted the ultimate agony on his own wife.

As part of this, Ken may also have wanted to have himself killed by the hitman, to end his emotional pain and depression. The bullets would do the job much more quickly than the heart troubles would. The only consolation was that Ken's neglected son Kent would inherit hundreds of thousands of dollars.

Another possibility was that Ken had hired a hitman only to kill Carolyn, and something had gone terribly wrong out on Ortega Highway.

Either way, the cash withdrawal, the depression, the tortured marriage, the strange conversation with Chris—it all pointed to Kenneth Stahl as the architect of this crime.

But who had pulled the trigger?

This former boyfriend of Adriana's, Greg Stewart, was a possibility. But they had no physical or eyewitness evidence linking him.

Another possibility was Adriana herself. She had lied to detectives in the days after the murders by denying having a sexual relationship with Ken. And it was questionable that she was now telling the truth when she said that that relationship had ended three years earlier and that they had remained platonic friends.

But at the same time, it seemed believable that Ken had given her money all those years—and had still been helping her financially up to the day he died. So why would Adriana want to kill her sugar daddy?

Unless she wanted the wife gone so Adriana could have Ken to herself—and things just hadn't worked out as planned.

In the end, the detectives felt Adriana hadn't had anything to do with Ken's murder. She may have known that he wanted to kill his wife, but then, she wasn't the only one. Chris Anaya, Ken's former lover Denise, his other friend Patricia—all had heard him speak of wanting her dead.

Adriana's grief seemed sincere. She'd lost a friend, confidant and source of ready cash. It didn't make sense that she'd want him dead.

By the summer of 2000, the case that had generated so much early attention now warranted only a small mention in a little Orange County paper called the *Sun Post News*. "Nothing new has developed," said Orange County Sheriff's Homicide Captain Steve Carroll in a story that appeared on August 1. "But it's still an active case."

Adriana Vasco was by now off the official radar. She was no longer being contacted by police, and got on with her life. Shortly after her police interview, she hit the Internet looking for companionship, finding a man named Steve in March of 2000. At the time, Steve was married but separated, with three children. After corresponding over the Internet for about three weeks, they had their first meeting in April at a Carl's Jr. fast food restaurant in Anaheim, about a block and a half away from Adriana's apartment.

They saw each other about a dozen times. They went out to lunch and dinner. Early on they started having sex.

On their dates, Steve always paid, as Adriana was struggling financially. She told him she was having a difficult time paying for car maintenance and making rent on her apartment in a second-rate complex called the Avanti Apartments behind the Anaheim police station, not far from Disneyland.

Steve was sympathetic. "It was very hard for a single mom to raise two children by [herself]," he recalled.

It also became increasingly clear to Steve that Adriana, while out dating again, was still coming to grips with the loss of a man named Ken. And while she told Detectives Homs and McDonald that she never spoke to anybody outside her close circle of family members about Ken, she opened up to Steve.

She told him she had known Ken for more than seven years, that they had met at work, that they once had been lovers but became close friends. Ken, she said, had taken care of her financially and that "No matter what she wanted, whatever she needed, he would always be there for her. He bought her a car. He gave her spending money to help her out." And while they had stopped sleeping together, her feelings for Ken were intense. "I think she loved him with her heart and soul forever," Steve recalled.

Adriana introduced Steve to her two children, then ages 3 and 12. He was particularly smitten by her youngest, the daughter—"so adorable," he'd say later. But the conversation always seemed to return to Ken.

Ken was not the girl's father, she told Steve. Rather, Ken had had an unhappy marriage to a controlling woman who'd refused to give him a divorce. When it became clear that Ken wasn't going to leave his wife, Adriana ended the intimate part of their relationship and got pregnant with her daughter to spite Ken, Steve recalled Adriana telling him. Then Ken was killed—murdered along with his wife, she told Steve.

Along with the emotional loss, Ken's death had hurt her already shaky financial picture. Adriana had been working part-time before the murders; now she was working full-time, and it still wasn't enough. "It is a big difference when somebody is helping take care of you and all of a sudden it changes," Steve recalled.

In time, Adriana confided that she had even spoken to Ken the day he was killed. She told Steve that Ken wasn't himself, that he'd been uneasy.

Then she explained why, telling Steve something she hadn't revealed to the police detectives just a few weeks earlier.

On the day of his murder, Ken had told Adriana on the phone that he was supposed to meet somebody, but he didn't want to do whatever it was he was supposed to do with this person. "He wanted to call it off or something," Steve recalled Adriana telling him. "He was very uneasy, unclear. He wasn't himself, and I think he wanted to change his mind."

She told Steve that during this phone conversation, Ken had been in his car—and somebody was with him. It wasn't Ken's wife.

Adriana never told Steve who that person was.

But Steve got the strong impression it was a man.

Chapter Ten

By the summer of 2000, it had been nearly a year since the Weasel slipped out of the police car into the Virginia woods—and still nobody could find a trace of him.

No one wanted more desperately to find him than Sergeant Ronald Wayne Smith. A deputy sheriff for Pitt County, North Carolina, with almost twenty years on the force, Smith had been dealing with the Weasel off and on for most of his career—since the Weasel's first brushes with the local law after his grandfather died.

Periodically, Smith would check the houses and mobile homes of people with whom the Weasel was known to associate. In July 2000, Smith got word that the Weasel may have hooked up with a new girlfriend, a woman who lived in the county. One day, Smith decided to pay the woman a visit. When he arrived at her house, the place was bustling with people. It was noisy and chaotic as he tried to talk to her, and he was distracted by having to keep an eye on a young trainee who had tagged along. The visit yielded no leads on the Weasel.

But later Smith got some unsettling news. He was told that one of the people in that crowded house may have been the Weasel.

Smith simply didn't recognize him.

The Weasel had slipped out from under him.

It was the first of two times in the summer of 2000 that the Weasel would get away from Smith. The second came a month later, in August, when the Weasel was tracked to a mobile home in Bellarthur, North Carolina, a rural area where he had grown up. As deputies arrived, the Weasel was seen climbing out of the trailer's bathroom window. One of the deputies tried to tackle him, but the Weasel kicked him in the head and then ran into the woods that, Smith was certain, the fugitive knew like the back of his hand.

What was particularly galling was that the Weasel never seemed to venture far from the Pitt County jurisdiction, hanging out with friends and family, making very little effort to hide. One day a 14-year-old high school kid named Kyle Alligood went with his friend, Reid Radcliff, to a small single-story home on Highway 99 in Belhaven, where an older guy named Ed Godley lived. Kyle was friends with Ed's son, Edwin. Kyle and Edwin went to high school together.

After they got there, Reid went into the house to pick up money for mowing Ed's grass, while Kyle stood outside Reid's truck. That's when Kyle saw a shirtless man covered in tattoos emerge from the garage. The man was drinking something brown, and he appeared to have a booze buzz going.

The man turned on a radio or CD player, then sat in a chair with his drink. "He just started talking, like where he was from and all that stuff," Kyle would recall. "And I told him where I was from and all that."

It turned out the man was Ed's son—Edwin's brother,

which was odd. Edwin hadn't spoken of having an older brother. What's more, the man didn't say he was from North Carolina. He told Kyle he was from California. He mentioned something about Orange County.

"I just had never heard of it," Kyle said. "We were just sitting there talking and everything. I reckon he had been drinking, and he just started mouthing off." The man talked about having recently come down from a small town nearby, and that he, too, knew Reid.

And then he casually mentioned something.

He said he had killed some people back in California.

"He didn't go into specific detail or nothing," Kyle recalled. "To my knowledge, I would think that he said Orange County, California, because that's where he said he was from, and that's where he came from at the time."

He also didn't say who he'd killed, or how many. He just said "a couple" of people.

"I really didn't ask him no questions," recalled Kyle. "I really didn't think much of it when he told me about it, because I didn't really think it was true. . . . I just never heard anything like that happen before in real life."

About this time, Reid came out of the house and that ended the conversation with the man. Kyle climbed into Reid's truck and as they drove off, Kyle told his friend what the man had said.

Reid didn't seem surprised, telling Kyle, "Yeah, I reckon he had been in a lot of trouble and stuff."

Chapter Eleven

It didn't take long for word to get out to local police that the Weasel was now living with his father, Ed Godley, in the house in Belhaven.

It took even less time for that word to get back to Ed.

News travels fast in rural North Carolina. A friend of Ed's, who worked for the sheriff's department, called him to let him know that authorities were planning to arrest his son.

"[He] told me that they were going to bring a squad or something," Ed recalled. "If he tried to run, that they would probably shoot him because he had already escaped from one thing and hurt a deputy sheriff, and that he was wanted for something in Virginia. He didn't tell me what."

About 10 p.m. the night of August 17, 2000, Ed called the Pitt County Sheriff's Department and asked to speak with an old acquaintance, Ron Smith. They had known each other from the many times the Weasel had gotten into trouble over the years.

Ed left his name and number, and Smith, who was on

duty that night, called him back a short time later. They spoke for about five minutes.

"He was telling me he was thinking about turning his son in, that he had feared that it got to the point that his son was either going to kill someone, kill an officer or someone would kill him," Smith recalled. "He didn't want that to happen. Also he didn't want us to harm his son. He was undecided what to do at the time."

Ed would recall: "My son, he's scared. Anybody would be scared of the law. He was running, and I didn't want him hurt." Ed also worried about his other two children, who were living there: his teenage son Edwin and his 10-year-old daughter—the half-siblings of the Weasel. He said he had to think about what to do and hung up.

Smith had the communications center trace the call. It had come from Ed's home. Smith needed a plan. "Everyone in the department knew I was looking for [the Weasel]" said Smith. "And I wasn't going to let him get away this time."

About ten minutes later, Ed called Sgt. Smith back. "He wanted to turn his son in and decided to do so, as long as we wouldn't hurt him," Smith recalled. Ed told the sergeant what authorities already knew: His son was staying with him in his house. He was staying there with a woman—the same woman Smith had interviewed earlier that summer while the Weasel may have been just feet away.

Ed said his son wasn't home at the time, but would be returning around midnight. "He again told me that he had got to the point that he feared his son was going to kill an officer or an officer [would] kill him," said Smith, "and he told me he [the Weasel] was armed and had two weapons"—a shotgun and a handgun in his room.

Ed said it would be best to wait until his son returned

home and fell asleep. Smith could arrest him then. Smith agreed, but he was still worried about those guns. He asked Ed if he'd hide them while his son was away. Ed said he didn't want to because it would tip off his son that something was afoot. Smith tried to reassure him. "I told him that we wasn't going there to hurt his son, and that we would do everything we could to see that no one got hurt," said Smith.

From sheriff's headquarters, the deputies drove about thirty miles east to a parking lot at a school near Ed's house to await word on when to move in.

At about 3 a.m., Ed called the sheriff's captain, who relayed the information to the arrest team: The Weasel had come home and fallen asleep.

Smith had already worked out with Ed how the arrest would go down. Ed would leave open a side door, through which the deputies would enter, go straight to the Weasel's room and arrest him. Ed would stay out of sight. He had left the guns alone, but did move his other two children out of the house.

It didn't go exactly as planned. When the officers arrived at the house, they found Ed standing in the front doorway with the outside porch light on. As the officers walked up the yard, Ed started yelling, "Don't shoot him! Please don't shoot him!"

The officers swept by him and stormed into the house through the side door. They went down a hall, turned right and ran down another narrow hall and into the back bedroom. There they found the Weasel asleep on a mattress next to a woman. In front of the mattress lay a single-barrel 20-gauge shotgun, pointed toward the bedroom door. An old Western-style handgun rested nearby.

The first two officers into the bedroom leaped on top of the Weasel. He awoke in a foul mood, struggling against the officers as they cuffed one hand behind his back, then the other. All the while he was shouting that they were "motherfuckers," lucky he couldn't reach the shotgun or he would have taken out two or three of them. At one point he said to an officer, "What the fuck are you looking at?"

As he was led out of the home, he screamed to his father, "Don't let them take me away, Dad!"

His father watched, helpless, yelling, "Please don't hurt my son."

The deputies put him in the back seat of Sergeant Ron Smith's patrol car, this time under heavy guard, with an officer next to him. The Weasel started pounding his head against the window.

With Smith at the wheel and an officer in the back, they returned to sheriff's headquarters. For some of the half-hour drive, the Weasel was "in a very violent state," recalled Smith, "and then he was in a calm state." His hands were cuffed in front of him, connected to a chain around his waist, and his feet were shackled.

"He would calm down and then he would get back violent," said Smith. "And we just tried to keep him calm."

But very early in the drive—perhaps even as they were pulling out of Ed's driveway—Smith couldn't help but ask the Weasel: What were you running away from so hard?

That's when he'd said something that hadn't made much sense.

The Weasel said he was wanted in California. He said they had some "lifer shit" on him—charges that could put him away forever.

Smith didn't know anything about crimes in California. As far as he knew, the Weasel was only wanted on the robbery and escape charge in Virginia and the assault charge in Greenville for kicking the deputy in the head. Nothing had popped up for the Weasel in the National Crime Information Center computer. "I didn't know anything about California," said Smith.

Smith didn't discuss the matter with the Weasel, whose behavior was erratic. Instead, he told him that it was time to get his act together, that he had two kids who needed a father to take care of them.

Hearing a gagging sound, Smith turned on the interior light and saw blood all over the Weasel, who complained that he suffered from a bleeding ulcer and needed to go to the hospital.

"You ain't done nothing but bit your tongue," Smith told him.

When they got to the sheriff's headquarters a medic examined the Weasel and found that he had in fact bitten the tip of his tongue.

The Weasel didn't make bail. But a couple of days later, Edward Godley called Sergeant Smith.

He wanted to know if there was a reward available for his son. Smith told him that as far as he knew, there wasn't, but to call the county's Crime Stoppers program, which gives out rewards of between $1 and $2,500.

It was the first of four or five calls. Each time, Ed inquired about a possible reward, and each time Smith told him to call Crime Stoppers.

Within a year, Ronald Smith would retire after twenty years on the force, finally having caught the man he had been wrangling with for some fifteen years. He did check the computer again: nothing about charges in California.

Smith took it for more of the Weasel's crazy talk.

Chapter Twelve

By the fall of 2000, Adriana Vasco's Internet romance with Steve had ended and she moved on to Jeffrey, another lover she had met online. Their first date was at a bar and they met six or seven times from late September through the end of October. One time, Jeffrey went to Adriana's apartment in Anaheim behind the police station. "It looked a little bit rough, but it was very nicely equipped inside," he said.

Jeffrey learned that she had two children—he met them once; all he would remember was that they were a boy and girl, young, but couldn't recall their ages.

Jeffrey said his relationship with Adriana became sexual, but not serious. "We were just dating. I mean, it was just a good time between the two of us," he said, though he thought "she felt a little stronger . . . but I don't know for sure."

As with her previous online lover, Adriana wasted little time in telling Jeffrey about Ken. "We were just talking about prior relationships and . . . how she was telling me that she was in this relationship and how much she loved him and vice versa," Jeffrey recalled. "She said she had one true love in her life and that was Ken, and that she loved him and that he loved her. And then I asked her a little bit more about him, and she said he has been deceased." She also told him that Ken was a doctor.

"At that point, it rang a bell about the incident on the Ortega Highway," Jeffrey said. "I saw it on the news."

Intrigued, Jeffrey asked Adriana about Ken's death, but she only wanted to talk about her relationship with Ken. "She just stated that she loved him, he loved her and that he was giving her a little bit of money on the side so she didn't have to work as much so they could see each other," said Jeffrey.

She also told him about Ken's wife. Adriana called her a "gold digger." "I was told that him and her kind of went their separate ways, but they were still married," Jeffrey recalled. "And she knew about Adriana. And I guess she called once and the wife picked up the phone, and they got into a big argument and Ken stepped in and broke it up. But I guess the wife knew about it and put up with it."

Looking back on his one-month not-serious relationship with Adriana, Jeffrey recalled something particularly strange that happened. One day, they were driving and he was "talking about other girls," he said.

That's when she bit him.

It was not, in his mind, a playful bite. "It hurt," he said.

Chapter Thirteen

Filipe "Phil" Villalobos had been a homicide detective for two weeks when his sergeant called him into his office.

"Hey, Phil," the sergeant said, "I want you to do something for me. I want you to take this case over."

Villalobos and his new partner, Brian Heaney, a former narcotics investigator who had spent about two years in the unsolved homicide unit before moving to the regular homicide desk, knew about the Stahl case from media reports. That was *all* they knew.

They were now the new lead detectives.

The case was shifted to them amid reorganization in the sheriff's department; leaders were changing and so were detective teams. McDonald and Homs were reassigned to another unit; a second detective team came in briefly to look at the Stahl case but didn't get anywhere, then it went to Villalobos and Heaney.

At first, the detectives were overwhelmed. Four veteran homicide detectives had given it their best shots and failed to make a case strong enough to prosecute. Still,

Heaney had been a cop for twenty-three years, with work in narcotics and the unsolved unit; Villalobos had put in fourteen years, including intense service on a career-criminal apprehension team—six cops and a sergeant who went out to find and arrest the toughest of the tough felons. "We were the guys they called in to do the dirty work," Villalobos said. Both detectives were also experienced in interrogating hardened criminals such as gang members and drug dealers. They didn't know it yet, but they would make a good team—Heaney the intense, type-A personality, Villalobos the more easy-going one, who actually spoke fondly of his patrol days working the mean streets of unincorporated Stanton—"Out of control," he said. "It was rock 'n' roll."

Their first order of business was to review the paperwork generated by the previous detectives—the crime-scene reports, the forensic science material, the photos of the crime scene and autopsies, the interview transcripts, including the one of Adriana Vasco, and the witness statements from everybody from electrician Chris Anaya to Ken Stahl's family members and former lover Patricia.

In trying to decide which way to proceed, they weighed three theories for the murders. The first, and least likely, was that Ken Stahl had been bumped off for business reasons. Reading the reports, Villalobos and Heaney found that their predecessors had toyed with the theory Ken could have been involved in insurance fraud or some financial shenanigans with other doctors. The detectives went down that road a little, interviewing business partners, but came up with nothing.

A second possibility was that the murders had in fact had something to do with Ken Stahl's sorry frame of mind—that he was depressed over his health and marriage and wanted to die, but wanted his inheritance to go to his son and not to the wife whom he hated. Therefore, he arranged Carolyn's murder and his own suicide, somehow finding a killer willing to work for $20,000.

The last possibility was the least attractive, but still very real: that Kenneth and Carolyn Stahl had been the victims of a random attack. They'd gone out to Ortega Highway for a little roadside lovemaking, as many have done before, and found themselves confronted by a deranged killer.

The more the detectives thought about it, the more they liked the second theory: that Ken had set this all in motion himself. The medical fraud angle had been heavily investigated without success, and if this were a random act, there was nothing to look for.

The murder-for-hire scenario started looking even better as the detectives dug deeper into the files. In reviewing Ken's cellular phone records, they found out he had made several calls to the same number on the day of his murder—a number that had also popped up on his pager.

The telephone number of Adriana Vasco.

It was now clear Ken had had more than that one conversation with Adriana that she said was about her computer. The records suggested he'd spoken with her— or someone using her phone—four or five times on November 20, 1999, including one call late that night, perhaps minutes before he'd died. Looking at the interview with Adriana, the detectives felt the computer story was bunk anyway, and the fact that she'd made no mention of any other conversations that day was a suspicious omission.

Villalobos looked at Heaney and said, "We have to focus on this gal."

The detectives decided that Villalobos would make the first contact. Since Villalobos and Adriana were both Hispanic, the detectives felt she might be more comfortable talking to him rather than Anglo Heaney. It wasn't easy finding her. The phone number listed for her home had been disconnected, and she no longer worked at the same place. The only phone number in the files that worked was an old pager for Adriana. Villalobos dialed the pager several times before Adriana called back.

Their initial conversation on October 4, 2000, was tense. Villalobos told her that he and another detective had been put on the Stahl case and they would like to talk to her about Ken. Villalobos didn't tell her about the calls they'd found in the cell phone records, or that the detectives felt she may be the key to jump-starting the investigation.

At first, Adriana was leery. She said that she didn't trust the police and she seemed suspicious about being contacted again so many months later. But she reluctantly agreed to meet. They set a time for the end of that week, but Adriana called it off, citing personal problems. Her car wasn't working and she didn't have money to fix it. They planned to meet the next week.

Detectives Villalobos and Heaney used the time to re-interview some of the other witnesses, starting with electrician Richard Christopher Anaya, who repeated his story about going to Ken's house late one night only to have him ask whether he knew of anybody who could kill Carolyn.

They also interviewed Tamara Parham, Ken's sister, who gave an even more bleak assessment of the Stahl marriage. "Parham stated that over the years Kenneth became moody and extremely depressed," Villalobos would later recount in a search warrant affidavit. "Parham stated that something was obviously wrong with Kenneth and Carolyn's relationship. Carolyn began gaining a lot of weight and became a compulsive eater. Kenneth was very cruel to Carolyn." After the murders, Parham learned that Carolyn had had $96,000 in credit card debts. Parham also "became aware" that Ken always carried a gun, but that the gun was never loaded.

Then, on October 11, 2000, the detectives spoke by phone with Linda Dubay, sister and confidante to Carolyn. "Dubay stated that Carolyn knew about Kenneth's infidelities," Villalobos reported in an affidavit. She'd even confronted one of Ken's lovers—the woman named Denise whom detectives had interviewed a year earlier—at Ken's medical office in Huntington Beach. In 1996, Carolyn had spoken of divorcing her husband and told her sister she had a safety deposit box that contained "dirt on Ken." Carolyn told her sister to check the box if anything ever happened to her. Dubay thought it was located near Carolyn's workplace in Newport Beach, but the box was never found.

While conducting these interviews, the detectives tried to get Adriana Vasco to sit down for a second interview. It wasn't easy. Villalobos and Heaney had paged her all day Monday and Tuesday, without reaching her. She finally called back October 11 and arranged to meet the investigators that night at the Stanton sheriff's substation on the corner of Beach and Katella boulevards. This was Villalobos's old turf, where he had worked patrol early in his career, one of the toughest neighborhoods in Orange County. He had tangled with a lot of hardened criminals. As the interview progressed and became more intense, Adriana would hold her own against all of them. "A very tough cookie," Villalobos would recall.

Villalobos and Heaney had agreed that Villalobos would take the lead—playing the good cop—on the theory that his gregariousness and shared Hispanic ethnicity would create a bond with Adriana. The steely Heaney would play bad cop. But from the moment Adriana entered the interview room a few minutes before 8 p.m., it was clear from her words and demeanor that she wanted nothing to do with Villalobos—and that she instantly warmed to Heaney, an attitude that would prevail throughout the investigation. The detectives changed gears and Heaney took the lead.

There's laughter between Adriana and Heaney at the beginning of a tape recording of the interview. Then Heaney got down to business, stating the date and time, eliciting Adriana's name and birth date, and explaining that he and Villalobos had been brought in to review the Stahl case anew.

"We don't mean to drag you through a lot of emotional stuff," Heaney told her. "But there are some particular issues we have we would like to talk to you about. So in general terms, I think if Phil agrees, we will just hear what you have to say about your relationship with Ken. And then we'll kind of go from there."

The detective told her that he and Villalobos had reviewed the tape of her interview with detectives Homs and McDonald back in February. Heaney didn't tell her he had found additional phone calls between Adriana and Ken the day of the murders, or that they had spoken to Chris Anaya again about Ken's odd request.

Then, under gentle questioning, she went over the same ground as in the interview eight months earlier: meeting Ken while working at the National Pain Institute, their first date—going out for a drink—in 1992 after he'd been asking her to go out for a long time. She spoke of how they'd shared their personal problems, how he'd treated her for the bruises left by her husband.

"From then on, we kept seeing each other," she said. "We kept going out to parks, to lunches. Sometimes at night he would tell his wife that he was on call and they called him and he used to go and meet me. We used to go to the movies. But, like the last few years, his wife found out."

Heaney asked her to clarify the timing.

"Maybe '96, '97, more close to '96," she said. "And the reason why is . . . she called Greg's parents' house and she found me there. She would press the redialer or the star 69 and she would tell me—"

"Who is Greg?" asked Heaney. He knew the answer, but he wanted to see what Adriana said.

"Greg is my daughter's father."

"So Carolyn, Ken's wife, found that number somehow? So she dialed it?"

"She dialed it and she called there. She even spoke to Greg's mom. And she was very nasty. There was other numbers that Ken had with him that were my friends. So he always wanted to know where I was."

Once, Carolyn had called around to Adriana's friends— Carolyn had apparently found the numbers among Ken's belongings—and first claimed that the friend had won some kind of tickets, but then "kind of blurted out that she was Carolyn Stahl."

Adriana repeated the story of how Ken had called her one night and put Carolyn on the phone, how it was clear they had been fighting—and how surprised Adriana was that Ken could get physical, too.

"He said, 'You know what? I am not this kind of a person, but she's making me do this.' And I said, 'What did you do?' He goes, 'I just pushed her around. I didn't really punch her or anything.' And he goes, he was apologizing to me, maybe because of all the things that I've lived through. . . . And I did speak to her. She did talk to me. And he was on the other line on the phone. And he said, you know— And I told him, 'You know what? We're just friends, and it's OK,' I said."

In the beginning, Carolyn called Adriana to tell her to stop seeing Ken. "And after that she's like, 'Well, I know about you,' and 'I know about you.' And I say, 'You know what? Stop calling.'"

She said that her relationship with Ken went from sexual to platonic in the fall of 1996. "For a while, I wouldn't want him even to, you know, to touch me in that way anymore," she said of Ken. "Because it was just hurting me emotionally."

She would explain that Ken didn't want to cut off the sex.

"He never stopped wanting. He used to bring it up. But I didn't want to," she said.

But, she added, "We know the love that was there. It was something that I will never experience again. He was like my husband, my friend—he was everything to me."

Nor did the communication stop between the two.

"He never, never, never stopped calling me," she said. "He called just about every day wherever I was, and I always told him where I was."

At the same time, she said, she was hurt and angry that Ken wouldn't leave his wife. It was around the time her romantic relationship with Ken ended that she started sleeping with Greg, and she soon became pregnant with their daughter. The pregnancy didn't scare Ken away.

"I noticed that when I was pregnant he would come even more, and especially late at night," she said.

"But Greg was there?" said Heaney.

"Yes."

"Greg was comfortable with Ken?"

"Yes, Greg was comfortable with Ken," she said. "I just don't understand why he will come late at night when he knew we were asleep or we were resting. I was just kind of shocked."

"But he would call?"

"No, he will show up."

Later in the interview, Adriana said that Greg actually was taken aback by Ken's late-night visits.

"I know Greg used to get upset, because he used to come at night, you know, late at night, and he would sit in our room with us," said Adriana. "And I was like, 'Oh, my God, this is not right.' But I don't know really what the motive was of Ken doing that. I never asked."

Listening to this, Detectives Heaney and Villalobos, like detectives Homs and McDonald before them, were intrigued by this three-way arrangement, and continued to wonder what kind of man would put up with that—or what he would do when he got tired of it. Greg was no angel; he had a criminal record for drug and domestic violence arrests.

Adriana explained that she had met Greg in a psychiatric facility where she was staying after trying to commit suicide, and he was being treated for schizophrenia. He had tattoos—a pair of panthers—but no gang past that Adriana knew of. She wasn't sure where he was from—she thought somewhere in the South, like Tennessee. Adriana said that although she would have a relationship with him—and a child by him—she came to see him as a lying, violent, drug-abusing, not-too-bright man.

The restraining order against Greg was due to fights between him and Adriana, at least one of them resulting in his arrest. She said that she had obtained a restraining order against him, though she thought it had expired.

Adriana said that after one fight with Greg, she, too, had been arrested, though she claimed it wasn't her fault.

"I was put in jail for defending myself and because I left Greg with scratches," she said.

"So you scratched Greg?" asked Villalobos. "You got in a fight?"

"To get him off my top," she said. "To get him off from top of me. He was suffocating me."

Despite these problems, she deliberately became pregnant by Greg. She said she did it, in part, because she knew that Ken Stahl wouldn't ever leave his wife and be with her. And still, Ken stayed in the picture and Greg stayed in the picture, with Ken coming by to visit the couple, even when Adriana was pregnant.

"It wasn't a problem for Greg?" asked Heaney of her continued friendship with Ken.

"No," said Adriana matter-of-factly, "because Greg knew how I felt about him."

She said she would later find out one possible reason why Greg didn't have a problem with Ken: During these visits, Ken had slipped money to Greg. "I had no idea," she said. "It was all done behind my back. And I told [Ken]—because he had lied to me. And I said 'I don't want to talk to you.'"

"Let me ask you," interjected Villalobos, "did Ken and Greg—Were they friends? I mean, would they go places?"

"Oh, no—Well, not that I know of."

Heaney resumed the questioning. He knew from the first interview that not only was Greg immersed in this unusual relationship—one, incidentally, that the upstanding people in Ken's family and the medical community would find unbelievable—but he was also surrounded by guns.

"Greg's family, I think I understand they like to go shooting?" asked Heaney. "Is that a pastime or a hobby?"

She said it was a hobby.

"And Greg?"

"Greg doesn't go."

"Never? Who had the hobby? Was it the father, his father?"

"By now it's his mom and his dad. They go every Sunday, shooting."

"Just target shooting?"

"Yeah."

"And Greg never got into that?"

"No."

"OK, did Ken go shooting with Greg's parents?"

"No."

Villalobos asked, "Did he take you to go shoot? Did he teach you how to shoot a gun?"

"Who?" Adriana asked.

"Ken."

"No."

"When you went out—I mean, I'm just asking when you went out on dates to the movies, to dinner or something, did he try to ask if you wanted to go out and shoot a gun or anything like that?"

"No," she said. "He took me to Montana. And he told me that's where he likes to go because of the deers and stuff."

Heaney circled back to Ken.

"Did Greg ever tell you what he thought about Ken? Or what Ken was doing that he thought?"

"He thought he was a nice guy," said Adriana. "A nice man, and that he cared for me a lot. He wouldn't say anything negative, because I wouldn't let anybody talk negative about him."

"Was Greg on drugs when you knew him?"

She said she didn't know it in the beginning, but she discovered he was using methamphetamine—speed. Discovered, but didn't witness it first hand. "I don't know," she said. "I never saw him do anything like that, and I don't remember."

Heaney paused and put on a good-cop face. "You know," he said, "as we talk about all this stuff, you're not in trouble for anything. And you're not going to be in trouble for this."

He told her she wouldn't be in trouble for seeing Greg do drugs and not reporting him.

"That's not our intent here," continued Heaney. "And I know that some of it maybe is hard for you to talk about, but it just exposes more of your life. But whatever we can learn from talking to you will help us know what happened, definitely, to Ken and to Carolyn—and ultimately catch the person who did it. Because whoever did it, you know, is a cold-blooded person and will do it again. And it's sad when you think about somebody who is suicidal, not being able to get help, and here is some cold-blooded person who's willing to take a life as opposed to saying, 'Hey, man, you need help.' That's why we ask you a lot of, maybe, very personal questions, but we are trying to figure out where this is going to go."

Adriana then told the truth. She'd known about Greg's drugs. She'd come to have a pretty good idea how he paid for the drugs—with the money Ken gave him. It was a bizarre and tawdry scene, and one that could cause problems in Ken's life if it ever got out: This respected Orange County doctor helping support the drug habit of his ex-lover's schizophrenic boyfriend.

"Do you think Greg could have been blackmailing him?" asked Heaney.

"I don't—I know that never came to mind. I don't know," stammered Adriana.

"OK, try," said Heaney.

"I— I don't think so. Because Greg has this thing that he plays that he's smart, but he's kind of—I'm sorry to say—kind of dumb."

Villalobos asked, "Towards the end, did Greg ever

show up with anything kind of out of the ordinary? Like something very expensive?"

"No," Adriana said simply.

"Maybe he would show up with nice clothes or, you know, a car?" asked Villalobos.

"No, nothing. Nothing out of the ordinary. Nothing at all."

"No jewelry?"

"No."

What was unusual, she said, was Ken's behavior near the end. Abruptly changing the subject, she said, "Before Ken had his surgery he was suicidal. He would tell me that he just wanted to end it all."

He never told her that he was going in for the bypass operation. It wasn't until he was actually in the hospital that he called to apologize for not being in touch with her lately. "When he called me he could barely talk, so probably it was very recent after the surgery," she said.

She rattled off Ken's problems with his wife—how he'd wanted to get a divorce for years—and with his beloved mother, who had adored Carolyn. "I saw the relationship that they had," she said of Ken and his mother. "He had a lot of respect. I don't know how to describe it, because I saw her come into the office and those minutes that I was in the office, it's like: 'Yes, Mother,' 'Yes, Mother,' 'No, Mother.' I'm like, 'Oh, my God, here we go—*Mommie Dearest*.' And I used to tell him, 'You know what, have you seen the movie *Mommie Dearest*? That is exactly what I got.' "

Heaney now decided to tell Adriana why they really needed to talk to her again, what they had discovered since the last time she'd spoken with detectives.

"We've done a lot in terms of looking at this case and trying to break down the last days and final moments," he said. "We know that you were talking to him on a regular basis, fairly regular basis. And we also know that there were a number of phone calls made to your home number and your cell number on the day—on that Saturday. And in having talked to some other people and looked at some other evidence that we have, it's our opinion that when he talked to you, it was more than just about the computer. It's important for us to know what he said to you. It will help us tremendously to understand what happened and give us direction."

Adriana broke into sobs. "That's the only thing I can remember," she said.

"Adriana," Heaney said, trying to reassure her, "you're not in trouble, and I don't want you to feel guilty about anything. Here's a man who struggled with his depression, a deeply depressed person probably most of his adult life, it sounds like. He had a lot of family support even though he probably felt like he didn't. So there were caring people there. But ultimately he got to a point where we think he felt there was no alternative. And he talked to you. And we know that his relationship with you was much more personal than simply a computer problem. This is something we need to know. You need to share with us what he told you that day."

Villalobos, who had been hovering, added bluntly, "Did he make you promise not to say anything? And you gave your word?"

Adriana didn't answer. Just tears.

"I want you to think about something as you think about what was told to you that day," Heaney said, resuming the good-cop role. "This investigation is affecting a lot of people, not just yourself. We know there's innocent people that are being looked at as suspects. There's personal lives that are being pried into, disruptions in families . . . We're really, not pleading, but we're very, very sincere and very, very in need of you sharing with us."

The detectives, who had promised to try not to drag her through any emotional stuff, were now laying it on thick.

"We just wish you would do it out of the goodness of your heart, for Ken's family, for Carolyn's family, and for your own peace of mind," said Villalobos. "Because if you don't come clean and tell us the truth, this is going to be bugging you for years to come. It is going to be a guilt inside of you that is just going to be tearing you apart— unless you get it off your chest."

He told her, "We can get you some assistance. We can get you some counseling, so you don't feel this guilt. 'Cause it's written all over your face. It is all over your face right now, Adriana, that you knew what he told you was going to happen. But I think he made you promise that you wouldn't say anything. Because it would ruin his life."

Heaney jumped in: "Did you help set this up? Yes or no?"

"No," she said.

"You didn't help arrange to have him and his wife murdered?"

"No."

Heaney turned up the pressure.

"Are you willing to take a polygraph test?"

"Why is there a need for that?" Adriana asked.

"Because I don't think you are being truthful with us, and it will tell us whether you are being truthful," the detective said. "If you are being truthful and the test says you are being truthful, then I'm wrong. But I don't believe you. I don't think Phil believes you."

He asked her, "Do you know who he cared enough about . . . to talk to on that Saturday?"

"His mom?" asked Adriana.

"*You*," he said. "Carolyn called her sister in Michigan and said, 'Ken's taking me out for a surprise. I don't know what it's about. He won't tell me.' She thought that was strange, because that just wasn't normal. So Carolyn calls her sister, and Ken calls *you*."

"Adriana," said Villalobos, turning up his bad-cop act, "who did this? Who killed Ken?"

"I don't know," insisted Adriana.

"What did he say?" shot back Villalobos.

"Just the same thing he always used to tell me."

"What was that?" asked Villalobos.

"He just wanted everything to end."

"What did he say, though?" Villalobos pressed. "What were his words? What were his words?"

Adriana paused. "He didn't use any particular words. He just only said the same thing."

Heaney asked, "And what was 'the same thing'?"

" 'I want to end it all.' "

Over and over they asked her, and she insisted she couldn't remember if he'd said anything more.

She cried for mercy. "I am truthful. I don't remember it. I don't remember it."

"You know you can, you can," said Heaney. "This will lift off your shoulder this burden."

"I don't remember it," she said between sobs.

"This thing that's going to ultimately burden you and hurt you for the rest of your life—you can release it by telling us."

"I don't remember," she cried.

"Let it go."

"I really don't remember."

"Just let it go. Tell us what happened."

"I don't remember. I don't remember what happened. I don't remember."

Heaney asked if she were trying to protect somebody involved in the killing.

"Did you help arrange it?"

"No," she insisted.

"Are you sure? Did you introduce him to someone?" He told her that he had talked to a person who had come forward and was afraid he would be accused of the murders. He didn't tell her that it was Chris Anaya, the electrician.

"Did you introduce him to somebody?"

"No," she said again.

"Did Greg?"

"No," she said, then, "I don't know."

"OK," Heaney said, "you didn't pull the trigger, OK?"

But, he said, she could still be held responsible. If she cooperated, they could help her.

"We could get you legal representation," Heaney said. "And we will sit down and make sure that not only do we learn the truth, but that you're also protected."

"I didn't do anything," Adriana said.

He asked her again: "Would you take a lie detector test?"

"No."

Villalobos asked, "How come, Adriana?"

She didn't answer. She only sniffled.

After a pause, Villalobos asked, "Did Ken give you ten thousand dollars?"

Adriana was indignant. "Would I be homeless right now? Would I be taking the bus for two hours? Come on! No, I wouldn't accept that money."

Heaney asked, "Did you help him in paying somebody? In other words, did you have control over some money for Ken to help pay somebody to do this?"

"No," she said, her voice breaking. "No."

The detectives now laid it out for her in the starkest terms.

"You're withholding information," said Heaney. "You know, when people withhold information, they become suspects in our minds."

"You don't leave us any alternative," said Villalobos.

"You're the closest person to the whole thing," said Heaney. "You are the last person other than his wife to speak with him. And we know that it was set up. We know that it was prearranged. We know that he was suicidal. We know that he was homicidal. You know, he didn't stand a chance of living much longer anyway because of his heart condition. We also know that he wanted everything to go to his son—that if his wife is left alive and he dies, his wife controls everything and the son gets nothing. We know he didn't want that to happen. We know that the only way for his son to get everything was to insure that his wife also died."

Heaney told her that Ken's family needed to understand why this happened—and police needed to see that justice was served.

"We need to find somebody out there who's willing to kill people," he said. "You're holding the key to all that. That burden rests on your shoulders. That burden is with you alone."

"Do the right thing, Adriana," said Villalobos. "Do the right thing. You know what's right. Who did this?"

"I don't know," she said, sobbing. "I don't know."

"Who do you think did it?" Villalobos asked.

"I don't know, I don't know," she sobbed.

"What happened that night?" asked Heaney.

"I don't know what happened."

On and on it went. The more the detectives pressed, the more she denied knowing anything—or remembering anything. If there was a burden on Adriana Vasco's shoulders, this interview wasn't going to lift it. She admitted to nothing incriminating, shed no new light on the case—only tearfully spoke of loving a depressed man in a rotten marriage, and making her own bad choices with men.

Everything the detectives tried—appealing to what they saw as a guilty conscience, offering her reassurance, appealing to her motherly instincts or invoking the pain of the murder victims' relatives—drew little more than denials and sobs. All the interview tricks Villalobos and Heaney had learned in those years dealing with gangbangers and drug dealers weren't working on this petite woman.

"Let's wrap this up tonight," Heaney told her about 10:15 p.m., "'cause it has been a long night and I think you're exhausted. And let's agree to make things better, OK? I'm not sure how that's going to happen, exactly, but we're going to agree to try to work things out. Yes? Yes?"

Through sniffles, Adriana said, "Yes."

They escorted her out of the substation to her car, a white Mazda—the approximate size and color of the car a witness had seen making a U-turn next to the Stahls' car out on Ortega Highway. Before the interview, Detectives Heaney and Villalobos had run a routine criminal check on Adriana and knew that she was driving with a suspended license. There was a warrant out for her arrest. They could have arrested her on the spot.

Instead, they wanted to know where she would go after the interview. They cooked up a ruse: They told her that she was upset and they were worried about her, that if she got into an accident on the way home, they would be held responsible. They told her that they would follow her home, for her safety.

Adriana led them to the same Westminster house where she had been interviewed months earlier by McDonald and Homs, the Stewart family home. The detectives led Adriana inside. She was sobbing, a total wreck. Inside the house, they found Greg Stewart and his mother, Nancy. As

Adriana went in the house, Heaney chatted up Nancy while Villalobos took Greg outside to the street in front of the house.

Greg was, in the detectives' minds, a key part of the investigation—potentially the gunman—and Villalobos was curious what he would see in the man. To his surprise, Greg—the former mental hospital patient with a crime record—was friendly, outgoing, helpful and, unlike Adriana, warmed to Villalobos immediately. Greg asked if there was anything he could do to help the detectives.

Villalobos took a shot.

"Hey, Greg," he said, "if you were me, who would you be looking at in this case?"

For all Villalobos knew, Greg would finger himself. Stranger things had happened.

Instead, Greg said, "Tony."

Nearly one year of investigation by six detectives and this was a name that had never cropped up.

"Tony who?" asked Villalobos.

"Tony," repeated Greg, "Adriana's boyfriend at the apartments."

Not once in the interview had Adriana mentioned him.

Villalobos decided not to push it. Greg seemed a helpful sort. No need to roil things too much just yet.

He bade Greg a good night and got into the car with Heaney.

"Brian," said Villalobos, "we've got to find out who this Tony is."

Chapter Fourteen

Detectives Villalobos and Heaney waited less than twenty-four hours before speaking again to Greg Stewart. This time the interview would be more comprehensive than a chat at the curb. As he had been the night before, Greg was open and helpful, confirming just about everything Adriana had said about the unusual arrangement between him, Adriana and Dr. Kenneth Stahl. Greg said he had in fact lived with Adriana even as she continued seeing Ken, who would stop by day and night, even when Adriana was pregnant with Greg's child. Greg told the detectives he simply accepted that Ken would always be a part of Adriana's life. Greg also acknowledged that Ken would slip him some money when Adriana wasn't looking. The money, between $500 and $2,500, was ostensibly for Adriana to help support herself, and some had gone to groceries and clothing and other expenses. He said he'd spent the rest on drugs.

The issue on which Greg differed from Adriana was the fighting at home. He said he did move out after Adriana's arrest in 1998 for domestic violence—though Greg insisted he was the victim, not her. He portrayed Adriana as much tougher than she appeared.

The detectives weren't as interested in that disparity as they were in something else Greg had said that Adriana hadn't. They asked Greg the same thing they had asked Adriana: Did he know anything about Ken wanting to kill his wife? Unlike Adriana, who said Ken had only spoken about getting out of his marriage in abstract, non-violent terms, Greg said that he and Ken had talked frequently—and directly—about the subject. During Ken's visits, he and Greg spoke about a variety of ways of murdering Carolyn, including shooting her with a sniper rifle, shooting her at close range, forcing her car off a highway in a national forest and poisoning her.

Greg said that as graphic as the discussions had gotten, they were always hypothetical. He strongly denied being involved in the actual murders.

That's when the detectives returned to what Greg had told Villalobos the night before about Adriana's "new boyfriend," whom he'd described as a light-skinned Hispanic man, about 5-foot-8, 160 pounds, who lived in the same Anaheim apartment complex where Adriana was living at the time of the murders.

Greg only knew the boyfriend's first name, Tony, but he did know that Tony was jealous and possessive of Adriana.

And he liked guns.

Chapter Fifteen

"Hello," said Detective Brian Heaney, sticking his head out his car window. "How are you doing?"

Adriana Vasco was walking through the parking lot of Hoag Memorial Hospital in Newport Beach. Wearing her clinic uniform, she was getting off her job as a medical assistant. It was the evening of Tuesday, October 17, 2000, six days after Adriana's interview at the Stanton substation. The detectives had waited in their car until she came out.

"I know you're sick and tired of us," Heaney told her, "but could we just have a minute of your time?"

"OK," said Adriana warily.

"A lot of things are coming together in a hurry for us. We want to believe you. We really do," said Heaney, and then he made his pitch: "Up, about a mile up the road, is a gentleman named Paul."

Adriana uttered an "Uh-huh."

"He does—He's not working with us on this case, but all he needs to do is talk to you," said Heaney. "And what he'll do is, you'll sit down and you will help him write the questions. This is the way it works. I want you to understand, he would simply talk to you about when you were born and where you grew up and those kinds of things. And he would ask you some questions about what we're interested in. You would actually sit down and talk to him. We won't be present."

The detective told her that when they were done, Paul would "just run through it" with Adriana, and this would all "help us when we go and talk to the DA about who's being truthful with us."

"OK," Adriana said.

Heaney told her all this would happen "just up the road, right up here off Newport. . . . We can go up there and be done within an hour, OK? I know you have car problems and other things, but there's nothing more important right now than convincing us that you're being truthful. We're here now, let's run up there. Why don't you just get in the car? We'll just run up there and do it with Paul, let you meet Paul, talk to him about it and see what you think, all right?"

After some more persuading, Adriana finally said, "Let me get a jacket."

She got into the detectives' car, sitting in the front seat with Detective Phil Villalobos, with Heaney in the back seat. They asked her if she wanted the heater on. She said she did, then added, "Somehow I knew you guys were gonna come."

After learning about Tony, the detectives felt they had to squeeze Adriana even more tightly than before. They were convinced she was more deeply involved in the murders of Ken and Carolyn than she was admitting—and that she was withholding critical information. They were starting to feel that these killings were not a murder/suicide-for-hire, but simply a murder plot gone awry. Ken had spoken of killing his wife, but not of killing himself in the process. What could have gone wrong?

Adriana might know and wasn't saying. She had already failed to say anything about Tony. What more could she be holding back? Other detectives were out looking for the boyfriend, and Heaney and Villalobos worried that Adriana might try to warn him. The boyfriend could flee—and possibly take Adriana with him. Or he could do something violent.

As they were driving with Adriana, Heaney told her that the upcoming session with this gentleman Paul was "going to be pretty interesting," that Paul is a "low-key guy," that he's "impartial" and "I think that will benefit you."

"Why are you guys pressuring me so much?" Adriana asked.

"I'll tell you, the reason is simple," said Heaney.

"Because I was the last person he called?" she asked, referring to Ken.

"No," said Heaney, "we think we are real close to solving this, and things are gonna start happening here real soon."

While secretly tape-recording their conversation in the car, they asked her if she wanted a soda, coffee, cigarettes or music on the stereo. Her reply wasn't audible.

Heaney called Paul and told him they were about fifteen minutes away.

Adriana asked Heaney what kind of questions she would be asked.

"Well, I don't know," the detective said.

Adriana started talking about Ken, and how he would share some things with her, but not everything. Heaney changed the subject, asking Adriana what was wrong with her car. She said the transmission was broken and the car wouldn't go in reverse.

"And I'm PMSing, too," she said.

"Uh-oh," said Heaney.

"Doesn't make it any better," said Adriana.

Heaney asked her again if she wanted anything: a soda, coffee or hamburger. She declined. As they continued to drive through Costa Mesa, Heaney tried to make small talk. He asked her about how she'd gotten her job in the medical profession, whether she'd had to go to school for it, what kind of retirement plan she had and whether she went to the swap meet.

A few minutes later, they arrived at their destination. That place "up there" that Heaney had spoken of was the Costa Mesa Police Department. The low-key guy named Paul was Officer Paul Beckman. His job was to administer a voice stress analysis—a test for signs that people are lying.

"Did they kind of explain to you what my role is?"

Paul Beckman was sitting across from Adriana Vasco in a large interview room.

"Yeah," said Adriana. "You're gonna help me write down some questions."

"Right," said Beckman. "Right."

This man assigned to see whether Adriana was telling the truth was fudging a little. Beckman told her that his "purpose" was "to get you to pass," and that once they "get this thing going, you'll be on your way."

In fact, she was to be hooked up to a machine to evaluate the stress in her voice. Beckman wasn't going to try to get her to pass or fail; he was just there to administer the test and analyze the results. As for whether Adriana would soon be on her way—whether she would have another day of freedom would depend on how she fared on that test.

An arrest warrant was still out for Adriana on the traffic

citations and suspended license. Police could lock her up at any moment.

Before the test began, Adriana called the home of Nancy and James Stewart. Her son came on the line.

"Hi, Mijo," she said. "I love you." Then she told him, "I have to go."

Beckman asked Adriana a series of questions she had been asked many times before, about the day of the murders, the phone conversations with Ken, how Ken was getting her computer fixed. He also briefly went through her relationship with Ken, the problems in Ken's marriage, Ken's suicidal thoughts, whether there were any hard feelings between Ken and Greg Stewart. It was all material she had covered and re-covered in the previous interviews, and Beckman didn't press too hard. He asked her whether she had anything to do with the murders, and, crying, she again said no.

Then, she took the voice test. He clipped a microphone to her shirt, explaining that the microphone was hooked up to a laptop computer with special software that analyzes her voice for stress and helps investigators determine whether or not she was telling the truth to yes-and-no questions. "It's been tested quite rigorously over the years, kind of state-of-the-art stuff," he said. "It definitely should help me to be able to convince the investigators that you've been truthful. So I have all the confidence in that."

He asked her to answer all of the questions truthfully, except two: When he asked her if the light-colored wall in the room was black, he wanted her to answer yes. And when he asked her if she had ever driven over the speed limit, he wanted the repeat traffic offender to answer no.

"All righty," he said. "Is your name Adriana?"

"Yes."

"Is the color of the wall black?"

"Yes."

"Is today Tuesday?"

"Yes."

"Did you know someone was going to kill Ken or Carolyn?"

"No."

"Is this the month of October?"

"Yes."

"Did you arrange for someone to kill Ken or Carolyn?"

"No."

"Are we in the city of Costa Mesa?"

"Yes."

"Have you ever gone over the speed limit?"

"No."

"Am I wearing a watch?"

"Yes."

"OK, do you suspect someone of killing Ken or Carolyn?"

"No."

"Are you wearing tennis shoes?"

"Yes."

"Did you know someone was going to kill Ken or Carolyn?"

"No."

"Are you sitting down?"

"Yes."

"Did you arrange for someone to kill Ken or Carolyn?"

"No."

"Are we in the state of California?"

"Yes."

That final answer ended the first part of the test. He then led her through the questions again. He told her that the second round of questioning showed the truthful people to be very truthful and the deceptive people to be obviously deceptive. When she went through the questions again, he made a printout of her voice stress results, little boxes with lines that form shapes.

He explained to her that the shapes that looked like Christmas trees denoted truth in the voice; those that didn't suggested lying.

Then he gave her the bad news.

Christmas wasn't coming early.

"I have a little concern with question number four," he said.

The test showed lots of stress in the voice when she answered.

The question was: Did you know someone was going to kill Ken or Carolyn?

"We're not going away. This case is going to get solved."

It was a re-run from five days earlier. Detective Brian Heaney was hammering Adriana with questions. Detective Villalobos would join in. Tears flowed down Adriana's face. She sat in another room at the Costa Mesa Police Station. By now it was about 9 p.m.

"You need to get rid of what you know," Heaney told Adriana. "Share that with us now, and that'll be the first day of the rest of your life right here and now. But we're not going to disappear or go away and we know that you have information."

Over and over again, they pounded her with questions. The machine had said she'd lied. Their gut told them she was lying. They even told her that if she wasn't comfortable telling them what Ken had said about his wife on the day of the murders, then she could write it down.

Adriana wrote: "I want her gone."

It was maddening for the detectives.

"What did 'gone' mean to him?" asked Heaney.

"Just to not have her there," said Adriana, sniffling.

"What does it mean to not have her there? To have her at her mom's house?"

"No."

"To have her dead? Yes or no?"

"Before I answer—"

"It's real simple," said Heaney.

"OK, but before I answer, can I say something?"

"Why don't you just say yes or no? Did he want his wife dead? Yes or no?"

"Yes," Adriana said.

Finally, an admission.

"Yes?"

"Yes," she said again, and burst into sobs.

It was the first crack in her story. Up till now, all she'd said was that Ken had wanted Carolyn out of his life, but didn't want a divorce. Now, they had the seeds of a murder plot.

But they needed more.

With Heaney doing most of the questioning, they asked if Ken had discussed this with Greg. She said no. They asked her if she was sure. Then she cracked again.

"I didn't believe any," she said. "I didn't believe any. I didn't believe him. I didn't think he could be that way."

Then she backpedaled. She said she didn't know if he'd talked to anybody about carrying out this thought.

"We've heard this. This is a broken record," Heaney said, disgusted.

Adriana started to say something, then Heaney hit her with a surprise question.

"How about Tony?" he asked, gambling that Greg had not told her about revealing Tony-the-jealous-boyfriend. "Did he ask Tony to kill her?"

Adriana turned white. Then she cried and said, "I don't know."

She quickly added, "I don't know who Tony is," but it was too late. Heaney seized on her admission.

"You want to go back on the machine?" he said. "Do you want to go back on the machine? Do you think we're coming in here with half a load?"

He asked her, "Did you talk to Tony about this? Did he ask Tony?"

"I don't know," she said.

"Where's Tony now?"

"I don't know, I don't know who—I don't know, I don't know."

"When was the last time you saw Tony?"

"I don't—"

"I'm going to get Paul, OK? We're going to start on this machine again and see if you want to try to tell us that you don't know Tony, you don't know where Tony is."

"I have to go to the restroom," Adriana said. "Please tell somebody."

Heaney said OK, she could go. "But," "he warned her, "we're going to talk about Tony when you get back."

A matron took her to the restroom. The officers made sure that Adriana left her purse in the room. She would have to come back to get that.

When she did return, she said, "I don't want to talk anymore," and burst into tears.

"OK, where's Tony right now?" asked Heaney, ignoring her sobs.

"I don't know," said Adriana.

"When was the last time you saw him?"

"I don't know. It's been a long time."

"Give us an idea: Ten years ago? Ten days ago?"

"No."

"Maybe in between somewhere?"

"It's a long time. I can't remember."

"It would help if you could remember."

"I don't want to talk anymore. Please, I'm tired."

"OK, what do you want to do?"

"I want to go to my kids."

Heaney continued to ask her about Tony. She told him she didn't know his real name, that he was in his early 20s, that he sometimes gave her drugs and that they didn't live together.

"Let me ask you this—Did Tony kill Ken?" asked Heaney.

"I don't know," Adriana answered.

Not a denial.

But not a confirmation.

"Did Tony kill Carol?"

"I don't know."

"Did Ken give Tony money to kill Carolyn?"

"I don't know."

He asked her again.

"I don't know, I don't know, I don't know," she repeated, her voice cracking.

Heaney was on a roll. The pieces were falling together. He just had to get Adriana to admit it.

"Did Ken know Tony? Did he meet him—Heaney paused and had a new thought. "Did Ken meet Tony through you?"

"No," said Adriana. "He didn't, never met him." Then she backpedaled again. "I don't know."

"You're absolutely positive?" said Heaney. "You can say for certain right here, that Ken never met Tony?"

"I don't—"

"So, the question is this: Can you say [with] one hundred percent certainty that Ken never met Tony? Absolutely never happened? Swear on it?"

"Not that I can remember. Not that I know."

Then she pleaded with the detective, "Brian, please, I want to go home." She wanted to lie down.

But she wouldn't leave. Heaney wanted her to answer some questions about Tony—when they'd met, how long they were together, whether he was a drug dealer. Finally, Adriana refused to answer anymore. "I'm tired," she said.

Heaney had had it. She wasn't giving the 100 percent cooperation that the detectives wanted.

"Here's where we're at right now," said Heaney. "And it's obvious you cannot tell us anything anymore. You want the shocker? Do you want the shocker?"

"What's the shocker?" Adriana asked.

"That you're gonna have to go to jail tonight."

She burst into tears, pleading, "Oh, please, no. Please, no. No, please. No, no."

"This case is getting solved," Heaney told her. "We can try to dance around all the reality of it, but this case is getting solved."

"But please don't," she said through tears, insisting she wouldn't run away, that she would just be going home. "I give you my word."

"Tell us the truth," said Heaney. "That would be good enough."

Heaney asked her more questions, but she didn't give any new information.

Then she had an idea, one that had never struck her before.

"What about my rights and stuff?" she asked.

Villalobos told her they could get her an attorney. But then Heaney repeated that they were taking her to jail. "You've chosen to bullshit us," he said. "You want advisement of your rights?"

Adriana said she did.

Heaney said that, sure, they could read her her rights, and then, "You're just going to jail. We're done talking."

She wanted them to do it anyway.

Villalobos read Adriana her Miranda rights—her

rights to remain silent, that anything she said could be used against her, to have an attorney during questioning, to have an attorney appointed if she couldn't afford one.

She said she understood her rights.

Then Villalobos said, "OK, can we talk about what happened?"

"Well, can I talk to an attorney first?" asked Adriana.

"Yeah, that's your choice," said Heaney.

"That's your choice," echoed Villalobos.

Adriana started to say something. "I mean . . ."

Then Heaney cut her off, saying, "Listen to me. Listen to me." He said that if she got an attorney, "Then we're done and we leave."

"And what happens to me?" asked Adriana.

"You go to jail."

She kept on answering questions, late into the night. At one point, she said she worried that if she talked, something could happen to her children. Heaney said that Adriana could sit down and talk to an attorney the next day, and "We'll all sit down and we'll talk about how we can protect you and your children." He said she could try to get an attorney now, but "it's so late that an attorney may or may not visit you."

No attorney came. The questioning continued. The detectives were pushing the envelope. Every time the question of an attorney came up, they were risking a Miranda violation. A judge could throw out everything Adriana said. A jury might never hear it. And yet the detectives pressed on. She was all they had. They had nothing to lose.

And so, in bits and pieces, in fractured order, in between crying spells, Adriana yielded key facts, the most important of which was that Tony and Ken had in fact known each other—and had both been pressuring her to do something she didn't want to do.

"I want[ed] to be left alone," she said. "I don't want it

anymore, to talk to Ken anymore. I don't want to talk to Tony anymore. I just wanted to be left alone with my kids."

But what were Tony and Ken pressuring her to do? Commit murder?

She wouldn't say, no matter how many times she was asked.

That was it. No more details about how Tony and Ken had met or what they'd talked about.

After another couple rounds of questioning, it was clear that the detectives could question her all night and she wasn't giving up any more information. From then on, she mostly asked for help, told them she was scared.

They got her some food. They let her call Nancy and James Stewart.

"I'm being detained," she told the Stewarts, then tried to devise some makeshift arrangements for the children's care. "I love you," she added. "Give the kids a kiss for me, OK?"

It was now about 10:30 p.m. The detectives brought in their supervisor, Sergeant Bob Blackburn, and Adriana was told that she was going to be put in jail on traffic warrants in Los Angeles and Orange County. It was a tough call. The detectives thought they could still get something out of her. But they also felt that now that they'd played their hand on Tony, she could get to him before they could.

Heaney cuffed Adriana's hands behind her back and told her, "Walk straight down the hall."

Chapter Sixteen

One name: Tony.

It might not even be his real name. But it was the best lead in the eleven months since Adriana Vasco's phone number had been found on Ken Stahl's pager the day after the murders. With Adriana now confirming that this Tony had known Ken—that they'd done something together and she hadn't wanted to be a part of it—Detectives Brian Heaney and Phil Villalobos set out to find him.

The search took them into Adriana's past—to the late 1990s when she'd worked in the front office of an ob-gyn clinic at Garden Grove Hospital. Adriana would greet patients, take phone calls, pull files, call for insurance authorizations and schedule appointments. Although she had told detectives that virtually nobody outside her immediate family knew about her relationship with the married Dr. Kenneth Stahl, the detectives would find that, on the contrary, Adriana had spoken at length about her tangled personal life to friends, co-workers and subsequent lovers.

"She didn't like Dr. Stahl's wife," recalled her friend and hospital co-worker Nicole Nguyen. "She said that Dr. Stahl would complain that his wife would not give him a divorce." Adriana had shared Ken's low opinion of Carolyn. "She called her a witch," said Nicole.

Adriana and Ken had been so open about their relationship that Ken frequently called Adriana at work and stopped by several times to take her out to lunch. Adriana had introduced him to Nicole there. During these visits, Ken would leave money for Adriana; once he gave her $800, according to Nicole. He also helped her make a household budget so she wouldn't squander the money. Adriana was so bad with finances that she would go to the mall and buy Beanie Babies and other presents for her children, then not have enough money left over for rent or car registration. She was so late with her automobile fees that her car would get impounded—then she'd have to scrape up more money to retrieve it from the lot.

Once, another friend and co-worker, office manager Susana Bivian, drove Adriana to the impound lot to get her car back. Adriana was open about her affair, as she'd been with Nicole. "At the very beginning, when she had just started for us, she had mentioned to me that she was seeing this doctor, Dr. Stahl," recalled Susana. "She just had mentioned to me that she had been seeing him for about eight years and that he was married and that he would help her financially whenever she needed some money. He was always there for her, kind of like a guardian angel that would help her when she needed, you know, some support, or kind of like a father figure, but at the same time he would help her."

Susana had also met Ken. "It was there at the office, and he had come to pick her up to take her out to lunch," she said. "I was just introduced to him and that is about it." When she'd returned from lunch, Adriana had said that Ken had given her $500.

Adriana told her all about Ken's marital woes, how he wanted to get out of his rocky marriage, but feared that a divorce would cost him too much money and ruin his reputation. In conversations that would have made Carolyn cringe, Adriana told her co-workers how Ken no longer was attracted to his wife. "I guess they had just, you know, grown apart," recalled Susana. "She wasn't an attractive woman, and she had gained a lot of weight."

And Adriana told her co-workers something she had failed to mention to the detectives: that she had once arranged a meeting with Carolyn. "Adriana showed up, but I guess when she got to the restaurant where they were going to meet, [Carolyn] just drove off when she took a look at Adriana."

It was in the summer of 1999 that Adriana first spoke at work of a new man in her life. She said his name was Tony and he did maintenance work around her apartment complex. At the time she was "still kind of seeing Ashley's father"—that is, Greg Stewart—but Tony had excited Adriana, and the relationship soon became sexual.

Susana met Tony three times, the first when she had lunch at Adriana's apartment and "he showed up to fix a leak or something that she had in her sink." She saw him again after she'd locked her keys in her car and Adriana called him to help get the door open. Then one last time when the two of them went out for the evening and Adriana dropped off her children with Susana to babysit.

Detectives Heaney and Villalobos also found that Greg Stewart wasn't the only member of his family to know about Adriana's lovers.

The Stewarts, the detectives found, had a complicated relationship with Adriana: they were the mother and father of her ex-lover Greg, but they were also the grandparents of Ashley, whom they adored. They would also, over the years, become close to Adriana—though not close enough to bail her out of jail.

In an interview on Wednesday, October 18, 2000, the day after she was arrested, the Stewarts said they'd been aware of Adriana's relationship with Ken Stahl while she still lived with their son, though they didn't know much about it. Once, Nancy Stewart was unwittingly drawn into the fray when she received a call at home in the late 1990s.

"I believe it was early in the morning one morning. I don't know when exactly. The phone rang and I answered it. And there was an irate woman screaming, 'Why are you calling my husband? Why are you calling Dr. Stahl?'" recalled Nancy. "I didn't know any Dr. Stahl. At that point in time I only knew Ken as Ken. And I said, "'I'm sorry. I don't know who you are talking about. Maybe it was a wrong number dialed to your house or something'. I said, 'There is [sic] other people at this house. I didn't call your husband.' And she hung up." Only later would Nancy find out that the irate caller was in fact Carolyn Stahl, who had apparently found the Stewarts' number in Ken's belongings or pressed star 69 to dial back the number from the last incoming call.

The Stewarts first met Tony in the late summer or fall of 1999, when they came by Adriana's apartment. Tony was sitting on the sofa watching television. They remembered him as being a white male, in his early 20s, with a thin build and brown hair. Adriana introduced him, giving only his first name.

"He was very unfriendly," James Stewart recalled. "And I went to shake hands with him one time and he turned around and walked away, that kind of thing. Very unpleasant person in my opinion, very short. He also had like a real ghetto demeanor kind of thing. I thought he was kind of a sleazeball."

Tony also had a habit of letting himself into Adriana's apartment without knocking. "It was probably the second time I met him," James said. "I thought that was kind of funny for him to come slamming in kind of like he owned the place, but I didn't see where he came from."

It was because James Stewart had such a low opinion of Tony that the events of the summer or fall of 1999 were so disturbing. Adriana had picked up James at the airport after he returned from a business trip. On the drive home to Westminster, he asked her to stop by a gun shop, Turner's Outdoorsman on Brookhurst Street in Fountain Valley. James, a gun enthusiast who shot skeet and hunted deer and rabbit, owned eleven pistols, seven shotguns and four rifles, all locked in a gun safe at home. He had won another shotgun in a raffle and wanted to pick it up from Turner's.

There was paperwork to be filled out in the store, and while they were there, Adriana was looking at the guns. She pointed to one of them. "She said that she had bought a gun like that for Tony," recalled James, "at which point I came unglued. We had an argument." He told her to never buy a gun for somebody else, "much less somebody I thought was a bad guy."

The detectives asked James what kind of gun it was. James, who obviously knew his firearms, said it was a "fairly large revolver," probably stainless steel. He thought it might have been a Taurus.

He was describing, exactly, one of the two possible murder weapons.

After the argument in the gun shop, James said, "She pretty much clammed up, because I get a little hysterical about people doing stupid things."

James said that one day, about two months later, he was reading a newspaper account about the murders of Ken and Carolyn Stahl. He realized that this was the same Ken Stahl with whom Adriana had had the love affair and subsequent platonic friendship. One detail from the story caught his eye—how no shell casings were found at the crime scene. As a gun enthusiast, he knew that revolvers didn't eject casings.

He confronted Adriana about the Taurus revolver she had said she'd bought for Tony. Adriana told him that she had returned it.

Something else that Adriana had said took on new meaning after the Stewarts heard about the murders. Nancy Stewart recalled that just a few days before the murders—it may have been the Thursday or Friday before the Saturday attacks—Adriana called Nancy at home from her apartment. Adriana said she had been "all stressed out" lately and, to unwind, she'd taken a drive to a beautiful wilderness area in south Orange County. Adriana couldn't recall the name of the road, but said it was a long, pretty highway. Nancy was familiar with the area around San Juan Capistrano. She asked Adriana if she had driven out to Ortega Highway.

Adriana said yes.

A year after the murders, the pieces were falling into place. The detectives could complete the circle, linking Ken to Adriana, Adriana to Tony, and Tony to Ken. One call to Turner's Outdoorsman and they might be able to link a murder weapon to Adriana. But the big question was still: Where was Tony?

The Stewarts said that he'd disappeared from Adriana's life in the months after the murders, but they had a good idea where to start looking. Just a week before the detectives spoke to the Stewarts, Adriana—who was living with the Stewarts—warned Nancy that the upcoming phone bill had some long-distance charges she'd rung up. Nancy was known to get miffed over big phone charges. Nancy asked Adriana which calls were hers.

Adriana said the calls had gone to North Carolina.

After speaking with the Stewarts, Detectives Heaney and Villalobos scrambled to follow up on the leads about Tony and the gun. They had the makings of a murder case against Adriana, and they wanted to get as much of it as they could wrapped up while she was still safely tucked away in jail. Assuming nobody bailed her out—and for now, the Stewarts, the only people in Adriana's life with any money, seemed wary of getting any more involved— the traffic violations would keep Adriana confined until December 23. The holidays were approaching, which meant limited manpower at the sheriff's department. It would be a stretch of resources to investigate what was now shaping up to be a case involving both California and North Carolina. In addition to that, someone would have to keep watch 24/7 on Adriana lest she flee to Mexico, where she had relatives, or somewhere else.

What looked to be the easiest lead to follow was the potential gun purchase at Turner's Outdoorsman. Detailed records are kept on handgun purchases, with buyers required to show photo identification. According to Turner's records, Adriana Vasco had in fact come into the store—on September 26, 1999. But she didn't get a revolver. Instead, she bought a serious piece of weaponry called a KBI Sporter, the standard issue semi-automatic rifle for Warsaw Pact soldiers—a gun almost as big as Adriana. It is a copy of the better-known AK-47 with a ten-round detachable ammunition magazine. The rifle was one step down from a machine gun; bullets could be fired as fast as the shooter pulled the trigger.

Adriana provided salesman Flynn Watton with her address, date of birth and driver's license number. Watton also made a photocopy of Adriana's license; the copy clearly showed her smiling face. Adriana paid for the gun in cash, $359.98 plus tax of $27.90 for a total of $387.88.

But as it turned out, she never actually took the gun out of the store. There is a waiting period for firearms to allow for a criminal background check, and three days later she canceled the purchase, probably because her arrest on domestic violence charges had been discovered, or she feared that it would be. Either way, she got her money back, minus a $30 processing fee.

Still, the transaction raised profound questions about Adriana's credibility. She had told detectives nothing of buying an assault rifle one month before the murders; in fact, she'd indicated that she knew very little about guns. So why was she in Turner's picking up a Russian Army rifle, unless it were for somebody else, like Tony?

The search for Tony's identity took the detectives to a public storage facility on La Palma Avenue in Anaheim, where, according to the Stewarts, Adriana kept some of her belongings. Cathy Barrial, property manager of the facility, confirmed that Adriana Vasco was renting storage unit B-110, but said a search warrant was necessary to see inside. The next day, armed with the warrant, Heaney looked inside unit B-110 and found utility bills, an address book and a vehicle title. He also found photos, newspaper clippings and rental receipts dating back to 1994 "connecting Vasco to Kenneth Stahl," according to a search warrant affidavit.

More interesting were phone bills, one showing two calls made from Adriana's cell phone to another 714 area code number on the night of the murders—one at 7:33 p.m. and the other at 9:42 p.m., shortly before and after the shootings. There also were several calls made from her phone to a number with a 252 area code: Greenville, North Carolina. Those calls were placed just days after Adriana was first contacted by Detective Villalobos.

And finally, there was the best find of all: photographs of a smiling Adriana embracing a dark-haired man with a goatee whom the detectives had never seen before.

Could this be the face of the man who'd killed Kenneth and Carolyn Stahl?

Chapter Seventeen

It was a police report that under other circumstances would have been forgotten. In October 1999, Adriana Vasco was pulled over and arrested by the California Highway Patrol on suspicion of drunken driving.

What made this interesting was that the officer's report made note of a passenger in her car.

The man's name was Tony.

Tony Satton.

When Detectives Phil Villalobos and Brian Heaney came across the CHP report, they hoped they now had a last name to go with the Tony mentioned by other witnesses. They ran a check of Anaheim police records and scored a direct hit: From September 14, 1999, to December 2, 1999, Tony Satton had lived at 650 W. Broadway, Unit 201—the Avanti Apartments, the same complex where Adriana Vasco was living.

A phone call to the apartment managers, American Landlord, found that Tony Satton had filled out an employment application on September 3, 1999, to work as a maintenance man. "I have plumbing experience and light elec.," Satton wrote. He provided two personal references, both people living in Anaheim, and listed as his nearest relative an Ada Smith of Wilson, North Carolina. As a previous address, he listed a number on Forbes Street in Greenville, North Carolina.

The interviewer was impressed. "Very nice, very eager to work, has experience, liked him," she wrote on the application. Under the sections for "neatness" and "personality," she wrote "Good." Under "ability," she wrote, "Has a lot." Tony Satton was hired.

The date of birth—April 20, 1970—and Social Security number on the application matched those found in police files for Tony Satton. There also was a photocopy of a California Identification Card: the picture was that of a dark-haired man who looked very much like the person standing next to Adriana in the photos found in her storage unit.

A second team of detectives, Brian Sutton and Dan Stack, went to the Avanti Apartments on October 25, 2000. There, they interviewed the complex's manager, Deborah Burns, who remembered Tony well. She said he was a bad man who liked guns.

Meanwhile, two other apartment residents, Raymond Ruiz and his brother Raul "Sean" Ruiz, went to the Orange County sheriff's headquarters in Santa Ana for questioning by Heaney and Villalobos. Raymond had hung out with Tony, and admitted to getting marijuana from him; his brother Sean had lived with Tony for a time in a spare bedroom, according to the detectives.

Sean said Tony was from the East Coast. He described him as a crack cocaine–using "sissy boy, like a white nigger." Tony, according to Sean, was into White Power, but listened to rap music. Tony was close to Adriana—and the two of them both used drugs. Sean said he, too, had taken drugs with them. In November, a teenage runaway girl, from Utah or Colorado, moved in with Tony and Sean.

Tony also had a thing for guns. He already owned a shotgun and a handgun, but he wanted more. Sean recalled accompanying Tony and Adriana on a gun-buying trip to a store in Garden Grove. Tony wanted a rifle, but for some reason couldn't get one from the store. Tony then asked Sean to get him a "throw-away gun" that he said he needed for his protection. Sean tried to acquire the gun from a man he identified as his Uncle Cooch, but couldn't get it.

Then, in early November 1999—about two weeks before the Stahls' murders—Tony was showing off a new firearm. Raymond told the detectives that he was inside Adriana's apartment with her when Tony entered.

"Look what I got, woman," Tony said, and pulled out a Western-type revolver and let Raymond hold it. It was a silver color with a long barrel. Heaney and Villalobos knew that this was the same kind of gun that could have been the murder weapon, and the same kind of gun that Adriana had pointed out to James Stewart in the Turner's Outdoorsman.

Then, on the night of the murders, Raymond went to a quinceanera party, a traditional Latin celebration for a girl's 15th birthday. This party was for a friend's sister. Raymond left about 6 or 7 p.m. with his mother, aunt and cousin. On his way out, he saw Adriana and Tony leaving Adriana's apartment. They were dressed in black, with Tony wearing a long trench coat, black shirt and black pants, and Adriana in similar dark clothing and possibly gloves. He thought they looked like ninjas.

Sean also saw them leave. He told Heaney and Villalobos that Tony had told him something to the effect that he was going on a mission or that he had something to take care of, Sean couldn't remember the exact words.

Raymond stayed at the party until midnight and never saw Adriana there, even though she had been invited. He didn't see Tony that night either.

Sean, however, did see Tony. Sean had skipped the party and instead walked to the nearby Five Points Liquor Store, returned to his unit, and drank the evening away with the runaway girl. At some point, Tony called the apartment, possibly in response to a page from Sean—Sean couldn't be sure.

"Is everything cool?" he asked Sean. "We'll be home soon."

About an hour-and-a-half later, Tony came home, sometime between 9 and 11 p.m.

Adriana wasn't with him. When Tony saw Sean, he flipped something to him.

It was a shell casing from a bullet.

"There's your souvenir," he told Sean. He also said that the mission had been completed—and that whatever it was he did, he had received about $30,000 in cash.

A couple of days after the murders, Raymond saw Tony and Adriana at the apartments. They offered him drugs and he accepted, according to an affidavit; it didn't say what kind of drugs. Raymond walked into Adriana's apartment, did the drugs and was confronted by Adriana and Tony.

They wanted to know what he knew, what he was talking about and to whom he had been talking. Raymond said Tony had stood behind him with his hand behind his back and he thought he'd heard a "click." Scared, Raymond ran out of the apartment.

After the murders, Raymond said, Tony had Adriana's son, Mark, carry some bullets from his apartment to

Adriana's. Adriana and Tony got into a big fight over that. Adriana was mad because Mark had become scared carrying the bullets.

Later, Tony approached Sean and asked him to hide a revolver. He agreed, secreting the gun—wrapped in plastic—in bushes at the complex. But an hour later, Sean had second thoughts and gave the gun back to Tony. Sean wasn't certain what Tony had done with it after that, but thought he may have tossed it in the ocean.

A week after Heaney and Villalobos interviewed the Ruiz brothers, Heaney tracked down two more witnesses linked to Tony and the Avanti Apartments. The first was Ryan Casas, whose mother lived in the complex. Talking to Heaney in the detective's car in the parking lot of a Carl's Jr. on the corner of Harbor and Broadway in Anaheim, Ryan said that between Halloween 1999 and the day of the murders Tony had approached him asking to obtain a gun for him "stat."

Ryan told Tony he might know of somebody who could help him: his friend Oscar.

Ryan led Heaney to Oscar, who spoke to the detective in his police car in front of Oscar's apartment in Anaheim. Oscar confirmed that he had in fact tracked down a gun for Ryan, and Ryan had brought him to Tony Satton's unit at the Avanti complex.

Oscar offered to sell Tony the gun for $225. Tony talked him down to $200.

Two weeks before the murders of Kenneth and Carolyn Stahl, Tony had in his possession a long-barreled .357-caliber handgun with soft grips.

In the course of one intensely productive week, Detectives Heaney and Villalobos gathered evidence and witnesses linking Adriana to a lowlife named Tony

Satton—and Tony Satton to the kind of gun that had killed the Stahls. The detectives also could produce witnesses who had seen Adriana and Tony leaving the apartment the night of the murders with plenty of time to kill the couple, then Tony returning within that same window of murderous opportunity.

All they needed was Tony.

They had a name, Social Security number and photo of Tony Satton—but still no Tony. None of the witnesses knew where to find him, or if they did know, they weren't saying. A computer search turned up no criminal record for a Tony Satton; in all likelihood it was an alias.

The final push to find Tony Satton shifted to the southeast. Adriana's phone records showed she had called a number in Greenville, North Carolina, shortly after she was contacted by Villalobos in October 2000. That was the same town that Tony had listed on his employment application for the apartments.

The detectives sent the driver's license photo and description of Tony Satton to the Pitt County Sheriff's Department in hopes that somebody there recognized him. The photo landed on the desk of Detective Corporal David Ricky Best, who showed the photo around the department.

In early November 2000, Pitt County Sheriff's Sergeant Ron Smith reviewed his paperwork. Staring up at him was the face of the Weasel.

Chapter Eighteen

"Tony Satton" was in fact an alias. His given name was Dennis Earl Godley, the son of Edward and Brenda Godley, long divorced, both still living in North Carolina.

As it turned out, Detectives Heaney and Villalobos had had their suspect's last name for days and didn't even know it. Several witnesses at the Avanti Apartments told them that the word "Godley" was tattooed across his belly. They didn't think it was his surname; they had thought it was the name of his old gang.

In a phone call to Ron Smith on November 13, 2000, Heaney and Villalobos got the lowdown on Godley. His rap sheet was long, with arrests in North Carolina and Virginia dating back to 1987, when Godley was still a teenager. The rap sheet read:

Juvenile Record

1. **Date:** December 18, 1987 (age 17).
Agency: Pitt County, North Carolina, Sheriff's Department

Offenses: Breaking and entering, larceny, possession of marijuana with intent to distribute.

Outcome: Convicted on August 2, 1988, in Pitt County District Court of breaking and entering; other charges dismissed.

Sentence: Three year suspended confinement; five years probation; $20 restitution; $125 court costs; 100 hours of community service.

2. **Date:** December 24, 1987 (age 17)

Agency: Hyde County, North Carolina, Sheriff's Department

Offense: Larceny

Outcome: Convicted as charged on March 23, 1988, in Hyde County Superior Court.

Sentence: Three years as a juvenile offender confinement by the North Carolina Department of Corrections in Raleigh; paroled on March 31, 1989.

Adult Record

1. **Date:** June 25, 1991

Agency: Farmville, North Carolina, Police Department

Offenses: Breaking and entering, larceny

Outcome: Convicted on December 12, 1991, in Pitt County Superior Court of misdemeanor breaking and entering, misdemeanor larceny; felony charge of possession of stolen goods was dismissed.

Sentence: Two years confinement. Paroled on February 25, 1992.

2. **Date:** Not listed.

Agency: Not listed.

Offenses: Parole violation, driving on a revoked license.

Outcome: Sentenced in Pitt County Superior Court on July 1, 1991, to 100 hours of community service and confinement in jail on the first weekend of each month over two years.

3. **Date:** Not listed.
Agency: Not listed.
Offense: Parole violation, possession of weapon at school.
Outcome: Probation revoked on August 22, 1991.
Sentence: Not listed.

4. **Date:** 1993
Agency: Not listed
Offense: Manufacture of marijuana, a felony
Outcome: Convicted as charged on March 2, 1994, in Pitt County Superior Court.
Sentence: Five years state prison; no release date or parole information provided.

5. **Date:** June 7, 1995
Agency: Greenville, North Carolina, Police Department
Charges: Possession of marijuana with intent to sell and deliver; possession of crack cocaine; carrying a concealed weapon; possession of drug paraphernalia.
Outcome: Convicted on January 25, 1996, in Pitt County Superior Court of felony possession of cocaine and felony possession of firearm by a felon; misdemeanor charges of possession of drug paraphernalia and carrying concealed weapon dismissed.
Sentence: Eleven to fourteen months in state prison. Paroled on March 12, 1997.

6. **Date:** November 7, 1995
Agency: Pitt County Sheriff's Department

Charge: Possession of a firearm by a felon.
Outcome: Convicted as charged on January 25, 1996, in Pitt County Superior Court.
Sentence: Not listed.

7. **Date:** March 3, 1998
Agency: Pitt County Sheriff's Department
Charge: Assault on a female.
Outcome: Convicted on May 20, 1998, in Pitt County District Court of threatened assault on a female.
Sentence: 150 days in jail, three years probation, $100 in court costs.

8. **Date:** July 3, 1998
Agency: Newport News, Virginia, Police Department
Charges: Assault and battery.
Outcome: Convicted on September 4, 1998, in Newport News General District Court of misdemeanor assault.
Sentence: Not listed.

9. **Date:** August 20, 1998
Agency: Pitt County Sheriff's Department
Charge: Larceny (felony)
Outcome: Convicted on November 20, 1998, in Pitt County District Court of misdemeanor larceny.
Sentence: 30 days confinement; one year probation; $90 in court costs.

10. **Date:** June 25, 1999
Agency: Isle of Wight County, Virginia, Sheriff's Department
Charges: Contempt of court, obstruction of justice, grand larceny
Outcome: Pending.

11. **Date:** July 25, 1999
Agency: Not listed.
Charges: No operator's license; defective equipment.
Outcome: Convicted as charged on August 19, 1999, in Isle of Wight General District Court.
Sentence: $150 fine and court costs.

12. **Date:** August 20, 1999
Agency: Not listed
Charges: Possession of cocaine, escape
Outcome: Pending.

13. **Date:** August 18, 2000
Agency: Pitt County Sheriff's Department
Offenses: Assault on law enforcement officer; fugitive.
Outcome: Pending.

14. **Date:** September 15, 2000
Agency: Suffolk, Virginia, Police Department
Charges: Robbery, wearing a mask in public.
Outcome: Pending.

15. **Date:** September 20, 2000
Agency: Isle of Wight County Sheriff's Department
Charges: Possession of controlled substance; escape without force by felon.
Outcome: Pending.

Smith filled in the details of Godley's final encounters with law enforcement, which related to the charges in August and September. He told them about Godley's 1999 escape from the patrol car, after he was arrested for robbing the Virginia convenience store. Godley had obviously made his way to California after the escape, getting the job at the Avanti Apartments just three weeks later, where he'd hooked up with Adriana and bought the revolver.

Smith said the next time Godley was spotted in the Southeast was in the summer of 2000 when he kicked a deputy in the head during an arrest attempt in North Carolina. Smith told the detectives that Godley was finally hauled in from his father's house in Belhaven on August 18, 2000.

While driving Godley to the jail for booking, Smith told the detectives, he had even spoken of "lifer shit" he was facing in California. It turned out that, as crazed as he was that night, the Weasel was telling the truth.

The second week of November 2000, Detectives Heaney and Villalobos packed up and flew from Orange County to North Carolina. There were witnesses to be interviewed, including Godley's father Ed, and search warrants to be served on places where Godley had stayed while on the run. Among them was the residence of Ada Smith, the woman whose name had been written on his apartment employment application. Ada turned out to be Godley's grandmother—the woman who had raised him until his grandfather died and his life went sour.

And, as a shot in the dark, they thought they'd try to visit Dennis Godley himself, now being housed in the Tidewater Regional Jail in Suffolk, Virginia.

Surprisingly, Godley agreed to see them.

Chapter Nineteen

The detectives decided to try an old interrogation trick.
With several people describing Godley, aka Tony Satton,
as deeply paranoid, Villalobos and Heaney thought they
would toy with him psychologically. As they entered an
interview room at the Tidewater Regional Jail, they en-
countered a tattooed man with the coldest, meanest eyes
they had ever seen. He'd come without a lawyer. Heaney
sat across from him; Villalobos hovered just outside the
line of sight, close enough so that Godley would know the
detective was there, but not what he was doing.

But if they thought they were going to rattle the
Weasel, they would be sorely mistaken. For more than
five hours they talked to him in the jail, and for more than
five hours Godley gave up virtually nothing. "Rhetoric,"
Villalobos would later recall. "A lot of bull. He was
good."

He did a lot of talking, about his troubled youth in
North Carolina, friends he knew, family problems. He
confirmed a lot the detectives already knew. He admitted

to living in California in 1999 and using the fake name Tony Satton. He admitted to living in Anaheim and knowing, among others, Ryan Casas, but denied getting a gun in a deal set up by Ryan. Godley said he'd returned to South Carolina in early 2000 and given most of his belongings, including a black leather trench coat and boots, to his mother, Brenda.

As for Adriana, he acknowledged that he'd known her while living in Anaheim. He said they'd gone to numerous places, including taking scenic drives. Godley downplayed his relationship with her. "She was extremely possessive of him, and he would sleep with her when he felt like it, but kind of didn't want to have a full-time relationship with her," Heaney said. Villalobos would put it more bluntly: "He basically described her as a pincushion," he said.

Godley told the detective that Adriana had a jealous streak, and was once so angry she'd thrown a bottle at him. Another time, he said, an evening at a nightclub with Adriana had gone sour when Godley started talking to another woman. Adriana stormed out of the club.

When Heaney asked Godley about Ken Stahl, "He had told me that he had never met anybody," Heaney recalled. "I think he said he had seen a picture of him, and Adriana had spoken of him."

When asked about the night of the murders, Godley offered an alibi of sorts. He confirmed that he had gone out with Adriana, but said it was a shopping trip to a nearby mall called The Block in Orange. Heaney said, "His recollection, I believe, was that he was at a mall for some period of time and that Miss Vasco was out of his sight, that they separated for a period of time." Godley denied being out on the Ortega Highway that night and denied being involved in the murders of Ken and Carolyn Stahl.

All this went on for hours. The detectives kept asking Godley the same questions, and he kept giving the same answers. As good as Adriana was under questioning, Godley was better. As the interview ended, the detectives made a last gasp attempt at getting Godley to talk.

"My attorney told me not to talk to anyone and not to make any decisions, anything involving my cases," Godley said, according to a partial transcript.

Heaney responded with an "Uh-hum."

"So he told me not to talk to anyone," Godley said.

"OK," said Heaney.

"Except to my psychiatrist."

"OK," said Heaney, "is there anything you want to say off the record? Would you have something to say if the record was turned off?"

"I'm just letting you know that I haven't done anything," said Godley.

"We're going to hear the same thing that we heard before: denial," groused Heaney. "And that's what you're going to live with, is the denial part of it. You know it was important to us to find out whether or not you had feelings at all about what happened."

"Nobody said I didn't have feelings."

"It's apparent that you don't," said Heaney.

"I do," said Godley.

"Well," said the detective, "what we're going to do is go home and tell them is: He has no feelings about it whatsoever."

"You don't have any jurisdiction," said Godley.

"We're done."

Then Godley said, "I got a question for you."

Villalobos said, "We're done."

Godley asked about a possible extradition to California to face capital murder charges if he were arrested in the Stahl case and "what I need to do about it." The detectives told him that was up to the local prosecutor and public defender, not them.

"Well, do you have any insight into it?" asked Godley.

They said they didn't and that it was time for them to leave.

"So, you all through harassing my people now?" asked Godley.

"No," said Villalobos.

"We're not through conducting our investigation," said Heaney. "Our investigation will continue until we're exhausted."

"We're not going away," said Villalobos.

"Well, I don't expect you to go away," said Godley.

"It's not harassment," said Heaney. "You know what?"

His partner answered him. "You're guilty," said Villalobos.

"No, I'm not," said Godley.

"You did it," said Villalobos.

"Hear me, whatever we do is not harassment. It's part of our investigation," said Heaney. "Dennis, I tell you, as long as there is work to do, we're going to do it and that's it."

With that, the investigators left him.

The trip to North Carolina and Virginia wasn't a total bust. The detectives did get some more details about the dangerous life and wily character of Dennis Godley. For one thing, he seemed to have moved on romantically from Adriana Vasco. Not even life behind bars cooled him. While in jail he continued to communicate with another inmate, Lisa Stone Snell—the woman at the wheel of the Blazer during the convenience store robbery.

Interviewed immediately after Godley by Heaney and Villalobos, Lisa first identified the picture of Tony Satton from the California ID as being Godley. Then she said that she was able to secretly correspond with Godley by mailing letters through other inmates and through a man on the outside, Dennis's cousin Eugene Carter. She offered them no useful information about Dennis's activities in California.

Heaney and Villalobos next met with Godley's father, Edward Lee "Ed" Godley, at his house in Belhaven, North Carolina. Villalobos recalled the elder Godley as being "very pleasant," and that "the only difficulty, if we had any, was just trying to understand his accent from North Carolina." In this interview and subsequent ones, Ed Godley gave a father's perspective on a son now suspected of committing a brutal double murder.

At the time of his interview, Ed Godley, his body battered by misfortune, was bedridden, recovering from steroid injections for his bad back. He was 49 years old, but a hard life had put many more years on him. In 1992, he was putting a new exhaust pipe in his wife's grandfather's car, when, just as he was finishing, the car rolled over him. The accident sent him to Belhaven Hospital with a severe back injury. Six years later, while working as a line supervisor at Fountain Power Boats, he was thrown from a boat into the Tar River. That accident placed him on temporary disability. He was also having some lingering problems with nerve damage from a car accident. This accounted for his lack of employment and need for bed rest.

Dennis Earl "The Weasel" Godley was the oldest of Ed's three children. Ed had gotten married at age 16 to Dennis's mother, Brenda Dell. The marriage ended in divorce while Ed was in prison on the safecracking rap. When Ed got out of prison, he married a woman named Michelle Burbidge, with whom he had two other children, Jessica and Edwin. Dennis lived with his father and stepmother from about age 11 to 13, then moved back in with his mother, then with grandparents.

When Dennis's grandfather died and Dennis started getting in trouble, his father never saw reason for alarm. "In my opinion, it was just doing fifteen-, sixteen-year-old kid things, you know, going out drinking, staying in trouble," said Ed Godley. "My understanding, he broke into places, but that doesn't make him hurt people."

He recalled the problems: Dennis once "took a gun" from somebody, Ed said. Dennis also got into scrapes with his cousin, Don Murray. "They were two kids that grew up and they fought all the time anyway," he said. Once, he heard they had gone into bars and beaten up gay men. "I had heard they did," said Edward. "They were sixteen-year-old kids. We all actually do things we really don't [mean] sometimes."

Although not living with his son, Ed did try to pay some of the legal bills. "He was my son, and if he had any problems, yes, I tried to be helpful," he said. But the money expenditures didn't go over well with Michelle. "It caused problems between me and my wife," he said. "Then my wife was going to school, and I had just came out of school and was on a tight budget and, you know, we just needed the money. And my wife just felt like it was more important to, you know, for the money to go into our household than me having anything to do with my son."

In 1999, after many years away from his father, Dennis started showing up more at his father's home, spending time with his half-siblings for the first time in his life, and getting on Ed's wife's nerves. The marriage ended after twenty-one years, said Ed.

At the request of the California detectives, local police searched Ed's home, looking for clothes, letters, even the gun used to kill the Stahls, but came up empty. Ed told the detectives that the woman in bed with Godley when he'd been arrested—was his girlfriend, and that a few weeks after Godley's arrest, she'd come back to the house and collected all of his belongings. Despite several searches of homes throughout the area, nothing was ever turned up.

Still, Heaney and Villalobos returned to California feeling good. These had been two of the most productive weeks of the year-long investigation. They felt they knew how and why the murders of Ken and Carolyn Stahl had happened: that a depressed Dr. Stahl had called on his former girlfriend from the other side of the tracks to find a hitman to kill his wife, Carolyn; that Adriana had hooked Ken up with a career criminal named Dennis Godley; that on the night of November 20, 1999, the black-clad Adriana and Tony had left their Anaheim apartment complex with a .357-caliber revolver Tony'd bought for $200, driven out to Ortega Highway to a pre-arranged spot and gunned down the Stahls. The payment was between $20,000 and $30,000.

There were still holes, to be sure. The biggest question was: Why was Ken also murdered? And who'd actually fired the shots—Dennis or Adriana?

The case was built on the recollections of the upstanding Stewarts and the Avanti Apartment denizens—some of questionable character—and supported, in a way, by Godley's statements in the North Carolina patrol car about the "lifer shit" he faced in California. But it was more information than the police had had to date. And might be all they were ever going to get. The detectives still lacked any physical evidence: They didn't have the dark clothes or gun casings that the witnesses had talked about, and they didn't have the .357.

Adriana and Godley were both in jail; arresting them on murder charges was merely a matter of paperwork. At

the end of November 2000, the detectives talked to prosecutors at the Orange County District Attorney's Office.

"At that point," Heaney recalled, "the DA was not willing to file."

Chapter Twenty

For Dennis Godley, there was still time. The escape and assault charges in North Carolina, combined with his lengthy arrest record, meant that he could be locked up for years. Returning from North Carolina to California, Detectives Heaney and Villalobos knew there was no urgency in trying to persuade the DA to charge Godley in the Stahl killings.

Adriana Vasco was another story. She was set for release from the Los Angeles County Twin Towers jail on December 23, 2000, when her stint for the traffic warrants ran out. After that, she would be set free, and the detectives ran the very real risk of losing her. It was hard enough to pin her down when she was cooperating with police. She moved around a lot, changed phone numbers and pagers and switched jobs. If she wanted to run, it would be very difficult to find her. If she fled to Mexico, where she was born and still had relatives, it might be impossible. That gave the detectives about four weeks to build a good enough case to convince the district attorney to file murder charges against her.

They had already interviewed everybody they could find who knew anything about Adriana Vasco and Dennis Godley, from James and Nancy Stewart to Adriana's two Internet lovers. They had searched Adriana's storage facility and a slew of houses and mobile homes in North Carolina. They had inspected Adriana's phone records and confiscated photographs.

Heaney discussed the situation with his supervisor and the DA's office.

There was one more plan of attack.

On Monday, November 27, 2000, a week after returning from North Carolina, Brian Heaney called Greg Stewart on his cell phone. When he answered, it sounded like he was driving. Heaney could also hear a child in the background.

"We found Tony," Heaney told Greg. "We have some concerns."

Heaney said he wanted to set up a meeting. Greg suggested they meet three days later, when both he and his mother, Nancy, would be available at home.

That Thursday, Heaney and Villalobos met Greg and Nancy at their Westminster house. What Heaney had to say wouldn't take long. He told them that they had found Tony Satton—that his real name was Dennis Godley, that he was in jail in North Carolina and that he knew Orange County detectives suspected him in the killings of Ken and Carolyn Stahl.

What they didn't know was how many of Dennis's dangerous friends were still on the outside.

For right now, the detectives told the Stewarts, they should consider taking simple steps to ensure their personal safety. They should keep their lights on at night and if they saw any strange vehicles in the neighborhood or re ceived any unusual phone calls, they should contact Westminster police. Heaney and Nancy discussed whether her husband should get a concealed weapons permit.

Heaney made it clear that he had no reports of any specific threats against the Stewart family. It was all just a precaution.

After the meeting, Greg followed the detectives to the car and told them that on that Monday, when Heaney had called his cell phone, Greg and his father were actually driving up to Los Angeles to visit Adriana. During their visit, they told her that Tony had been found.

Greg quoted Adriana as saying: "Oh, my God, he can put me away forever."

Heaney and Villalobos drove back to their office in Santa Ana. Later that day, as Heaney stood outside his office, somebody told him that he had a phone call. He went back in his office and picked up the receiver.

"Hello there," came a familiar voice.

It was Adriana Vasco.

Chapter Twenty-One

Detective Heaney asked her how she was doing in jail.

"Surviving," Adriana said. "Taking one day at a time here."

But that wasn't why she'd called the morning of Monday, November 27, 2000. She had spoken to Nancy Stewart.

"I just was kind of shaken," she said.

Heaney now spoke carefully.

It was his responsibility, he said, to warn everybody "when there's a potential for threat." The man whom Adriana knew as Tony Satton hadn't specifically threatened the Stewarts, the detective said, but "he did insinuate" that he could "take care of things." Heaney told Adriana that he hadn't really believed her at first when she'd said at the Costa Mesa police station that she was scared of Tony. Heaney told her he'd thought she was trying to get some sympathy out of him.

"It wasn't until Phil and I went back to North Carolina," Heaney said, "that we realized he is a dangerous person."

They were on the phone for some time, with Heaney doing most of the talking. He gave an account of his visit with "Tony"—real name Dennis Godley, he told her—and what it meant for Adriana.

"We didn't tell him this, but he absolutely believes that you've cooperated fully with us," said Heaney. "What he actually told us at one point was, if he had done it right, he would have left no witnesses, and that included you."

In fact, Godley had admitted to nothing more than losing track of Adriana during a shopping trip the night of the murders. But Heaney didn't tell her that. The detectives had tried to scare the Stewarts to smoke out Adriana. That had worked. Now they wanted to put the fear of Godley into Adriana herself.

Heaney told her that Godley had said that he and Adriana had driven out to Ortega Highway a day or two before the murders, and that the night of the 20th, they had gone to the mall but "you guys separated . . . and he doesn't know where you went."

"Oh, my God," Adriana said.

"He's trying [to imply] that you're capable of committing these murders," the detective said. "You're the one with the motive. He had no motive. You had the motive and the opportunity, and that you were trying to buy a gun, a handgun, for him also."

"I'm listening to you and I'm not even believing what you're telling me," said Adriana.

The detective tried to seize the moment and question her in detail about the murders—about what kind of role Tony and Ken had played—but Adriana, while upset, couldn't answer. She spoke of hiring an attorney and repeatedly expressed fear of the man she still called Tony.

Heaney said, "For us to begin considering how to protect you, we need to know what your involvement . . . . What we have now, we can use to file charges against you and against Tony. That's your risk. That's what you should be scared of."

They spoke a while longer, with Adriana asking for help and assurances of protection, and Heaney linking his assistance to her telling all she knew.

He later told her that he had pictures of her with Tony, taken at a Halloween party, that had been found as part of the investigation. This rattled her.

"If he has my pictures over there, then I'm in danger with my kids," she said.

Heaney didn't tell her that he'd found the pictures in Adriana's own storage facility.

Finally, Heaney said that he and Villalobos would drive up to the jail that day and talk to Adriana in person. She asked him not to get mad at her if she didn't answer the way he wanted her to.

"I promise you, I won't get mad," said the detective.

Adriana ended the conversation by urging Heaney not to file murder charges against her " 'til you talk to me," she said. "Please."

The jail was forty miles north of Santa Ana. The detectives arrived at 7 o'clock. They went to the basement and into a small room, about 8 feet by 5 feet, with table and three chairs, and a door with a glass window that opened onto a corridor. A female deputy sat at guard station outside.

Heaney and Villalobos waited in the little room. Heaney stood as a deputy opened the door and escorted Adriana into the room. She ran up to Heaney, buried her head in his chest, hugged him and began sobbing uncontrollably.

"I'm sorry," Adriana cried.

"It's OK," said Heaney.

"I'm sorry. I'm so sorry. So sorry."

"I'll be OK. I'm sorry for you," the detective said. "This makes us all feel very, very sad."

"I wasn't bullshitting you when I told you that I was scared," she said.

"We know that now," said Heaney. "You want to sit down here?"

She took her seat. She said "Hi" to Villalobos, who asked, "How you doing, sweetie?"

"Taking it one day at a time, I guess."

Heaney then told her they needed to conduct "a little official business."

He read her her Miranda rights.

Then he asked Adriana to tell her whole story.

She paused. "You said you weren't going to get mad if I didn't answer some of the questions," she said.

"There's one thing I want you to understand tonight," Heaney said. "There's nothing that you can say tonight or do tonight that I will get upset about, OK? Do you understand that?"

"I want to believe you."

They gave her a glass of water.

The questioning started slowly and gently, going over well-trodden ground, with Adriana talking about her long relationship with Ken and Ken's problems with Carolyn. Only this time, Adriana made it clear that Ken wanted Carolyn dead.

She quoted Ken as saying, "That bitch, I can't stand her anymore. I want her gone. Can you make her disappear? Do you know anybody?"

Adriana said she'd told Ken she didn't know anybody.

But then Tony Satton entered her life, letting himself into her apartment one day with his maintenance man's passkey to fix the sink. She told him not to barge in like that; he responded by going into her bedroom.

"Well, it began that way [and] every day after that he started coming," she said. At first it had been civil. They'd just talked. Then one weekend, he'd asked her if she could get some marijuana. She didn't want to—she had started going to church again and had been clean and sober—but eventually she relented, finding him a drug connection.

"That's how he started," she said. "And then he wanted some speed. So then I got that for him too."

One night, she smoked a joint with him and "before you know it, I started using again."

While they were high, Tony told her about his violent past and his troubles with police in North Carolina. He told her to keep this information to herself. If she told anybody, "He'd take Ashley"—her daughter. "He goes, 'I personally won't do it, but I'll have somebody come and get her and you'll never see her,' " Adriana recalled.

"So what happened?" asked Heaney. "[At] what point did he know about Ken and what Ken was talking about?"

"I think it was one time that Ken came to my place," said Adriana. "Like I said, I was on and off with drugs. I can't remember."

Adriana had never been so open with the detectives. The fear of "Tony Satton" had her talking with ease.

Heaney told her that he had spoken to two people whom Ken had approached asking if either could kill his wife.

"So Ken asked you to ask Tony the same thing, yes?"

"Yes," said Adriana simply.

The case now blowing wide open, Adriana confirmed for the first time the beginnings of the murder plot.

She'd told Tony about Ken—and regretted it immediately.

"I wanted to call it off," she said. "I told Ken, 'I don't

want this anymore. I don't want to be involved in this. This is wrong.' "

But Ken wouldn't listen. She quoted him as saying, "Look at these things I've done for you. I've treated you good. Have I ever let you down? You know about all these other men? They all let you down. I've never let you down. I show you that I care. I'm the only one that has been there."

Heaney asked, "How about Tony? How did Tony come to decide 'Let's go do this thing'?"

"It was Tony's decision," said Adriana. "Tony and Ken spoke on the phone."

She said that Tony had asked her to "drive him somewhere" shortly before the murders, so she took him out to Ortega Highway, where she had gone one time to clear her head after a fight with Greg.

Heaney said that witnesses had seen Adriana and Tony, together, leaving the apartment building the night of the murders.

The memory brought Adriana to tears.

"I did not want . . . I wanted to talk, I just wanted to just, like, 'Please don't,' " she said. "I told Ken, 'Please, no. Please no. Please don't do this.' I begged him not to do this. I begged him not to. I begged him to just leave me out of it. I didn't want—I have my kids. I had everything. It's not me. I begged him not to. And then, then I had Tony over here telling me, 'I'm going to blow you [away] and your kids.' "

"If you didn't do this thing?"

"If I didn't follow it."

She said when they'd left the apartment on the night of the 20th, Tony had been carrying a silver "Western-type" revolver like the one in a picture that Heaney had shown her—a gun similar to the one used in the murders—that he was "loading and unloading in front of me." Tony wore gloves; she didn't.

At this point in the interview, Adriana was crying. She interrupted the narrative to tell Heaney, "I want to be home for Christmas."

The detective made no promises, and Adriana resumed her story.

She said that she and Tony had driven down to San Juan Capistrano in her car and that they'd followed Ken and Carolyn out to Ortega Highway.

"When I saw Ken driving out there, I couldn't believe it," she said, sobbing. "I was thinking, 'Shit. What the fuck is he thinking?'"

They drove to a spot on Ortega Highway and stopped.

"What did Tony do?" asked Heaney.

"Just got out," sobbed Adriana.

"And then what?"

"And I didn't want to," she said, crying. "I was just, like, looking straight."

"Did you realize what happened at that moment?"

"No."

"In other words, did you realize that he had shot both people?"

"No, I did not know what was happening," she said. "I just heard the shots and I was like, 'Oh, my God.' And I wanted to take off."

Finally, she spilled.

Now, all the detectives needed were the details, which they got out of sequence, between many tears from Adriana.

"What did Ken offer you to do this?" asked Villalobos.

"Ken didn't offer me anything," she said.

"What did he offer Tony to do this?"

"Money."

"How much money? Was it a lot of money?"

Dr. Kenneth Stahl, from his California Driver's License found in his wallet. There was no sign of robbery in the killings. *Orange County court file.*

Kenneth Stahl's wife, Carolyn Stahl, an optometrist, from the driver's license photo found in her purse. None of her jewelry was taken in the attack. *Orange County court file*

A security guard on late-night patrol found the car but at first didn't see the bodies inside. *Orange County DA*

Police found no physical evidence at the scene to suggest who the killer or killers could be. The only clue was that the lack of gun casings was evidence the couple were killed by a revolver. *Orange County DA.*

The entrance to the Huntington Beach, Calif., gated condo community where Kenneth and Carolyn Stahl lived. An electrician who did work on the house said Stahl eerily spoke of murder. *Michael Fleeman*

The Avanti Apartments in Anaheim, where Adriana Vasco and Dennis Godley lived—and where much of the murder plot was allegedly hatched. *Michael Fleeman*

Godley allegedly walked around the apartment complex with guns—even though it's located just behind the Anaheim Police Department. Patrol cars drive by every few minutes. *Michael Fleeman*

Adriana Vasco met Kenneth Stahl while working in his pain clinic. *Orange County DA*

By day, the murder scene on Ortega Highway, just outside San Juan Capistrano, is a place of rugged beauty. *Michael Fleeman*

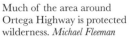

Much of the area around Ortega Highway is protected wilderness. *Michael Fleeman*

The electronics store parking lot where Kenneth Stahl allegedly made a monetary transaction that led to murder. *Michael Fleeman*

The Stahls' car was still running and the headlights were on when police found the bodies. *Orange County DA*

The Huntington Beach pier where a witness says Dennis Godley claimed to have disposed of a gun into the Pacific Ocean. *Michael Fleeman*

The Orange County Superior Court building in Santa Ana, Calif., where Adriana Vasco's trial was held. *Michael Fleeman*

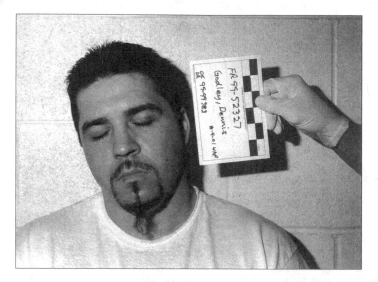

Dennis Godley, after his arrest. North Carolina authorities had been tangling with Godley since he was a boy. *Orange County DA*

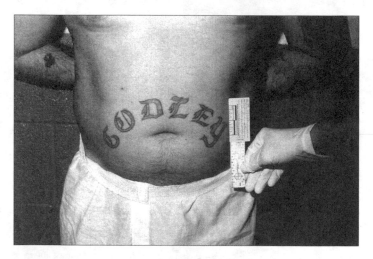

Although he went by the pseudonym Tony Satton, Godley actually had his real name tattooed across his stomach. People thought Godley was a gang name. *Orange County DA*

"To me it was."

The total: $30,000, in three payments, which Ken made to Adriana, and which Adriana gave to Godley. This was the same amount related by one of the residents of the Avanti Apartments.

Adriana said she wasn't sure exactly when the payments had been made, except that at least one was before Halloween 1999, one or two after. At each point, Adriana said, she'd begged Ken to drop the plan. She'd told him how much she feared Tony. Ken, she said, wouldn't listen. She quoted him as saying, "Just give it to him and tell him, after it's done, I'll give him more."

Ken had had a few ideas about where the murder should take place. "This man that's so righteous had all these thoughts about [murder]," she said.

Adriana was fuzzy on what she'd known about the planning, saying she'd only gotten parts of it from overhearing conversations between Godley and Ken. She had known that Ken originally wanted Carolyn murdered at the end of September 1999, then said October. Adriana kept urging them to stall, playing one off the other.

"He didn't care," said Adriana. "He didn't say anything. He just wanted it done."

Finally, they settled on a date—November 20, 1999.

The day before, Ken, Adriana and Tony had met in a Circuit City parking lot in Huntington Beach. Tony ordered Adriana to get out and talk to Ken.

"I'm watching you," Tony warned.

She walked over to Ken's van. They talked and then she got back in her car and led Ken down to the freeway to the Ortega Highway exit in San Juan Capistrano. They drove a few miles east on the highway and parked along the road—at the spot where the murders would occur the next night.

Godley, carrying the revolver, got out and talked to

Ken. Adriana said she didn't know what they'd said. Then Godley started shooting at random into the bushes. He got back into the car and Adriana drove them back to their apartments in Anaheim.

The next day, Saturday, Ken called her. Adriana insisted he did in fact talk to her about fixing her computer, just as she had said days after the killings.

Later that day, Tony came into Adriana's apartment and told her they were leaving. He wore a long leather coat, gloves and no hat. She had on bell-bottoms and "a top," she said. In the evening, Adriana drove Tony down to San Juan Capistrano in her white 1987 Mazda 626LX four-door, which Ken had bought her.

"Piece-of-shit car," she said.

They pulled off the 405 Freeway into a gas station next to a Jack in the Box, where they waited for Ken and Carolyn in Carolyn's car. Ken had earlier shown Adriana a picture of the car so she'd know which one it was.

"It seemed like forever," said Adriana of the wait.

That night, the Stahls had gone to dinner at the El Torito Grill in Mission Viejo, where Ken had taken Adriana before. While Adriana waited in the Jack in the Box parking lot, Ken called her on her cell phone to tell her that he was leaving.

"I was like, 'Shhhh, don't say anything,'" she recalled. "And that's all I said. But he hung up."

Adriana then told Tony that Ken had called. About ten minutes later, Ken arrived in the parking lot. Tony pulled out the revolver and said, "Come on."

From the gas station, Adriana followed Ken's car out to Ortega Highway. Ken drove very slowly, at one point letting a car pass him. When Ken pulled over to the side, Adriana, under Tony's orders, passed by Ken's car, made a U-turn, and pulled alongside it.

"I just wanted to block it out," she said, "like, 'OK, it's

not happening. It's not happening. I'm not here. I'm not here. I'm really not here.' "

As she told this to the detectives, she cried and then didn't say anything for a moment.

"Take a deep breath," said Villalobos.

"I didn't want to be there," she said.

"Here, take some water," the detective said.

But the memory sent her into further convulsions of tears.

"Why did I stop?" she cried. "If I didn't stop this wouldn't have happened and I wouldn't be here and I would have been OK. I would have been OK. My kids would have been OK, and I wouldn't be here. For crying out loud! I was raised better than this. I'm so sorry, I'm sorry. I just had it in me for so long, I didn't have anybody to talk to. I just feel so bad about it."

Continuing her story, she explained that Tony had gotten out of the Mazda, slid across the hood carrying the revolver, and walked up to the Stahls' silver car. She recalled that Tony had yelled something like, "Are you OK? Do you guys need any help?"

"And then you heard shots?" asked Heaney.

"And then I heard shots," said Adriana.

She didn't see anything. Only heard.

"Did you hear anything other than gunshots?" Heaney asked.

"Yeah."

"What?"

"Carolyn yelling," said Adriana.

"What did she yell?" asked Heaney.

"I think she was saying just: 'Oh, my God,' and yelling."

As she heard this, Adriana said, she'd started moving her car forward slightly, taking her foot off the brake. Then she stopped. Tony, looking nervous, returned to her car after the shooting and asked her: "Where were you going?"

She told him, "Nowhere." She quoted him as saying, "Good, because I was going to blow you [away] first."

He got in the car with her. They drove off. After a while, Tony told Adriana that he had also shot Ken.

It was the first time she knew that Ken had also been killed.

She asked Tony why.

"He said, 'Because he didn't follow orders,'" said Adriana.

She recalled that Tony had told her that he'd shot Ken first, then Carolyn.

"He had to put her down," she said. "She wouldn't stay down."

This would account for the smears on the car, the blood drops outside, the shoe by the back wheel.

Adriana said that when she got home to her apartment, "I just, like, cried and cried and cried."

Heaney asked her if she'd helped get rid of the gun.

She didn't answer.

"This is not happening," she said. "This is not happening."

"Relax," said Villalobos. "Relax."

She ignored Villalobos. She was in Heaney's thrall. She looked at Heaney.

"Brian," Adriana said, "please don't keep me here."

"Adriana" was all he said.

"Keep my kids safe," she said.

Again, no promises. Instead, the detectives returned to the subject of the gun, asking her what had happened to it. It took a long time to draw it out of her, but she finally said, "Off the pier."

A few days after the murders, Adriana explained, she'd driven Tony to the Huntington Beach Pier, not far from the Stahls' condo. Tony had walked to the end, past Ruby's Diner and tossed it in the Pacific Ocean.

In the weeks after the murders, Tony's mood, always volatile to begin with, grew even more unpredictable. He started acting paranoid, said Adriana.

"I think towards the end I felt sometimes, the way that he looked at me, that he was thinking of getting rid of me," she said.

The money that Ken had given him for the hit didn't seem to last long. Adriana said Tony spent the money mostly on drugs, particularly rock cocaine.

Then, one day, he left.

"I was relieved for him to be gone," she said. She helped him pack his stuff in her car and then he drove her to a corner somewhere on Brookhurst Street in Anaheim.

"That was the last time I seen him," she said.

Heaney asked her, if she could do it over again, "what do you think could've been done differently?"

"Gone to the police," she said.

"And why didn't you?" he asked.

"I felt like I was too deep into it," Adriana said. "And I thought that nobody would help me."

By the end of the interview, Adriana stopped crying as hard.

"I feel better," she said, sniffling. "I feel so much better. I feel like I've had such a big weight taken off of me."

She said that she had been praying. There was a passage in Proverbs that she had read the day before. "It says something about an accomplice is its own enemy, something like that," she said. "God forgave and He's with me, for He says He's with me. I had to tell man about this and ask for forgiveness."

The detectives bought her a Coke from the machine, something she normally wasn't allowed to have in jail. Adriana brightened. Suddenly, having spoken to the detectives, the burden that Heaney had told her about was now gone.

"Oh, my God, this is going to taste so good. Soda!" she said. "You can't get no soda. Nothing—bad, nasty milk, Nestlé Crunch."

"You look happier now than you did when you first walked in," Heaney said.

"It's because of the Coke," she said.

She laughed.

"And you gave it to me in front of the deputy," she said. "It felt so good."

The session neared its end with everybody now laughing. Adriana was becoming giddy. When the detectives said they had to leave, she started guzzling the rest of her Coke.

"I can't help it," she joked. "My throat is asking me."

Then she burped.

Villalobos joked that they should turn off the tape recorder every time she belched.

They spoke a while longer about people whom Godley may have known and where they might live. She spoke about her daughter, Ashley, and how at first she hadn't been told that her mother had been jailed—she was told Adriana was "vacationing"—but that Adriana had finally told Ashley everything.

"I said, 'Mommy is in time out,'" she said, explaining that when Ashley was bad, Adriana would tell her she had to have a time out. "'Well, Mama is in time out in a big, big, big house.' And I said, 'I can't come home yet 'cause I'm being punished.' And I told her, and she's like, 'Why?' And I said, 'Well, 'cause I was driving my car when I wasn't supposed to.'"

As for her son, Mark, a teenager now, he was upset over losing the man he knew as Uncle Ken.

And, Adriana told the detectives, "He doesn't think

very highly of you right now, because I've been kept here . . . because of Uncle Ken."

Heaney ended the session by thanking Adriana for "inviting us up here."

It was 11:05 p.m.

"You spoke to us freely of your own will?" Villalobos asked.

"Yes," said Adriana.

"We didn't threaten you? We didn't make any promises?"

"No promises, but I do want you guys to protect me."

"Right," said Villalobos. "Yes."

"We have an obligation," added Heaney.

"We're not going to walk away and leave you hanging," said Villalobos.

Adriana said she just had one last question: "What will be my charges?"

Heaney said, "Call us on Tuesday and we'll talk to you about that."

"But can you give me an idea?" she asked.

"Well, yeah, what we talked about from the beginning," said Heaney, "and that's murder."

Chapter Twenty-Two

The investigation was nearly complete; just one more task for the detectives—and one more pleasant surprise. On the night of Wednesday, December 6, 2000—two weeks after Adriana Vasco had told all about the Stahl murders—Detective Phil Villalobos called Dennis Godley's father, Ed, to confirm their meeting for the next morning at his home. Villalobos was making a second trip to North Carolina.

Ed Godley said the meeting was still on. And, he said, there was somebody else whom Villalobos might want to talk to while he was in town: a boy named Kyle Alligood.

It was cold and gray in North Carolina on December 7, 2000. Ed Godley's right leg hurt like crazy—nerve damage from when the car had rolled over him—and he had to interrupt the interview occasionally to go to the bathroom for medication. After speaking with Ed, Villalobos drove with him to the local phone company to pick up records of Dennis's calls while he was living at home. Then, they drove to North Side High School to speak with Kyle.

Dennis Godley's half-brother, Edwin, who was friends with Kyle Alligood, had already told him that California detectives were in town and wanted to talk to Kyle about Dennis.

"Just tell them the truth," Edwin said.

The detectives met Kyle in the principal's office. His grandfather was with him. So were local police officers.

Kyle related why Dennis's father, Ed, had led police to him. Just a few days before, on December 4 or 5, Kyle was at Ed's house watching television with him. A report came up on The Weather Channel about temperatures in Orange County, California.

Kyle asked Ed, "Isn't that where your oldest son killed those people?"

Alarmed, Ed Godley tried to contact a detective he knew at the Washington County Sheriff's Office, but couldn't find him. Then, when Villalobos called just a day later, Ed led the California detective to Kyle.

The Orange County reference on The Weather Channel had reminded Kyle of his encounter with Dennis Godley that summer, when he'd come out of the house without wearing a shirt, said he was from Orange County and boasted of killing "a couple" of people.

Villalobos wrapped up the interview and got back into his car. Ed Godley was waiting—he hadn't been in the room when Kyle spoke to police.

They got back to Ed's mobile home. As they walked toward the front door, Ed asked Villalobos, "Did Kyle tell you everything?"

Villalobos said yes.

Ed Godley then got upset. He told the detective he couldn't understand how his son could have done something like this.

Then he started crying.

"I blame myself," Ed Godley said. "I should have been there for him."

Chapter Twenty-Three

Carolyn Stahl's family was given the news before it was released to the public. They were "not particularly surprised," according to Orange County Sheriff's Captain Steve Carroll, head of the homicide unit, by the revelation that police believed that Kenneth Stahl had ordered the hit on Carolyn. Carolyn's family had divulged to detectives the uglier secrets of the marriage of Ken and Carolyn Stahl.

On Tuesday, December 12, 2000, authorities announced that murder charges had been filed against Dennis Earl Godley, age 30, and Adriana Vasco, 33, in the double murder on Ortega Highway that had stumped investigators for the better part of a year. With this announcement came the airing of the dirtiest of the Stahls' laundry.

"Our whole family is just so upset about this," Carolyn's mother, Ophia Sokolowski, told *The Orange County Register*. "I can't imagine Ken being in on this. It's so hurtful to think he would do this to her." But in the next breath, she indicated that she actually could imagine it, graphically. She said that her daughter had been bothered by Ken's frequent extra-marital affairs, even once walking in on him while he was with a woman from his workplace. Ken had physically abused Carolyn several years earlier. Photos showed injuries to her face and back. "I saw the pictures," Sokolowski told the newspaper, "and it was really bad."

Ken's family had little to say. They released a terse statement: "Ken's family is devastated with the revelation of these allegations. We will be following . . . further information either from the Sheriff's Department or the potential upcoming trial."

In a press conference receiving heavy local media coverage, officials released to the public the highlights of the investigation. Homicide detectives, they told reporters, had uncovered a murder-for-hire scheme with a deadly twist: the hitman had killed both the intended target and the man who hired him.

Sheriff Michael Carona, the highest-ranking lawman in the county, said that the upstanding Dr. Kenneth Stahl had "wanted to have his wife killed for some time" and solicited other possible hitmen before settling on Dennis Godley—an apparent reference to Ken's discussions with Chris Anaya and Greg Stewart. The conduit had been Adriana Vasco. "Ms. Vasco had been involved with a number of people who were involved in criminal activity," Carona told reporters. "Mr. Godley was in Orange County for criminal activity unrelated to the assassination." In going to Adriana for help, Carona said, Ken had "found the right person."

It wasn't clear what that activity was, although it may have been a reference to Godley's alleged drug dealing or flight from robbery and assault charges in Virginia and

North Carolina. Either way, Carona revealed, Ken had offered Dennis "a large sum of money" to kill Carolyn on Ortega Highway. Carona didn't give the dollar amount, but the *Los Angeles Times* got wind that it was $30,000.

Authorities told reporters that Godley had recently arrived from North Carolina—having escaped while police tried to arrest him for a robbery—and lived in the same Anaheim apartment complex as Adriana. The two were involved romantically, authorities noted. The *Register* tracked down Sergeant Ron Smith of the Pitt County Sheriff's Department, who said that Godley had a long criminal record that included larceny, robbery and assault on a police officer. Smith would later tell *Time* magazine of his long efforts to get Dennis Godley. "The Weasel—that's what we call him here, because he keeps escaping," Smith told the magazine. "In twenty years of service, he is one of the meanest men I have met. You look into his eyes, and they look black."

Carona described how the Stahls had had dinner in Mission Viejo, then driven out to Ortega Highway. "He pulled over, knowing that the other two—Vasco and Godley—are going to go up and shoot her," said Carroll. "He's not expecting to get killed." But he was, shot several times like his wife.

The outstanding question that couldn't be answered on or off the record was why Ken had been killed. Authorities at the time didn't reveal Adriana's statement that Godley had killed Ken because he wouldn't follow directions. If Adriana were to be believed, she too was surprised that Ken was killed—that his death was not part of the deal. The *L.A. Times* said some of the theories included Dennis's possible jealousy over Ken's relationship with

Adriana, the desire to eliminate witnesses or simply panic.

The charges had come more than a year after the murders, a fact not lost on the media. The investigation—described by the *Register* as "seemingly stalled"—had resumed when it was assigned to a new detective team, Carona said, without offering any details. The big break, he said, had come when detectives reviewed Ken's cellular phone records and found calls to Adriana.

It was indeed, as Carona told The Associated Press at the time, "a tale of intrigue, a tale of murder." It was also a family tragedy, this crime laying bare secrets that had been hidden for years. "They had a rocky marriage," Carolyn's sister, Linda Dubay, told the *Register*. "I know [Carolyn] was very unhappy and she talked about getting a divorce." But, Dubay told the *Times*, "Ken's mom encouraged them to go and get marriage counseling. That was four or five years ago." In the end, Carolyn's family said in a statement read to reporters by Carona, these problems still couldn't answer the ultimate question. They remained "baffled as to why Ken, or anyone else, would choose to end a marriage in this way," for Carolyn was a "gentle, soft-spoken, beautiful lady."

Authorities had now told just about everybody about the details of the Stahl killings, from the theory of the case to the names, ages and backgrounds of those charged—everybody, except Adriana Vasco.

In the television room at the Los Angeles County Twin Towers jail, she watched in shock as news reports asserted that she had been charged with killing Ken and Carolyn Stahl. They even had her picture on the screen.

"I couldn't believe it," she said later.

Hadn't Detectives Heaney and Villalobos promised to

protect her? Didn't they have a deal: She would talk and they would help her? Where were they now?

Twenty minutes after the TV reports aired, jail officials transferred Adriana from her dorm-like area to isolation.

Chapter Twenty-Four

On Wednesday morning, January 3, 2001, Detective Brian Heaney was reading an *Orange County Register* article about the Stahl case. By now, Adriana had already been charged with double murder and transferred to the Orange County Jail. She had made her first court appearance before Judge Pamela Iles. Adriana had attended the brief proceeding on Friday, December 29, in a chain-link–enclosed holding area. She didn't enter a plea—didn't say anything—as Iles ordered her held without bail.

As Heaney read his paper that morning, he could rest assured that the bulk of his detective work was done; all that was left was to appear in court and testify.

That's when he saw the story headlined, "Till Death Did They Part" with the bylines of Tony Saavedra and Bill Rams, the police reporters for the paper, who had been following the case almost from the start.

Heaney picked up his phone and called Rams at the paper. He got the answering machine.

"How did you pull that off?" Heaney said on the recording, then left his name and number asking Rams to call him back.

The story—as well as a second one elsewhere in the paper—featured jailhouse interviews with Adriana Vasco and Dennis Godley.

That afternoon, Rams returned the detective's call. Heaney complimented him on the scoops and asked him how he'd gotten the stories. Rams said that after the charges were announced, he'd sent a letter to Godley at the Western Tidewater Jail in Virginia, where Heaney had interviewed him. Rams told Godley that he was a reporter in Orange County writing a story about the Stahl murders and asked him to call collect if Godley wanted to comment. Reporters commonly seek comment from defendants, knowing that they almost never reply, usually on the advice of their lawyers.

But Godley called Rams back and they spoke.

"I've done a lot of things in my life," Godley told Rams, according to the story that appeared in the paper, "but taking another person's life is not one of them."

According to the articles, Dennis denied being out on Ortega Highway the night of the murders, and denied knowing Ken and Carolyn Stahl. "I've never met the man in my life," Rams quoted Godley as saying. "I never spoke to him. As far as me being jealous, I was in relationships with over seven women. [Adriana] was just another one."

He said he knew of Ken from a picture that Adriana had of him on the television set. "She said she used to date him," Dennis said. "I didn't really care. She was just another girl in the apartment complex as far as I was concerned."

Godley denied ever receiving any money, from Stahl

or anybody, noting that he had been evicted from his Anaheim apartment a month after the killings because he couldn't come up with rent money. "If I was paid $30,000 to do harm to someone, why would I be evicted for not paying rent?" he told Rams. "I had nothing to do with it, and that will be proven."

He questioned the strength of the case against him. He said he'd never owned a .357-caliber Magnum revolver, and had an alibi in a former roommate who'd told police that he came home within an hour of the time police say the couple were killed. "That's an hour off from where I [was living]," he said. "How could I be home?"

Godley speculated that he had been blamed for the killings because of his long criminal past, including running from the Virginia robbery. "They are making it look like we were in this mad love affair and plotting all these things," he told Rams. "That's complete [baloney]. I think it's a huge conspiracy, and I'm the scapegoat."

Rams told Heaney that after interviewing Godley, he'd gone to the Orange County jail and requested a visit with Adriana. At first, she refused to see him. Rams asked the visiting-station deputy to send in the request a second time, this time handing Adriana a note saying that Rams had already spoken with Dennis Godley.

It was the same thing that Heaney had done, and again it worked. Adriana agreed to talk to Rams. (Rams never mentioned the other reporter, Saavedra, being part of either interview or explained why his name was on the stories, though frequently reporters who help with the writing or background share bylines.)

Adriana provided Rams with much of the same key information that she had given Heaney and Villalobos in the Twin Towers interview a month earlier—and now directly implicated her former lover Dennis Godley.

She acknowledged that she had been with Godley the

night of the killings, at the murder scene and during the planning process, but said it was Godley who'd pulled the trigger. She said he'd killed Ken because Ken "didn't follow instructions"—before opening fire, Godley had warned them both to "always keep your hands where I can see them"—and to eliminate witnesses.

"For some reason, he spared my life that day," she told Rams. "I don't know why."

She said she'd had an affair with Ken in the mid-1990s, but that it had ended and they'd remained good friends. Although she denied having anything to do with the actual murders, she said she couldn't stop them, because Ken was obsessed with having Carolyn killed and because Godley had threatened her if she interfered.

"He kept toying around with the gun and told me he was going to pop me any time," she said.

It was Dennis's threats against her and her two children, ages 11 and 3, that had stopped her from calling police until just before Thanksgiving 2000, long after the murders.

She said that Godley and Ken had met, but she agreed that Godley wasn't jealous of him. The two men had spoken several times on the phone, and met a few days before the killings in a Huntington Beach parking lot, where Ken had given Dennis $30,000 in cash. Adriana told Rams she had been at that meeting.

Adriana said that out on Ortega Highway, as Godley had shot the couple, she'd covered her eyes. Godley had run out of bullets while Carolyn was still alive, and gone back to the car to reload and finish off Carolyn.

"He was very, very pumped," Adriana said of Godley, whom she said she still feared. "He has no conscience. He's cold-blooded. He has no feelings. He should admit what he did and be sorry."

It was an interview that Adriana would forever regret giving.

Chapter Twenty-Five

At the end of March 2001, more than three months after she was arrested and ordered held in jail without bail, the legal defense of Adriana Vasco began in earnest. With Dennis Godley's case put on hold while he faced the escape and assault charges in North Carolina, Adriana appeared in court with a new attorney, Huntington Beach lawyer Robert Viefhaus. Well-known at the courthouse among prosecutors and other defense lawyers, Viefhaus was a new face for reporters. "Orange County's best-kept secret," one prosecutor said of him. A former public defender, Viefhaus had a thriving firm that handled everything from DUIs—one of his specialties—to capital murder cases. He was thorough, scholarly—he taught law at Western University College of Law in Fullerton—aggressive when he had to be, but never strident, and never, ever, a self-promoter. Although he was taking on a case that had garnered national publicity, Viefhaus's comments to the press were measured and rare. He let his lawyering do the talking.

The prosecution was represented by a veteran of homicide cases, Orange County Deputy District Attorney Walter Schwarm, a rising star in the office who was being mentioned for a promotion.

Both lawyers had a lot of work to do. The year-long investigation had generated more than a dozen banker's boxes full of statements from witnesses in California and North Carolina, lab reports, phone and bank records, search warrant affidavits and grisly photographs of the crime scene and of the autopsies, the bodies of Ken and Carolyn Stahl lying naked on the coroner's table. It was the standard working materials of a double murder case of this complexity, minus one important thing: physical evidence.

The boxes being stored on the ninth floor of the Orange County District Attorney's Office in downtown Santa Ana, where Schwarm's office was located, contained no gun, no shell casings, no fingerprint cards, no shoeprint casts, not a single hair or fiber. Schwarm's case against Adriana was being built on her own incriminating statements. It wasn't until she had acknowledged her role in the killings, in the tearful jail interview with Detectives Heaney and Villalobos, that DA officials felt they had enough evidence even to file.

For Adriana, regrets and remorse wouldn't be enough to save her. Although she claimed that she hadn't wanted to be involved in the killings, that she'd even urged Ken to pull out, and that she'd only gone along with it all because she feared Dennis would harm her or her children, California law still allowed for her to be tried and convicted as if she herself had pulled the trigger with no regrets whatsoever. The legal device at work was the principle of natural-and-probable-consequence theory. The DA could argue before a jury that the natural and probable consequence of Adriana's actions—and inactions—was that Ken and Carolyn Stahl would be murdered by Dennis Godley. Not only does this theory make her the same as a cold-blooded murderer in the eyes of the law, she also faced three special circumstances—multiple murder, murder for financial gain and lying in wait—that upped the legal ante.

She was now eligible for the death penalty.

Still, this case was no slam-dunk for the prosecution, which is why the DA had waited so long to file. Adriana's words weren't enough; even confessions don't warrant a prosecution unless they're backed up with corroborating evidence. Schwarm had some independent evidence of Adriana's activities leading up to the murders, including James Stewart recounting that Adriana had spoken of buying a handgun similar to the murder weapon for Godley, as well as statements from the Avanti Apartment residents about Adriana's relationship with Godley and her black-clad departure the night of the murders. But the only one who'd said anything about hooking up Godley with Ken, or transferring the money in the Huntington Beach parking lot, or of driving out to Ortega Highway and being present during the shootings—was Adriana herself.

That's why, for defense attorney Viefhaus, it was critical that no jury ever be allowed to hear Adriana's words to the detectives that night in the Twin Towers jail. If the defense could get that interview thrown out of court, the case might not even go to trial and Adriana could walk free. In reviewing the hundreds of pages of transcripts of Adriana's interviews, Viefhaus found ample reason for hope. In both the interview at the Costa Mesa police station and the interview at the Twin Towers, Adriana had repeatedly spoken about wanting an attorney. In fact, sections of the interviews could be interpreted as the detectives linking any help for Adriana—from counseling to legal assistance—to her confessing everything she knew.

As with the prosecution's case against Adriana, getting her statements to police suppressed was no sure thing.

But in reviewing the transcripts, the instances of arguably unconstitutional behavior by Villalobos and Heaney mounted, Viefhaus felt. As he put it in legal papers, "In this case, the police offered the defendant promises of leniency and intimidated her to force her to make the statements in question." He then listed page after page of examples, including this statement at the Stanton substation in their first interview:

> *"We'll help you as much as we can with counseling, some place to stay," Heaney told her.*
>
> *"Arrange, too, for legal counsel and for emotional counsel," Villalobos had added. "We will do what we can to help you."*
>
> *"But before that will take any effect," Heaney said, "you need to start tonight by helping us."*

During the next interview in Costa Mesa, Adriana had repeatedly said she was tired and wanted to leave. Then, when she asked, "What about, you know, my rights and stuff?" Villalobos replied: "Remember the last time we spoke to you, and Brian told you that if you wanted to talk to a district attorney or you wanted to talk to counsel, we would get counsel for you?" Adriana said, "Yeah," and Villalobos said, "And that can still happen, if you feel that you need—" Heaney finished his partner's sentence, "That will happen if that's what you want."

But it didn't happen, not even close. Instead, Adriana was carted off to jail on the traffic warrants.

Then, Adriana had only spoken to the detectives at the

Twin Towers after they'd told her that they had tracked down Dennis/Tony and that the Stewarts should take precautions for their safety. Viefhaus felt that the detectives had not only scared the wits out of Adriana, but had implied to her that Dennis/Tony believed she was cooperating with authorities. Isolated from her children, in fear of her life, and believing the detectives were the only ones who could help her, she talked. This, Viefhaus believed, violated her Miranda rights and her rights to due process.

On Tuesday, March 27, 2001, lawyers appeared before Superior Court Judge Everett W. Dickey for a preliminary hearing to determine whether Adriana's statements to detectives would be admissible. As judges go, Dickey was a wild card, at once considered tough on defendants, yet also showing an independent streak. It was Dickey who'd earned headlines in 1997 for throwing out the murder conviction of Black Panther leader Geronimo Pratt, ruling it improper. Pratt was released after serving nearly 30 years in prison.

For the hearing, Adriana didn't have to stand behind the chain link as she had at the earlier appearance, but now sat at the counsel table next to Viefhaus. She wore a dark jail jumpsuit; no jury was present, so there was no reason to make her look less inmate-like.

With Adriana's interrogations the focus of the hearing, the prosecution called as its most important witness the man primarily responsible for eliciting those statements. Detective Brian Heaney testified to some of the key developments in the case, which until now had not been revealed to the public. The reporters in the courtroom heard for the first time about how Adriana and Dennis had been seen leaving their apartment complex the night of the murders wearing dark trench coats, black pants and possibly gloves.

"He told a young neighbor he was going on a mission," said Heaney.

Afterwards, Dennis had seen the neighbor's brother, Sean.

"He took a shell casing and threw it to Sean," said Heaney. Dennis had remarked, "Here is a souvenir."

But it was the interviews that most interested Judge Dickey. The transcripts had been placed under seal, so the public didn't know the tone, extent or substance of them, only that there was an argument by the defense that they violated Adriana's Miranda rights and rights to due process.

After the attorneys had questioned Heaney, the judge said that he, too, wanted to ask some questions of the detective.

"Did you talk with any of her family members who were visiting her during that period of time she was in the Los Angeles County jail?" asked Dickey.

"Yes, I did," said Heaney.

The judge asked if the investigator had asked the family to convey "any particular position to her."

"No," said Heaney. "I did tell them she could call me any time collect at my office."

"Did you ask them specifically to tell her it would be better to talk with you, or something along that line?"

"No, I did not."

Later, the judge homed in on the most critical issue: whether Adriana had been given the opportunity to talk to an attorney. Looking over a transcript of the November 30 jailhouse interview with Adriana, the judge noted that the detective had flat-out asked her: "Why didn't you call an attorney?" and Adriana responded, "I did. Not before I talked to you, but I did and I already talked to someone regarding the case and everything."

The judge then told the detective, "I can't find anywhere in the transcript where you followed up on that to inquire in any way whether she had an attorney who might be interested in being present before any further questioning. You just apparently went on to something else. Did you follow up on that in any way?"

"I'm trying to recall," Heaney said, suddenly in very dangerous legal waters. Sitting in the courtroom, watching his partner on the stand, Villalobos's heart sank. He feared that Dickey was siding with the defense—that at least some of Adriana's statements wouldn't get in. The question was just how many were doomed.

"She gave me no name of an attorney," Heaney continued, "and she didn't retain an attorney. I think she explained it to me that she had talked about what it would cost, but ultimately didn't retain an attorney."

The judge pointed out to the detective that, again, Adriana makes reference to possibly getting an attorney.

"And you basically, according to the transcript, just ignore that and go on with the questions," said the judge.

Heaney said that from his recollection, "it's a bit confusing" and, "I'm not sure. I'm a little bit confused by what she says."

The judge wasn't confused. He said the transcript showed that Heaney had even told Adriana's former boyfriend Greg Stewart and his mother, Nancy, that Adriana was considering hiring counsel.

Heaney acknowledged, "I could have conveyed that to Greg or Nancy."

Returning to the issue the judge had first raised— Heaney's conversations with Adriana's family—the detective said he had spoken to Greg Stewart after returning from North Carolina.

"I said, briefly, 'We found Tony. We have some concerns. We would like to meet with you and share with you what those concerns are regarding your personal safety,'"

Heaney testified. He told the judge about the meeting in which he'd advised the Stewarts to keep their lights on and, if they saw any strange vehicles or received any strange phone calls, to contact the local police.

"We didn't know at that time if there was anyone in the area that could threaten them," the detective continued. "Godley hadn't threatened the Stewarts, but I did feel compelled to share with them that information, because up until then, as far as I know, Dennis Godley didn't know what we were doing. . . . Prior to visiting with him, he didn't know that this investigation had gotten to the point it had."

The detective said he'd gotten word that Adriana had reeled at the news that police had found Godley. Greg Stewart had quoted the jailed Adriana as saying either, "Oh, my God, he can put me away for life" or "put me away forever," the detective testified.

Greg also told the detective that his family was looking into how much it would cost to get an attorney, according to Heaney.

"All right," the judge said, "thank you. Counsel, I don't believe I have any other questions. You may have some as a result of the court's questions."

The attorneys didn't have any follow-up questions for Heaney. But that didn't end things. After the prosecution rested its pre-trial hearing case, defense attorney Robert Viefhaus had his own witness: Adriana Vasco.

It is rare for a defendant to take the stand, in either a pre-trial hearing or a trial, and calling Adriana—whose mouth had already gotten her into so much trouble—was particularly risky. But Viefhaus had to make a case that Adriana's rights had been trampled by the detectives, and that the transcripts—while obviously making an impression on the judge—didn't tell the whole story. While there were poten-

tial pitfalls to putting Adriana on the stand, the benefits—
getting her statements thrown out, perhaps avoiding a
trial—seemed worth the gamble.

With the questioning narrowly focused on the circumstances of her police interviews, and not what she'd said to
the detectives, Adriana made it clear that she'd talked to
Heaney and Villalobos in part out of fear. She related
Heaney's visit to the Stewarts in which he told them about
seeing Dennis Godley in North Carolina. "At that point I
was scared," she said.

She'd felt, though, that, Heaney would believe her—
that Godley was a bad, bad man and that Adriana and
her family needed protection. Having heard from the
Stewarts, Adriana said she now felt she could rely on
Heaney and took him at his word.

She said she'd believed "if I talked to him and I told
him what I knew, that he was able to protect my kids and
myself. He will give me legal counsel, you know, somewhere where I can stay because I had lost my home, and
counseling for my depression."

Her understanding had been that if she talked to him,
"that I wasn't going to be charged with anything, anything at all." And so, when they'd read her her Miranda
rights, telling her that she had the right to an attorney,
she'd thought it was just a formality. "Maybe I should
have paid more attention of really the meaning of it," she
said.

When she finished her direct testimony, prosecutor
Schwarm rose to cross-examine her. He began by eliciting an acknowledgment that she hadn't told police the
whole truth in her first interview at the Stanton sheriff
substation.

"You lied to them?" asked Schwarm.

"I misled them," Adriana countered.

Schwarm suggested in his questioning that Adriana had a self-interest to mislead Detective Heaney, the truth betrayed only by her emotions.

"When you first saw him, you were sobbing very heavily, weren't you?" asked Schwarm.

"Yes, I was," she said.

"That's because of this heavy knowledge that you had about witnessing the murders of Ken and Carolyn Stahl?"

Viefhaus objected—the questioning was veering into the substance of the interviews, not the circumstances surrounding them. The last thing the defense attorney wanted was Adriana testifying to the very material Viefhaus was trying to get suppressed. But Judge Dickey overruled him and allowed the question to stand.

"It was the heavy burden of everything combined," Adriana said of her tears, "especially living every day in fear [for] my life and my kids'."

"But you also, Miss Vasco, felt a lot of remorse for your participation in the murders of Ken and Carolyn Stahl at the time you spoke with Investigator Heaney on November thirtieth, 2000?" asked Schwarm. "True, that's one of the things you were worried about?"

"I didn't want to keep living in fear, and I wanted to stop seeing a loaded gun in front of my face."

"You wanted to admit to the officers what happened in order to clear your mind, correct?"

"I wanted them to protect me and my kids."

"You also wanted to clear your conscience of this terrible thing that you participated in?"

"I didn't really feel like participating."

"About your knowledge of this terrible thing that you had, you wanted to share that with him?"

"Yeah, probably."

It was as far as Adriana got to speaking about the secrets

she held. Although prone to emotional outbursts, as the police interviews showed, Adriana proved to be a good witness on her own behalf. Adriana wrapped up her testimony and took a seat back at the counsel table next to Viefhaus.

Schwarm then made his final pitch to the judge to allow the police statements into evidence. He had covered the matter extensively in court papers, but he'd hit the important points in his oral argument. Schwarm contended that the reason Adriana had called Detective Heaney from jail was to help relieve the guilt on her shoulders, a guilt born from knowing she was responsible for the murders of two people. She had even made reference to a Bible passage about confession that helped convince her to tell the truth to Heaney and Villalobos. Nobody, Schwarm insisted, had tricked her or coerced her with false promises of attorneys, protection for her family or mental health counseling.

"She is the one that initiated this," he said. "She is the person. She never had to call the police on November thirtieth of 2000. She never had to invite them to the Los Angeles County jail Twin Towers facility. Those are choices she made. . . . I'd ask the court to find that those statements were voluntary."

But Viefhaus countered that throughout the case, the detectives "keep telling her they are going to either do certain things or help with certain things, but only after she talks." Hitting every emotional weak spot, the detectives had isolated her from her children, put her in jail, played on her fears of Godley, then dangled promises of helping protect her and her children. "He [Heaney] is simply utilizing her fear and his power," said Viefhaus. "It seems clear the reason she talked with them is she thought Heaney was her only salvation. She thought she could only go to him. . . . Therefore, I think the statements ought to be excluded."

With that, the matter went to Judge Dickey. It only took him a day to come to a decision.

On Wednesday, March 28, 2001, Dickey had barely exchanged good mornings with the attorneys when he made his feelings about Adriana's treatment at the hands of police starkly clear. "As I listened to the tapes pretty much over the last two weekends," Dickey said, "I was struck by the flagrant disregard of the defendant's rights by the sheriff's deputies in this case."

In the courtroom, Villalobos and Heaney felt like they had been hit in the stomach. The judge expressed shock in learning that the detectives had picked up Adriana at her workplace without notice and without charging her with a crime, taken her to a police station and "subjected her to a three-and-a-half-hour interrogation," essentially telling her that if she didn't disclose everything she knew, she could face the death penalty.

"And then when she wouldn't answer the questions the way they wanted her to—or at least as completely as they wanted her to—then they told her she was going to go to jail," said Dickey. "When she asked if she could answer questions with an attorney present, the investigator repeated, 'You are going to jail tonight.'"

Adriana's situation must be put in perspective, the judge said. "She is a thirty-three-year-old immigrant from Mexico who was abandoned by her mother as an infant and who came to the United States. She has no father in her life. She has no experience with a history of police interrogation as far as I can tell from these records," he said. "She is—vulnerable, I think, is the accurate way to describe it—a vulnerable person to overreaching by the law-enforcement officer."

That officer—Heaney—had played on her vulnerability by raising the specter of Dennis Godley, said Dickey. The judge expressed doubts that Heaney had really been worried about Adriana's and the Stewarts' safety when he'd warned them about the jailed suspected gunman. "I can conceive of no possible reason other than what happened: to call Ms. Vasco and increase the pressure on her to cooperate," he said.

Heaney and Villalobos ultimately did read Adriana her Miranda rights, but by then, the judge said, it was too late. "To be later given her rights cannot be given a lot of significance when she's already had her rights ignored by the same deputies," said Dickey.

"Of course," the judge continued, "these are extremely serious crimes, and it's understandable why they devoted the time they did to it. When you have a high-profile serious crime like this, the sheriff's deputies are probably under pressure to get the crime solved, as well," said the judge. "But that does not justify transferring that pressure to a defendant or a person who may be a possible suspect in the case. They simply have to follow the law, which includes the law regarding the defendant's rights, constitutional rights as well."

With that, Dickey handed the defense a major pre-trial victory. Adriana's statements to police—the heart of the prosecution's evidence-slim case—were cut out. The preliminary hearing was abruptly adjourned. Viefhaus told reporters the break was needed "to give both of us time to look at all of the evidence."

Schwarm declined to comment.

The hearing, meanwhile, had an ironic footnote. This same week, the sheriff's department announced that Heaney and Villalobos had just been honored with Medals of Merit for their homicide work.

"We are surprised and disappointed at the court's ruling," said a statement from their boss, Sheriff Mike Carona, who'd handed them their medals a day before the judge's decision was reached. "Our investigators did an outstanding job. . . . As always, we need to wait until the case is fully adjudicated to see what happens."

Chapter Twenty-Six

Each day at the Orange County jail, Deputy Christina Brown would read letters written by maximum-security inmates. The letters would get as far as the mail room and Brown had to clear them for release outside the jail. The practice is a security precaution—to get an early word on escape plans, root out gang affiliations or even protect suicidal inmates. If the letters don't have any sensitive information—and don't contain drugs or weapons—they're resealed and sent on their way.

On Friday, March 30, 2001—two days after Adriana's big win in court—Brown received a six-page letter that Adriana had sent to another inmate. The letter had been written that day. Looking back, Brown couldn't remember why the mail room had directed the letter to her. It could just have been because Adriana was in maximum security. In any event, Brown gave this letter a close read.

"Adriana had written that she was happy that her part of her testimony had been thrown out in court," Brown recalled. Adriana griped about the police, spoke of her children, and mentioned how optimistic she was that the case might turn out well. None of this stood out to Deputy Brown—until she got to this line in the letter:

> Now that I got rid of the cops, all I have to do is get rid of Bill Rams.

Deputy Brown had followed the Stahl case in the *Register* and knew exactly who Rams was and what his role might be in the case. Brown didn't save the letter; it was resealed and delivered. But she did discuss it with another inmate and write a report while the matter was still fresh in her mind. Then she spoke to Heaney about it. In reading the letter, she said, it wasn't clear whether Adriana was speaking in terms of legal strategy, or whether she wanted to get rid of Rams the same way Ken Stahl had wanted to get rid of his wife, Carolyn.

After the stunning loss in the fight over the police statements, the prosecution's case against Adriana now rested on the shoulders of a news reporter for *The Orange County Register*. Bill Rams's articles of January 3, 2001, contained the only other instance of Adriana Vasco admitting to being part of the murder plot and of being on Ortega Highway while Dennis Godley had allegedly gunned down Ken and Carolyn Stahl. With Godley staying mum, and Ken dead, the DA had no other witness— no friend, family member or inmate—to bring into court to say they'd heard these statements.

In the end, despite the apparent threat in Adriana's letter, Rams faced nothing worse than aggressive lawyers. On Wednesday, April 11, 2001, he came to court—not as a professional observer from the audience section, but as a subpoenaed witness for the People of the State of California. Prosecutor Walt Schwarm needed to call Rams in order to introduce into evidence the two *Register* articles. Under court rules, one side or the other can't simply introduce a newspaper article unless there's a stipulation. The lawyer needs to call the article's author or some other relevant witness to vouch for the article's authenticity.

In most cases, this is an innocuous enough event. But in this case, the defense strongly objected to introducing Rams's articles unless Viefhaus would be allowed to cross-examine the reporter. The defense had a long list of questions, most of them focused on what Adriana had said that never made it into the articles. The defense suggested that Adriana could have made statements favorable to her side and they simply never got into print. Viefhaus also wanted to raise questions about Rams's accuracy—he could have misquoted Adriana or shaded her statements inaccurately while paraphrasing her remarks in the articles. In short, the defense wanted to treat Rams like any other witness, preserving Adriana's right to confront the reporter under oath.

The problem, from the standpoint of *The Orange County Register*, was that Bill Rams wasn't just any other witness. He was a newspaper reporter, and in California, as in many states, reporters are protected by a shield law. California's is even written into the state constitution. A key part of the law are protections against peeking into reporters' notepads for unpublished material. Normally this would mean the names of confidential sources; in this case, it could mean material that wasn't included in the articles.

The situation created a constitutional clash between a reporter's First Amendment rights and protections under the state constitution and a defendant's rights to due process and a fair trial. But this was no mere scholarly discussion; Adriana's life was literally at stake. If Rams's articles were admitted into evidence, she faced possible conviction and death by lethal injection.

Both the *Register*'s attorney, Gary Bostwick, and Adriana's defense asked Judge Dickey to settle the fight before it even started, by quashing the subpoena and refusing to let Rams take the stand in the pre-trial hearing. But Dickey wanted to proceed, albeit slowly and carefully, and he gave the prosecution the green light.

"I will call Mr. Rams at this point, Your Honor," said prosecutor Walt Schwarm.

Rams took the stand.

After saying and spelling his name, Rams was asked a seemingly harmless question: Schwarm wanted to know if Rams had co-authored the story that bore his byline and that of the other reporter, Tony Saavedra.

"Objection on the grounds of journalistic privilege," said *Register* attorney Gary Bostwick.

The judge bristled. He couldn't see how answering that question would in any way violate a reporter's privilege by revealing unpublished information. He ordered Rams to answer.

"My name appears on the byline," Rams said.

Now Schwarm objected. He complained Rams didn't responsively answer his question.

"Sustained," said the frustrated judge.

"Mr. Rams," Schwarm said, "with respect to that article . . . entitled 'Till Death Did They Part,' did you co-author that article with Tony Saavedra?"

"I respectfully decline to answer that question," Rams said.

The judge had heard enough. "You are ordered to answer the question, Mr. Rams," he said.

Rams then huddled with his attorney, then answered, "I'm sorry. I worked on the story with Tony Saavedra and I reported on it."

The court hearing would lurch ahead at this agonizing pace, with the reporter and his attorney pettifogging at nearly every question.

Eventually, Judge Dickey ordered Rams to simply confirm that quotes in the article were in fact quotes from Adriana, and that some information was paraphrased by Rams. Beyond that, the judge sided with the *Register* and didn't allow Rams to testify about anything that wasn't directly mentioned in the article.

As difficult as it was for Schwarm to deal with the reporter, the net result was a big victory for the prosecution. Quote by quote, paraphrase by paraphrase, the prosecution was able to get into evidence statements similar to those the judge had barred just two weeks before.

For the defense, it was a crushing blow—and Viefhaus couldn't contain his disappointment when he started questioning Rams.

"Mr. Rams, how are you today?"

"Fine, thanks," the reporter said.

"That was a trick question," Viefhaus said.

From then on, it was all uphill for Viefhaus. The defense attorney tried to show that Rams had spoken to Adriana earlier by phone and told her that if she talked to him, it would help her get a lawyer. But the judge allowed Rams to remain mum on those issues.

Bostwick objected to virtually every question Viefhaus asked. The judge sustained virtually every objection. Rams provided nothing more than what was in the articles. As Viefhaus kept trying to cross-examine the reporter, the judge finally said the effort was futile.

"I didn't write the law," the judge said. "It's my job to

try to figure out what it is. That's what I've tried to do and rule accordingly."

There was little left for Adriana and her attorney to do but watch and worry. Rams ended his testimony and the prosecution recalled Detective Brian Heaney to fill out the rest of the prosecution's case. Heaney spoke of his interviews with Nancy Stewart and apartment neighbor Raymond Ruiz. He said that a couple of days before the murders, Nancy had talked about the phone call in which Adriana had said that she was feeling stressed out and took a drive down Ortega Highway. And Heaney recalled how Ruiz had seen Adriana and Dennis Godley leave their apartments the night of the murders dressed in black. "He described them as being dressed like ninjas, or undercover," Heaney said.

When Heaney finished testifying, Schwarm said, "Your Honor, at this time, the People would ask the court to hold Miss Vasco to answer on the charges contained in the felony complaint and the special allegations."

Viefhaus had won the fight over the police statements, but lost on the newspaper statements. He argued that the net result was that the prosecution had failed to put on enough evidence to hold Adriana to the charges.

"The only information we have that really links her at all is the newspaper reporter's statements, and that seems simply to indicate that she was present at the scene of the crime," said Viefhaus. "I don't think that is sufficient enough."

The judge took no time to even think about it. The burden of proof at the preliminary hearing level is low and he issued his ruling, if somewhat grudgingly.

"For the purposes of a preliminary hearing, I think the evidence is sufficient," he said, then added, "It certainly may not be for trial, if the case goes to trial."

The judge's reservations notwithstanding, charges were filed against Adriana a week later. She and her attorney received the information:

The District Attorney of Orange County hereby accuses the aforenamed defendant of violating the law within the County of Orange as follows:

COUNT 1: On or about November 20, 1999, Adriana Vasco, in violation of Section 187(a) of the Penal Code (MURDER), a FELONY, did willfully, unlawfully and with malice aforethought murder Kenneth C. Stahl, a human being.

COUNT 2: On or about November 20, 1999, Adriana Vasco, in violation of Section 187(a) of the Penal Code (MURDER), a FELONY, did willfully, unlawfully and with malice aforethought murder Carolyn M. Oppy-Stahl, a human being.

The information also contained the three special allegations of multiple murder, murder for financial gain and lying in wait. These made her eligible for the death penalty. And while the case did move forward, the DA did scale it back somewhat. On April 24, 2001, a week after the information was filed, attorney Robert Viefhaus received a letter reading:

Dear Counsel:
    After careful consideration of the facts presently available in this case, it is the decision of the Orange County District Attorney's Office not to pursue the death penalty against your client, Adriana Vasco. If, however, upon review and consideration of any new facts, there is a change of position by our office

regarding whether to seek death, you will be notified immediately.

Sincerely yours,
Walter Schwarm
Deputy District Attorney

With this letter, the worst that Adriana Vasco faced was life in prison without the possibility of parole.

Chapter Twenty-Seven

It was a sad sight.

Ed Godley slumped in the witness chair, struggling at times to stay awake. He spoke so softly he could barely be heard. He had recently undergone shock treatments and returned from a sixty-day stay in a mental hospital. His prescription pill diet included Percocet, Xanax, Celexa, Seroquel, Remeron, Pepcid and Adalat, as well as injections of Vitamin B12 and steroids.

When asked his address, he said, "My wife may have to tell you. I don't know."

It was Tuesday, February 26, 2002—ten months after Adriana Vasco had been charged with murder with special circumstances in the deaths of Kenneth and Carolyn Stahl. Now, Orange County Judge Christopher W. Strople was being asked to bind her one-time lover Dennis Godley over on the same charges, for a separate trial.

Dennis had been shipped from North Carolina to Virginia via a private prisoner transport service. Ed Godley had been summoned to the Santa Ana court from his home in North Carolina to testify in the preliminary hearing for his son.

Ed was a witness for the prosecution.

As mean and nasty a person as Dennis Godley had been described to be, the case against him was not that strong—arguably even weaker than the one against Adriana. The prosecution had no physical evidence—they'd never found the gun or any blood or fiber evidence on Godley's clothing or other belongings. They also didn't have his own statements to use against him; when Godley had spoken to Bill Rams, he'd denied having anything to do with the murders, confirming only having a relationship with Adriana that hadn't meant much. When Detective Brian Heaney interviewed him in jail, Godley said little more, again denying being involved in the murders.

The prosecution did have witnesses at the Avanti Apartment complex who could speak of Godley acquiring a gun similar to the one used to kill the Stahls, and of his having gone on what he called "a mission" the night of the murders. They had the statements from the people in North Carolina. And, if need be, they had Adriana Vasco.

It wasn't clear how much of Ed Godley's behavior on this day—his memory lapses, his lack of understanding of the questions, his deficits in attention—was due to a hard life and the mighty medication cocktail he was taking, and how much was due to his reluctance and discomfort in testifying against his son. Prosecutor Walt Schwarm suggested repeatedly that Ed Godley could have done a lot better on the stand. This was, after all, the same Ed Godley who'd turned in his son to authorities, then openly chatted with detectives from California. But that was about a year-and-a-half earlier, before the shock treatments, before the mental hospital stay.

"Do you remember," asked Schwarm, "your son getting arrested at your house in Belhaven, North Carolina, in August of 2000?"

"No," Ed said.

"You have no memory of that?"

"No."

"Did your son live with you in August of 2000?"

"I don't recollect."

As he spoke, his son sat just a few feet away at the defense table. Dennis Godley wore a jail jumpsuit and sat next to his attorney, Denise Gragg, widely regarded as among the best criminal defense attorneys in California. Once named Public Defender of the Year in the state, Gragg was aggressive and passionate—and a staunch opponent of the death penalty. Gragg taught at Western University College of Law and supervised her office's death-penalty caseload. Her résumé included representation in a number of high-stakes murder trials.

She watched as Schwarm pressed Ed Godley on the details of his son's arrest. "I remember a lot of commotion and a lot of people running all around the house," Ed said in his thick North Carolina accent. He said he also remembered his son's voice as he was being hauled off by police. "It's always been stuck in the back of my mind," he said. "I remember my son screaming, 'Don't let them take me away, Dad!' It's always been there and it never leaves."

Under cross-examination by Gragg, Ed spoke of his own deterioration starting around the time his son was arrested. He'd had his driver's license taken away, he'd stopped cooking for himself, stopped cleaning the house, stopped paying bills.

"Why was that?" asked Gragg. "Why did you have other people taking care of all that for you?"

"Because I couldn't do it."

"Couldn't do it physically or mentally?"

"Mental."

The testimony would continue in this vein, adding little to the prosecution's case.

During the morning court recess, Ed Godley fell asleep on the witness stand.

The preliminary hearing took a month recess—Ed Godley was sent home—then resumed on March 28, 2002, with the prosecution calling Ronald Smith, who testified that he'd spent much of his twenty years as a Pitt County, North Carolina, deputy sheriff responding to calls about Dennis Earl Godley—and said he had been there for Dennis's last arrest in August 2000. Smith recalled how Ed Godley was far from the addled, drug-popping forgetful case on the witness stand in California, but a man who had not only turned in his son, but then asked several times about a reward.

Under cross-examination, Smith acknowledged that as bad as the younger Godley was, his reputation often was worse than reality. What Smith didn't witness firsthand, he'd gotten by word of mouth from other lawmen; he didn't carefully read too many police reports. This only seemed to make the legend of the Weasel grow. For example, by the time word had gotten to Smith about Godley's escape from the Virginia patrol car, the episode had become more dramatic, with Godley knocking out a window and assaulting an officer, rather than just slipping away into the night through a door carelessly left unlocked.

The most important witness of the preliminary hearing was Kyle Alligood, just a few days shy of his 16th birthday, who was called to recount how Dennis Godley, in the first and last time they ever spoke, had strolled into the garage shirtless and tattooed and claimed to have killed a couple of people in California.

And then Detective Brian Heaney recounted his interview with an apartment neighbor of Dennis's who helped him acquire a .357-caliber handgun—the same kind of handgun that could have been used in the Stahl murders.

Having met their low burden, prosecutors got what they wanted: Judge Strople found grounds to hold Godley on murder charges. Only, unlike Adriana, there would be no letter from the prosecution sparing him the death penalty. The prosecution felt that Dennis Godley had pulled the trigger—and should therefore pay the ultimate price.

That decision, however, would have to wait.

Adriana Vasco's trial was about to begin.

Chapter Twenty-Eight

On Tuesday, November 12, 2002, Superior Court Judge Francisco P. Briseno took the bench, issued a good morning to jurors, and said that the day was already off to a bad start.

"I have been advised that there's a problem with the power box that operates the elevators, and so they're not working as they should," he said. "I mean, they are working, but they're very independent today. They might or might not come up to the eleventh floor, they might or might not take you to the third floor."

As Briseno's court was on the eleventh floor, this was a particular problem. He told them "the situation" would likely last for another day and that it was being worked on. It would not be the last inconvenience for jurors, who, over the course of the trial, would find themselves often spending as much time sitting in the hallway outside the court as they did in the jury box.

With that, he announced, "This is the matter of *People*

vs. *Vasco*. We're in open court with counsel, defendant and the jury."

The trial of Adriana Vasco was about to begin under the firm, experienced and dignified watch of Judge Briseno. Highly respected by both prosecutors and defense attorneys, Briseno was a former Marine who'd risen through the legal ranks in the Orange County DA's Office, where he'd tried homicide cases. Briseno remained in tip-top shape from his military days—lean and trim, with no trace of gray in his dark hair. As a judge, he was no stranger to high-profile cases. At the time of the Stahl trial, he was in fact juggling two, also hearing motions in the Samantha Runnion murder case, in which a man named Alejandro Avila was accused of the July 2002 kidnapping of 5-year-old Samantha from her condominium in rough-and-tumble Stanton, where Detective Villalobos once patrolled. The girl's body had been found along Ortega Highway, where the Stahls' were discovered. The parallels didn't stop there: The defense lawyer for Avila was public defender Denise Gragg; she would also represent Dennis Godley.

It had been eighteen months since Adriana had been charged with double murder and received the letter sparing her the death penalty. In the interim, Dennis Godley had been convicted of robbery in Suffolk Circuit Court on April 4, 2001, and sentenced to 20 years in Virginia state prison for the convenience store holdup. He had also been convicted of escape without force in another court and sentenced to an additional month in jail for slipping out of the patrol car. In August 2001, he was shipped by a private convict-transport company to California to face murder charges in the Stahl killings, and placed in the Men's Central Jail in Santa Ana. On September 4, 2001, he appeared in court with the assistance of a public defender and pleaded not guilty to the charges, his trial put off while Adriana's went first.

At Adriana's trial, jurors were each given a notepad and a single-page copy of the law that spells out their basic responsibilities. The judge had had jurors read it earlier and asked them to keep it with them. "I know you've already read it," said Briseno, "but it wouldn't hurt for you to take another look at it."

"We'll make our best efforts to keep you informed as to the pace of the trial, the availability of the witnesses, and how current we are with our time estimate," he said. "If there's any problems, we'll try to advise you as quickly as we can."

The judge then told the jury that the information—or charges, as they're called in California—alleged two violations of the law by Adriana, both murder. He told jurors that Adriana had pleaded not guilty to both charges.

"And that's why you have been impaneled," he said. "It's your job to determine whether the charges are true or not, consistent with the law that you'll be given and the evidence that will be presented."

He also told them that three special circumstances had been alleged. The clerk read the information, telling jurors that Adriana Vasco had been charged with two counts of murder in the deaths of Kenneth and Carolyn Stahl, with special circumstances. If they found her guilty, this jury would have the power to lock up Adriana for the rest of her life.

"So with that," Briseno said, "People have an opening statement?"

A new voice said, "Yes, Your Honor."

The prosecution of Adriana Vasco had been handed over from Walt Schwarm. Just six weeks before the trial started, he had been promoted up to the tenth floor to management and gave the case to Deputy District Attorney Dennis Conway, a street-smart litigator who for years had cut his legal teeth on gang cases before being moved to homicide. A single father originally from Massachusetts, Conway got to the DA's office the hard way, skipping college and going straight to law school in the late 1980s. He took night classes at Western State University College of Law in Fullerton—where Viefhaus would later teach—while working as a bartender at the Studio Café in Corona Del Mar. Before the Stahl case, he had handled about ten murder trials, though this was the first that didn't involve a gang killing.

Conway had had to scramble to bring himself up to speed on the case, relying heavily on guidance from Schwarm—a meticulously organized lawyer, who'd written brief synopses of all the important police interviews—and his investigator, Pat O'Sullivan, to wade through the thousands of pages of reports and pre-trial transcripts. But very early in his preparation, Conway knew he had an advantage that other prosecutors might not. The very difficulties of trying this case—proving a conspiracy between unsavory characters with little physical evidence—played to his experience at the DA's office. Conway had tried countless gang cases with the same dynamics.

There were only two things Conway didn't review: transcripts of Adriana's police interviews in Costa Mesa and at the Twin Towers. He knew that the statements had been suppressed; he didn't want to accidentally quote from them or ask any questions based on them—particularly if he were ever to cross-examine Adriana. Conway didn't want to provide appellate fodder.

"Good afternoon, ladies and gentlemen," Conway said to the jury.

"Good afternoon," jurors said back.

"You've heard the information and the charges, and in anticipation of your attention for the next week or so, I thank you in advance," he said.

He would need every ounce of their attention. The People had built a case marked as much by what it didn't have as by what it did. The prosecution would present no eyewitness to the murders and no physical evidence from the murder scene or anywhere else tying Adriana Vasco to the shooting deaths of Kenneth and Carolyn Stahl. They had no police confession from Adriana, and they had no friend, co-worker or relative of hers who could specifically say that she had planned, helped carry out or even talked about the murders after the fact. The case would hinge entirely on two things: circumstantial evidence linking Adriana to a very nasty man named Dennis Godley, and her statements to newspaper reporter Bill Rams.

In his opening statement, which by law is supposed to be a straightforward, non-argumentative presentation of what the DA believes the evidence will show, Conway asked the jurors to consider some questions: Did Adriana conspire to kill Carolyn Stahl? Was there an "overt act" committed to further that agreement?

And then he asked them to consider this legal mouthful of a question: "Did the defendant, with knowledge of the unlawful purpose of the perpetrator—that would be the person that pulled the trigger—and with the intent or purpose of committing or encouraging the unlawful purpose or the commission of the crime of the perpetrator, either by any of her actions or advice, aid, promote, encourage, or instigate the commission of the crime of murder?"

Courtroom poetry, this was not. But this case was going to be as much about legal principles as it was about anything else, and such statements would become common in this trial. The evidence would show, he said, that Adriana may never have pulled the trigger, but she was a killer just the same in the eyes of the law.

In laying out this circumstantial case, Conway asked the jury to keep an open mind, not just about the evidence, but about some of the people involved in the case. "There's a segment of society out there that may not think and act like you do," he said. "You are going to hear about a segment of society that you only read about in books or made-for-TV movies, but it exists out there." He didn't say it at first, but this was Adriana Vasco's world, the world that Dr. Kenneth Stahl was strangely drawn toward.

Adriana's lawyer had heard enough.

"Your Honor, I object," he said, interrupting the prosecutor's opening argument before it was even five minutes old. "I think this is an improper opening statement. I think this is more argument"—argument that is saved for the summation when lawyers draw inferences from the evidence and testimony.

It was one of several objections that Viefhaus had to the presentation. The judge cautioned the prosecutor, and he moved on.

From here, Conway introduced the jurors to the major players in this crime drama: Adriana Vasco—seated at the counsel table—as well as Dr. Kenneth Stahl, Dennis Godley, aka Tony Satton, and Stahl's wife, Carolyn Oppy-Stahl. Giving a brief biography of the Stahls, Conway noted that Ken was a doctor and Carolyn was an optometrist, and he made no effort to gloss over their problems. "The marriage of Carolyn Oppy-Stahl and Dr. Kenneth Stahl was not a good one, and that's an understatement," the prosecutor said.

He went on to say that Ken had had an affair with Adriana for "five years, if not more," and that at some point Carolyn even knew about it. But Ken was smitten with Adriana—"like a moonstruck teenager"—and the relationship, be it an affair or a close friendship that had Kenneth financially providing for Adriana, had continued up until the day the Stahls died. It was, Conway said, a sad life.

"He didn't like his home life. He didn't like his wife. All he did was work," Conway said. "But the one constant in his life was always Adriana Vasco."

Entering the picture, Conway told jurors, was Dennis Godley, who became Adriana's boyfriend—and Ken's partner in murder. "Even though Dennis Godley is from a completely different world than Ken Stahl, he's a guy that, you'll see, is exactly the kind of guy that will do a murder for money," said Conway. "Adriana Vasco found the person that will complete the plan for her and Ken Stahl." The plan, he said, "is concocted to do away with Carolyn Oppy-Stahl.

"They hook up and they pick a spot out on the Ortega Highway that's very remote. They pick a time, at night," he said. "And that is where the arrangement is done to murder Carolyn Oppy-Stahl."

Just after 10 p.m., he said the murder scene was discovered. Only instead of one body, there were two—Carolyn's and Ken's. And that's about all that's found. "The murders are done at a location where there's no eyewitnesses," said Conway, conceding the limitations of his case. "There's not even a shell casing; a revolver is used. There's no fingerprints. There is no tire tracks or footprints. There's no evidence out at the crime scene."

And so the prosecutor called on jurors to listen to the evidence, stay focused and consider the circumstantial evidence that the defendant—Adriana—had shared the murder motive with Ken, been involved in some of the planning, helped get the revolver, and been out on Ortega Highway when the murders were committed. And even though she hadn't planned on killing Ken, she was responsible for his murder just the same.

"He was killed to eliminate the only witness that can implicate [Dennis Godley] and Adriana Vasco," said Conway. "You see, one of the other pieces of evidence you're going to hear about, one of the most important pieces of evidence that corroborates her hooking Stahl up with Godley and cooking up this murder of Carolyn Oppy-Stahl is the fact that she's sitting here. That piece of evidence speaks volumes."

The cover-up after the murder had nearly worked, Conway said. With no evidence at the scene, it wasn't until she was booked in December of 2000—more than a year after the murders—that she'd played her hand, the prosecutor said.

"You're going to hear about a limited interview that she gave to the *Orange County Register* reporter," he said.

It was the heart of the prosecution case. And Conway gave no clue of the tough three-way battle between the defense, the prosecution and the *Register* over whether jurors would hear anything about that story reported by Bill Rams. He also made no mention of Adriana's jailhouse interview with Detective Brian Heaney in which she gave a much more detailed explanation of her role in the killings.

With that, Conway wrapped up his opening statement by again asking jurors to use their common sense—and realize the unique role that Kenneth Stahl had played in his own murder. "Even though in your minds you might think Ken Stahl's not really a victim, in the eyes of the law he is," said Conway. "And I'm confident you'll find [Adriana] guilty of his murder as well."

As Conway took his seat, Judge Briseno looked to the defense table and asked, "Mr. Viefhaus, did you wish to make an opening statement or did you wish to reserve it?"

In the first surprise of the trial, Adriana's lawyer said, "The defense would reserve opening statement at this time."

The prosecutor began by painting a picture of the crime scene, first calling Rancho Mission Viejo security guard Tony Castillo to recount how he'd found two bodies late at night on November 20, 1999, while patrolling the open land outside San Juan Capistrano in his cruiser. He described how the car was parked on the side of Ortega Highway with the high beams still on and a man who appeared to have been shot through the eye still strapped in his seatbelt, and next to him a woman slumped over with one foot sticking out the open passenger door.

Orange County sheriff's crime-scene investigator Laurie Crutchfield followed on the stand, and described how she had processed the scene, noting evidence before and after the bodies were removed by the coroner—particularly the damage to the car caused by bullets and the blood trail along the passenger side.

As Conway displayed grisly photographs to the jurors, Crutchfield identified the bloody bodies of Ken and Carolyn Stahl and explained how it appeared they had been killed. She noted that Ken had been shot from close range through the passenger side. One bullet had entered his head, exiting his eyeball, and one passed through his right arm and upper chest. She said Carolyn had taken shots to the body and the head.

The bullets were .38 caliber and appeared to have come from a revolver. By counting the wounds and recovered slugs, Crutchfield was able to conclude that the revolver had been reloaded and fired again—and that Carolyn didn't die at once.

"It appears that she made an effort to go to the back of the car," said Crutchfield.

For both witnesses, defense attorney Viefhaus had only a few token cross-examination questions, a signal that the defense was going to make its move later in the case.

Judge Briseno sent the jurors out for their afternoon break, which they spent mostly in the hallway. He apologized for the "limited facilities and limited space out there," and reminded them to steer clear of the witnesses, investigators, attorneys and audience members. When they returned, the judge said that the elevator situation was improving, to a point. They were now stopping on every floor. "So they're running," he said. "However, they won't be able to fix it until around ten or eleven tomorrow." He also noted the news reporters in the courtroom and reminded jurors to refrain from reading newspaper accounts or watching TV stories about the case.

The prosecution case resumed with the first—and only—of Ken's family members to testify: Tamara Stahl Parham, his sister and, now, executrix of his estate, who gave a brief history of Ken and Carolyn, noting that he had "had a very close relationship" with his mother. She also was one of the few witnesses to say anything nice— or at least not bad—about Ken, joking about his health and fitness fixations and how he "really cared about his body."

But the crux of Parham's testimony was about money. She said that after Ken was murdered, she'd discovered, while going through his financial papers, the $20,000 cash withdrawal from Union Bank of California shortly before the murders.

In the first lengthy cross-examination of the trial, Viefhaus elicited from a visibly nervous Tamara Stahl Parham more details about Ken's marriages, education and finances—and tried to get her to reveal one of her brother's secrets.

"You found his address book, didn't you?" he asked.

"Yes," she said.

"And it was mainly all women's names and addresses and phone numbers, right?"

"Nothing in that book stood out for me in any way."

"Well, do you recall what the percentage was of women?"

"No," she said, doing more than anybody else would at trial to preserve what little dignity her brother had left, "I do not have any idea."

The next day, Wednesday, November 13, 2002, prosecutor Dennis Conway put into evidence the most important part of his case: the *Orange County Register* story quoting Adriana Vasco from jail.

After all the fighting over its admission and the lofty arguments over First Amendment rights versus rights to a fair trial, the ultimate presentation before a jury was unexceptional. Bill Rams took the stand; his only purpose was to confirm that his article had said what it said. Nearby sat *Register* attorney Gary Bostwick to make sure that that reporter's shield remained in place.

"Did you have published, in the January third, 2001, edition of *The Orange County Register*, excerpts from an interview you had [with] the defendant, Adriana Vasco?" asked Conway.

"Yes," Rams said, and his testimony would get no juicier than that, confined mostly to monosyllabic answers in the affirmative.

The one time the prosecutor tried to get something more out of Rams—asking if he tried to be as accurate as possible when paraphrasing—Bostwick immediately objected on the grounds that a journalist's privilege holds that he doesn't have to speak about anything that isn't in the paper. The judge predictably sustained the objection, and Conway returned to eliciting answers that amounted to "Yes" and "That's a paraphrase."

But as terse, rehearsed and formal as Rams's testimony was, the net result for Adriana Vasco was devastating.

In front of the jury, Rams attested to the fact that in his interview, Adriana had tearfully acknowledged being in a car on Ortega Highway just a few feet away while Kenneth and Carolyn Oppy-Stahl had been gunned down by her boyfriend, Dennis Godley. He also confirmed that he'd paraphrased Adriana as saying that Carolyn was still alive when Dennis ran out of bullets, prompting Dennis to hustle back to the car where Adriana was seated, to reload and finish the job. And he confirmed that he'd paraphrased Adriana as saying she had been with Dennis and Ken during some of the planning to kill Carolyn.

"Did she further tell you in that interview that 'I'— referring to Miss Vasco—'told Ken, "please call it off," and he wouldn't listen. I cried, "Please, please"'?"

"That is a quote," Rams said.

Rams confirmed that she'd told him that Ken had hated his wife and spoken as early as 1993 about killing her; that he'd loved his mom and didn't want her to be mad at him; that he had hated doctors' parties and high society because it was so phony; that the murder plan, with $30,000 paid to Dennis, had been in place for months and that she had tried to stop them, but was only successful in delaying it.

Finally, Rams confirmed that Adriana had given him details of the murders and that Ken, in Dennis Godley's words, "didn't follow instructions"; and he confirmed that Adriana had told him that she'd wanted to go to authorities but was afraid, because Dennis had threatened her and her children.

"And did you quote her as telling you, he—referring to Godley—'has no conscience. He is cold-blooded. He has no feelings. He should admit what he did and be sorry'?" asked Conway.

Rams replied, "That's a quote."

At last, through a newspaper reporter, prosecutors got Adriana's confession before a jury.

Defense attorney Robert Viefhaus had no questions.

"Thank you, sir," the judge told Rams. "You may step down."

From here, the prosecution outlined for the jury the nature of Adriana's relationship with Ken Stahl, calling first her Internet-met lover Jeffrey, who had dated her from September to October 2000, ending the relationship just weeks before she was arrested for the murders. Jeffrey recounted how after only a few dates Adriana had told him about this important man in her life. "She said she had one true love in her life, and that was Ken, and that she loved him and that he loved her," Jeffrey said. As Adriana spoke about Ken, it dawned on Jeffrey that this was the late Dr. Kenneth Stahl, whom he had heard about in the news. Jeffrey recounted for the jury how Adriana had said that Ken hated his wife, but didn't want to get a divorce for financial reasons, and that Adriana considered Carolyn Stahl a "gold digger." Jeffrey also recalled how, to his surprise, Adriana had suddenly bit him in the arm one day when he was talking about other women.

"How tall are you?" asked Viefhaus on cross-examination.

"Five-eleven," Jeffrey said.

"And how much do you weigh?"

"Two hundred and thirty."

"And at this time she was four-eleven?"

"Uh-huh."

"Weighed about one hundred and six?"

"Uh-huh."

"Did you feel somehow—what?—that she was a threat to you when she bit you in the arm?" asked Viefhaus.

"No, but it hurt."

Jeffrey was followed by Adriana's former co-worker Susana Bivian, who also recalled conversations with Adriana about Ken. "He was always there for her," Susana told the jury, "kind of like a guardian angel."

In contrast, Ken's marriage was a mess, Adriana used to say, but Ken couldn't get a divorce. Susana told jurors that Adriana had claimed to have arranged to meet Carolyn at a restaurant once, but that Carolyn had driven off when she saw her husband's longtime mistress. And Susana spoke of how Ken had called for Adriana at the office the day before he was murdered.

On the Monday after the killings, Susana told jurors, Adriana had been in a state of shock as she spoke of how "they killed Ken."

"Was she crying when she was telling you this?" asked Conway.

"No. She was like in shock, like her eyes were like real glossy," said Susana. "She wanted to cry but no tears came out."

Still, Adriana didn't want the police to know about her relationship with Ken, even though Susana had urged Adriana to tell the truth.

"She didn't want me to say anything, if they had asked me, and that she wasn't going to bring up their relationship, because now that Dr. Stahl was no longer around, she didn't want his reputation to be, you know, ruined."

As for Carolyn's reputation, Adriana left no doubt for Susana how she felt.

"She told me that [Ken] had called her on Saturday sometime in the morning and had mentioned that he was going to take out—well, she used the term 'bitch'—for her birthday."

The next witness, a very uncomfortable Scott—the other man who'd dated Adriana in 2000 after meeting her on the Internet—also said that Adriana had spoken about Ken. "I think she loved him with her heart and soul, forever," he told jurors. But Ken had been married to a very controlling woman who'd stayed with him just to get back at him, Adriana had said.

"He wanted to get out of his relationship—get rid of his wife."

"And you use the word 'eliminate'?" Conway asked.

Viefhaus promptly objected. "He is leading the witness, Your Honor."

"Withdrawn," the prosecutor said.

"The words," said Scott, "were 'get rid of.' "

As he slumped on the witness stand, at one point speaking so softly lawyers couldn't hear him, Scott made no secret of what was in his heart.

"That look on your face," prosecutor Conway observed. "I take it you are not too thrilled to be here?"

"I'm a little uneasy, that is correct."

Conway asked if he would feel more comfortable if news reporters didn't put his name in the paper.

"Absolutely," he said.

Still, Scott spoke with kindness toward Adriana, one of the few who did at the trial. He mentioned how he'd sympathized with her plight as a single mother, and twice mentioned how adorable her daughter was. He said his discomfort on the stand had nothing to do with the fact that she was being tried for murder—just the intrusion into his personal life.

Like Susana, Scott had listened to Adriana talk about the days leading up to the murders and that phone call between Adriana and Ken the day of the killings. But

Adriana had given Scott even more information, recounting how Ken had told her "he was supposed to meet somebody and he didn't want to be there." That somebody was a man—not Ken's wife. She told Scott that Ken's mood had darkened in the two weeks before the murders. "I didn't know what she was talking about," Scott said on cross-examination. "Whatever [Ken] was talking about, he wanted to change his mind."

For the next witness, James Stewart, the judge held a hearing outside the jury's presence to make sure nothing improper was asked. James was the father of Gregory Stewart, the man whom Adriana had met in the mental hospital and later had a relationship with, producing a daughter—allegedly out of spite for Ken. James Stewart and his wife Nancy were now in a sensitive position: they had custody of Adriana's daughter, Ashley—their grandchild. Adriana's son was living with his father.

Judge Briseno wanted to make sure the jury heard nothing from James Stewart of the tumultuous, drug- and violence-plagued relationship between Adriana and Greg. The judge considered that information irrelevant to Adriana's guilt or innocence in the Stahl killings. During the hearing, James took the stand and the judge assured him, "The attorneys are going to be asking you certain questions in a very limited area, and they have already been cautioned about what areas they can ask you questions about, and they've also been cautioned about questions that they cannot put to you." He warned James not to volunteer any improper information.

When the jury was brought back in, James Stewart steered clear of any problems with his son and instead painted a nasty portrait of Dennis Godley. Stewart told the jury about the day he and Adriana had gone into the gun shop in 1999, when Adriana mentioned that she had bought Godley a gun that looked like a stainless-steel–barreled Taurus revolver, the same model of gun that crime lab investigator Laurie Crutchfield had testified earlier could have been used to kill the Stahls. Stewart said he had been so angry at her that "I came unglued.

"And I take it you didn't think too much of him?"

"No," he said, adding, "I thought he was kind of a sleazeball."

The same precautions against allowing negative testimony about Greg Stewart were taken with another witness, Greg's mother, Nancy, who'd also sat for a hearing to hash out her testimony before facing the jury. Nancy spoke of two phone calls. After the murders a call had been placed to North Carolina, where Godley was living at the time. The other was the call from Carolyn Stahl that had come to Nancy's house long before the murders.

"I believe it was early in the morning," Nancy said. "I don't know when exactly. The phone rang and I answered it. And there was an irate woman screaming, 'Why are you calling my husband? Why are you calling Dr. Stahl?' I didn't know any Dr. Stahl. At that point in time I only knew Ken as Ken."

Nancy said she'd apologized to the angry woman, who hung up. Only later did Nancy realize she had spoken to Ken's wife, Carolyn.

The jury next heard about Adriana's reaction to the murders. While her co-worker and friend Susana Bivian had said Adriana was in shock and couldn't cry, another co-worker, Nicole Nguyen, said she'd spoken to Adriana the next day and said, "She was crying hysterically."

Like the other witnesses, Nguyen had also met Ken when he would pick up Adriana at work, and knew about his financial support. Adriana had once returned from lunch with $800 he had given her. Nguyen also knew that, as upset as Adriana was after the murders, she'd had no use for Ken's wife over the years.

"She said that Dr. Stahl would complain that his wife would not give him a divorce," Nicole testified.

"And did you ever hear her ever use . . . any derogatory-type names in referring to Dr. Carolyn Stahl, the wife?" asked prosecutor Conway.

"Yes," said Nicole, "she called her a witch."

After the witnesses had been called to talk about the relationship between Ken and Adriana, the trial took a grisly turn as three forensic specialists gave graphic details of wounds to the bodies of Ken and Carolyn. Using crime-scene and autopsy photos that had jurors wincing, prosecutor Conway led crime-scene analyst Maria Golonski, Deputy Coroner Elizabeth Kinney and forensic pathologist Dr. David Katsuyama on a shot-by-shot re-creation of the murders.

The gunfire, according to the witnesses, had come from the open passenger seat and riddled the couple with bullets, some of which had traveled straight through their bodies. One bullet, according to the testimony, had caused the gruesome eye injury to Ken that the first man on the scene, the ranch security guard, had seen—the bullet had come from behind Ken's ear and exited through the eye.

At this point, Adriana started to cry. The judge called a recess so she could regain her composure, but the testimony continued to be graphic. Katsuyama explained how Kenneth had died of a bullet to the chest that punctured the aorta, while Carolyn had died of wounds to her head and several internal organs. Most chillingly, the witnesses spoke of how Carolyn hadn't died immediately—had even managed to move around for a while, perhaps even leaving the car—before being finished off with shots to the head.

"It is my opinion," he continued, "that she could have moved around for, say, anywheres of up to ten, fifteen seconds, perhaps longer, after sustaining those wounds."

Adriana lost it again. As the pathologist was explaining that Carolyn had been shot so many times—up to ten bullets—that he couldn't tell from her remains exactly where all the bullets had come in and where they'd come out, defense attorney Robert Viefhaus stood and said to the judge, "Excuse me, could we have a short recess?" By now, Adriana was uncontrollably sobbing.

It had been a long morning of trying testimony for all involved, and the judge was happy to oblige. "Sure," said Briseno, and he turned to the jury. "Ladies and gentlemen, is it all right if I ask you to step into the jury room? And we'll call you out when we're ready to proceed."

Court resumed for more testimony about Ken's and Carolyn's injuries, until Adriana started falling apart again as the pathologist spoke of how Carolyn could have moved around for a number of seconds after suffering the body wounds. The judge called another break and Viefhaus asked if Adriana could be excused for the rest of the coroner's testimony.

The judge asked if the prosecutor had any objection.

"No, Your Honor," said Conway.

"Miss Vasco?" the judge said. Adriana was crying, her head down. "Can you hear me?"

She nodded without saying anything.

"OK," said the judge, "we took the break at eleven o'clock because it appeared to myself that you were struggling keeping emotional composure when the doctor was testifying about the cause of death as it pertained to Kenneth Stahl. And we took a bit longer break than normal at your request to give you a chance to regain your composure. And obviously to all who are present—and I'm not trying to make less of you—but I need to make a record: You're having difficulty as the doctor continues his testimony."

Adriana dabbed at her eyes with a tissue.

"What I want to have clear on the record," the judge continued, "is, you're entitled as a matter of right to be present here in court. You understand that, don't you?"

She nodded without saying anything.

"And you wish to waive that right for the purpose of allowing us to complete the taking of the testimony as it pertains to the cause of death of the two victims, is that correct?"

She couldn't find words.

"You're nodding yes?" the judge asked.

She forced out, "Yes, yes, Your Honor."

He told her that he would take a break to help her regain her composure, but it might not do any good. "It would still be tough and difficult if we just put it over to this afternoon? Am I correct about that?"

"I'll try," Adriana said, "but, yeah, it's hard to hear. It's just hard. Really hard."

"OK," the judge said, "with your permission, then, we'll continue, but I'm going to have you step into the holding cell. Will that be all right?"

"Yes, Your Honor," she said, and deputies escorted her out of the courtroom.

With that, the coroner wrapped up his testimony. Adriana didn't hear how Carolyn had had more noodles in her stomach than her husband. She also missed another brief and uneventful cross-examination, as Viefhaus asked the coroner more about the timing of the couple's last meal based on how much food had been in their stomachs. It was a minor point, and it became increasingly clear that the defense was not going to challenge the major facts in the case, or the performances of the various investigators and technicians, or the coroner.

Jurors clearly had noticed both Adriana's struggle to contain her emotions, and her absence. The judge told them: "Miss Vasco was ill and asked to be excused from the courtroom."

The prosecution's case now shifted to the investigation, calling the first detective on the scene, James McDonald, who told jurors how police had found Adriana by calling the numbers left on Ken's pager. He recounted that in their first brief interview two days after the murders, Adriana said they were only longtime friends, not lovers, and that she had tried to reach him about a computer repair. McDonald then was led through the second, longer interview in which Adriana had admitted having an affair with Ken, though it was long over, and revealed details of their long relationship and Ken's deep unhappiness in his marriage. Unlike subsequent interviews, the details of this one were allowed by the judge, sparing Adriana from the most damaging statements.

Still, the prosecution made it clear that Adriana, while more forthcoming on February 29, 2000, had kept information from police.

"Did she ever tell you Ken Stahl wanted his wife killed?" asked Conway.

"No, she didn't."

"Did she ever tell you about a guy named Tony or Godley?"

"Neither of those names were ever mentioned, no."

"Did she ever tell you that she went out to Ortega Highway a couple days before the murders?"

"No, she didn't."

"Did she ever tell you anything about purchasing a .three-fifty-seven revolver?"

"No, she didn't."

"Did she ever tell you about being involved in the planning of the murder of Carolyn Stahl?"

"No, she didn't."

"Did she ever tell you about being present when Ken Stahl paid a guy named Godley thirty thousand dollars to kill his wife?"

"No, she didn't."

"Did she ever tell you about driving this Mr. Godley out to Ortega Highway to kill Carolyn Stahl?"

"No, she didn't."

"Thank you."

Jurors next heard details of Adriana's second extensive interview, the one she had with the new detectives on the case, Phil Villalobos and Brian Heaney, on October 11, 2000, at the Stanton sheriff's substation. Villalobos testified that the detectives had wanted to press her on the phone conversations she'd had with Ken the day of the murders, with Adriana still insisting that the talk had centered on computer repair and not murder. Although she answered their questions, her memory seemed to escape her, the detective testified. "She stated, 'I don't remember,' 'I don't know,' 'I don't remember,' 'I don't know,' more than a dozen—more than twenty—times," he told jurors.

This time, however, she did acknowledge having spoken to Carolyn, telling her, "I know about you, and you know about me, just stop calling me." But, as she had in February, she denied knowing anything about a plot to kill Carolyn Stahl, the detective testified.

"She told you that he hated her and he hated her for a long time, right?" asked Conway.

"Yes. Yes," Villalobos said.

"But never mentioned that he ever talked about wanting her killed?"

"Correct."

Also not mentioned in court were the interrogation tactics employed by Heaney and Villalobos—their pleas to her to clear her guilty conscience by talking to them, their constant hammering on her that she knew more than she was saying, and her tearful resolve in the face of all of it. Never was the jury told that these tactics would later escalate to the point that a judge had found that the detectives had violated Adriana's constitutional rights and that later interrogations were deemed inadmissible.

Seeking next to show that Adriana wasn't the helpless victim, the prosecution called Orange County jail Deputy Christina Brown to tell jurors about the letter Adriana had written to another deputy mentioning the key remaining witness against her.

"Adriana had written that she was feeling optimistic about her case, hopeful for the outcome of her case, and she wrote that now that she'd gotten rid of the cops, all she needed to do was get rid of Bill Rams," said Brown.

It was a tough break for the defense. Due to a ruling earlier by Briseno, jurors were never told that her reference to getting rid of the cops related to the pre-trial ruling throwing out statements from her police interviews at the Costa Mesa station and in the Twin Towers jail. This lack of context made the statement sound more ominous than it might have otherwise.

Dennis Conway wrapped up his case by doing something the prosecution rarely does: trashing a victim. After a weekend break, jurors came back to hear from gang member–turned–Christian-electrician Chris Anaya, who recalled the doctor's fascination with Anaya's gang past—and Ken's very unusual late-night proposal.

"He just said, 'I need somebody to take care of my wife, you know, she's making my life hell, and, you know,

I was just wondering if you knew anybody,'" Anaya re-counted for the jury. "And I was like, 'Wait a minute, man, are you joking around?'"

But by the look on his face, Anaya knew Dr. Stahl was serious. So they prayed together, and by the end of that, Anaya felt that Ken's outlook had improved, though his needs for electrical work had apparently ended.

"And he never called you any time after that?" asked Viefhaus on cross-examination, seeking to show that the conversation with Anaya had had no direct link to what had happened on Ortega Highway.

"Never called me after that."

"And sitting next to me," Viefhaus said, "is the defendant, Adriana Vasco. Do you see her?"

"Yes, I see her."

"Ever seen her before?"

"Never seen her before."

"Ever heard her name mentioned before?"

"Never heard her name," said Anaya, "never seen her."

Prosecutor Conway had a few follow-up questions, then said he was done with Anaya.

"Thank you, sir, you may step down," the judge said to Anaya, then to Conway, "Any further witnesses on behalf of the People?"

"No, Your Honor."

As promised, the prosecution had presented a case with no eyewitnesses and no physical evidence, just testi-mony linking Adriana to Kenneth Stahl and to Dennis Godley, evidence that Ken had wanted his wife dead, Adriana's lies and omissions to police and the most im-portant piece of all, her interview with Bill Rams of *The Orange County Register* in which she'd admitted being present during key parts of the murder scheme and out at the crime scene.

Forced to accept the article, and not allowed to question Rams's accuracy or credibility—or even ask him about the circumstances in which the interview had been conducted—Adriana's defense had essentially conceded every fact presented by the prosecution. He hadn't even made an opening statement.

So as the trial shifted from the prosecution's case to the defense's presentation, the question was, what exactly did Viefhaus plan to do?

Chapter Twenty-Nine

Throughout the trial, defense attorney Robert Viefhaus had kept the question of whether Adriana Vasco would testify a tantalizingly elusive one. He was not required to disclose that decision until the moment he called her to the stand. Through much of the trial, Conway—who would have to cross-examine Adriana—had tried to guess what was in his adversary's mind, through the attorney's words and body language, through his legal filings, through his careful comments to the judge about upcoming witnesses and exhibits. Viefhaus betrayed nothing.

By mid-trial, however, it appeared that the defense was angling for a way to get Adriana's account, if not some of her exact words, to the jury without calling her at all. It was a clever move. Adriana could get her side in and not risk the damage from cross-examination.

The first clues to this strategy actually came early in the case when Viefhaus had said he wanted to posit before the jury that Adriana suffered Battered Women's

Syndrome, a subset of the post-traumatic stress syndrome often associated with soldiers returning from battle. Under the defense theory, Adriana's actions—and inactions—before, during and after the murders were not due to her being a murderer under the definition of the law, but to being a victim of repeated emotional and physical abuse by men her entire life.

The judge had initially ruled against allowing testimony about her suffering this syndrome, but did so without prejudice, meaning he could revisit the issue later on. Now that the prosecution had rested its case, "later on" had arrived. A psychologist had examined Adriana in jail and was prepared to testify that she did, in fact, suffer Battered Women's Syndrome, which would explain why she'd fallen under Dennis Godley's spell and hadn't done more to stop, or report, the murder plot. The defense would argue that Adriana never reached the point in which, legally, she could be considered an aider or abettor to the crime.

To back that argument up, Viefhaus submitted a report from his expert, Dr. Nancy Kaser-Boyd of UCLA, who wrote:

> Ms. Vasco was less able than the average person to understand and accept that Dr. Stahl really did intend to kill his wife; that Mr. Godley was in fact a very dangerous person who would and could kill people; that Dr. Stahl probably would show up [at Ortega Highway]; and that she was probably not going to get stopped by police on the way there or have any other sudden rescue from these events as they marched forward towards their conclusion.

Upon more reading and reflection, the judge said on Friday, November 15, 2002, that he was inclined to change his mind, and was "prepared to grant the request by the defendant to have the expert testify as to her opinions and observations concerning the existence of this particular psychological aspect." But the testimony would come under strict limitations, he said. "She makes some conclusions that the defendant didn't think Dr. Stahl really meant to kill his wife. I think that's beyond the lines of what she is permitted to testify to," said the judge. "In other words, she could testify to the mechanics in this case of denial as it might pertain to a person that has the characteristics of the disorders that she's found. But for her to make any opinions about the defendant's state of mind, I think would be inadmissible."

The defense attorney said he understood. It was a natural reading of the law: Only a jury can decide what a defendant's state of mind and intent were—that's the point of a trial.

Viefhaus asked if he would be allowed to "speak in the abstract" about a Battered Women's Syndrome victim's comprehension of danger and the psychological phenomenon of denial—blocking out things that other people would immediately respond to, like murder plots. The judge said that the lawyer could argue that in summation, and that the expert was allowed to speak generally about denial. "But that would be the extent of it," said Briseno.

Predictably, prosecutor Conway took issue with this evidence being allowed, portraying it as a back-door ploy by the defense. "One of my perceptions—no offense—is this had a way of keeping Ms. Vasco off the stand," said the prosecutor. "The bulwark of it seems to be a lot of unsubstantiated, self-serving claims by the defendant herself."

The irony is that it's usually prosecutors, not defense attorneys, who call a Battered Women's Syndrome expert. In cases of domestic violence, a woman will often claim, under oath, that despite her injuries and previous accusations that her husband or boyfriend had beaten her, nothing had really happened. The expert would then be called to help the jury understand why a battered woman would still love her attacker to the point of lying.

Another prosecutor, Deputy District Attorney Jo Marie Escobar, called in to help Conway argue this issue, told the judge: "It's not used [to prove] that the defendant is a battered woman and, therefore, take her syndrome as a defense. That's a misuse of the syndrome. As a person who prosecutes domestic violence cases, it frightens me if the syndrome gets abused in that way."

Escobar told the judge that "it hit me in the middle of this hearing" that "not a word Ms. Vasco said to the doctor should come in." She said the judge should only allow the doctor to testify about the definition of Battered Women's Syndrome—and let the jury decide if that's what Adriana suffered.

As for anything Adriana may have said to the doctor, "not a word of it" should reach the jury, said Escobar. "And that's my last word."

"Well," the judge said, seeking to calm the prosecutor, "I need to talk to you a little further." He noted that while he doesn't normally preside over domestic violence cases, in this trial the expert had in fact talked to the defendant and therefore could give an opinion, as long as the jury is instructed that they could ignore that opinion if they didn't think it fit the evidence.

After the weekend, lawyers returned to court on Monday, November 18, 2002, with the defense making a final push for the judge to allow not only the expert's abstract testimony about Battered Women's Syndrome but also "everything she [Adriana] told the doctor, because all of those statements are relevant and important to the doctor's conclusions."

Briseno, after having a weekend to think about it, issued his ruling: "I will permit the doctor to testify . . . as to what constitutes a Battered Women's Syndrome," he said, acknowledging this was a "modification from my earlier ruling.

"However," he added, "I will preclude any reference to the underlying statements made to her during the interview."

It was a blow to the defense and seemed to catch Viefhaus off-guard.

"I'm sorry—as to the underlying statements, the court will what?"

"Exclude," the judge said. "And I will exclude any opinion by the doctor as to whether the defendant suffers from Battered Women's Syndrome."

It was a sweeping ruling. The defense could call witnesses talking about how nasty Dennis Godley was—to show how Adriana could have suffered Battered Women's Syndrome—but it prevented the defense from calling the psychologist, or any other witness, to testify about Adriana's traumatic past, from her abusive childhood to her violent marriage to Victor Vasco.

Any witness, that is, but Adriana Vasco.

The defense was painted into a corner.

Robert Viefhaus began Adriana's case by calling the few witnesses he was allowed to produce to show the psychological power Dennis Godley wielded over women. The first was Adriana's apartment neighbor, Belen Lopez, who spoke of Adriana's actions in the hours before the shootings. Lopez said that on the night of the murders, Adriana had actually planned to go to a quinceanera party. They had even spoken of what dress Adriana might wear. But that morning, Lopez told jurors, Adriana had argued loudly with Godley. At 6 or 7 p.m., Adriana unexpectedly canceled on the party plans and told Belen she was going out with Godley for what Adriana had called "a prior commitment."

Although the implication was that Adriana had left under duress, on cross-examination, Belen said that Adriana hardly seemed upset.

"You told the police that she appeared to be in a good mood?" asked Conway.

"Yeah, they [Adriana and Dennis] weren't mad."

"She seemed OK?"

"Yeah, she'd calmed down."

Conway also elicited that when Dennis and Adriana had been in Belen's kitchen, Dennis had seemed to be carrying something inside a shotgun case.

Then came the sad testimony of Kimberly Brady, the mother of Godley's two children, whom Viefhaus called to show that Adriana wasn't the first of Godley's psychological victims. Kimberly said that even though over the years she'd accused Godley of hitting her, knocking her down, pushing her, giving her a black eye and sending her to the clinic with a nervous breakdown, their relationship was actually "healthy" and that she'd made up those allegations to get back at him for cheating on her.

Next up was Melissa Tossey of Virginia Beach, to talk about how Godley had called her cousin, his girlfriend at the time, a bitch, slut and whore, and had been known, in front of others, to say to the cousin, "I'm going to get your pussy later." She also told jurors there'd been a bullet hole in the TV screen at the home where Godley and Tossey's cousin lived.

The last witness to speak to Godley's character was Paula Banks, another resident of the Anaheim apartment complex where Godley and Adriana had lived, who spoke of how Godley had carried around a shotgun concealed under his long coat.

The next morning, Judge Briseno called a hearing outside the jury's presence to make an announcement. "I've been advised informally that apparently the defendant does plan to take the stand."

Chapter Thirty

Judge Briseno had the reputation of treating everybody in his courtroom with the same respect and deference. And so he was taking care with his words.

"Miss Vasco," he said, "my next comments are not to be construed as being critical of you in any fashion. But I think we all understand that at various times throughout the proceeding that the proceedings have been difficult for you.

"And what I'm addressing," he continued, "is, if you start to cry, I'm prepared to take a break so that you can get an opportunity to regain your composure, if that's your desire or if that's a desire of your attorney. But each time we break, that means you're on the stand a tad longer. You understand that?"

"Yes," Adriana said.

Briseno said he didn't want to interrupt the flow of her testimony and that he would leave it up to her or Viefhaus to signal for a break.

"It's a difficult position for the court to be in," the judge said. "I don't want to interrupt your presentation of your evidence. On the other hand, if you're unable to proceed, I'm prepared to give you some time to recover and then continue."

"I thank you," Adriana said.

After some housekeeping matters were addressed, including dismissing a juror and replacing him with an alternate, the jury was brought into the courtroom and defense attorney Robert Viefhaus said, "The defense would call Adriana Vasco to the stand."

After taking the oath and spelling her last name, Adriana sat in the witness chair. The court was silent, all jurors' eyes on her.

"Miss Vasco," her lawyer said, "do you have water up there?"

"Yes," she said softly.

"Why don't you pour yourself a cup first?"

She poured herself some water into a paper cup, then Viefhaus asked, "How are you today?"

"Hanging in there," she said.

And with that, she began what would be two long days of testimony and cross-examination. She spoke quietly through much of it, so much so that her attorney had to repeatedly remind her to lean forward and talk into the microphone. But her words carried a punch. There would be no bored jurors, nobody nodding off as one juror notably had during the coroner's testimony.

"How old were you when you came to this country?" Viefhaus asked.

"I was thirteen years old."

Through gentle questioning, Viefhaus elicited from Adriana the testimony he was barred from getting from any other witnesses, the story of a girl—conceived as the result of a rape—who'd come to the United States from

Guadalajara, Mexico, to be raised by a violent stepfather and a beaten-down mother who didn't care.

"He would mostly, like, hit my mom, like the weekends," Adriana told jurors. "It was really bad. You know, all the yelling and things being smacked around. There was times where I would get between them and my stepfather would—was going to smack me away. There was times I wanted to call the police, but my brother and my sister, they begged me not to because they said, 'Well, he's not your dad, so you don't care.' So I didn't call."

Her mother also didn't take her side. "My mom never showed any sign of love, and she never told me she loved me. She never really did anything for me, like things that I would see her do with my brother and sister, like cuddling and kissing and even cutting their toenails. . . . I was not allowed to have conversations on the phone with friends. I was mostly just cleaning and making dinner for everybody after school. And then after that I could do my homework."

"Was there also some sexual abuse?" asked Viefhaus.

"Yes, there was," Adriana said.

"Would you describe that for the jury?"

It started, she said, "with spanking my behind, pinching my butt," and turned into her stepfather getting into bed with her and "start rubbing himself against me when he had a hard-on." Once, while her mother was at work, he had come into Adriana's room and fondled her breasts under her shirt.

"I pretended I was still asleep, and I kind of moved around a little bit," she said. "He stood there for a little while. He was in his underwear and he went back to the room, to my mom's room."

"Did you ever tell your mother about this?"

"Yes, I did," she said. "When she used to see [him]

pinching and I used to get mad, she says, 'Why are you getting mad? Don't you see he's showing you affection?' "

At age 16, Adriana said, she'd run away from home, first to a shelter recommended by one of her teachers, then into an apartment with Victor Vasco, whom she'd started dating while still in high school. They married shortly after graduation, when she was 19, and life was good—until their son, Mark, was born about two years later. Her husband changed.

"He began to drink, began to drink more," she said. "He didn't want to get up and help with the baby. There were some times that I don't forget where I was really sick and the baby was crying and there was no food, and I asked him if he could go get milk for the baby."

Her voice trailed off, and her attorney said, "I'm sorry, would you talk louder?"

"It was two or three o'clock in the morning," Adriana continued, "and he said, 'No, you go get it.' And I said, 'But the baby's crying, you need to help me.' He didn't want to get up and go get milk for the baby. So I had to go and get up and do it myself."

The drinking got heavier, then he started using cocaine, which Adriana also started doing. At times she didn't want anything to do with the drugs, but if she tried to hide them, her husband would get mad and "throw me around, like pull my hair." Sometimes she just gave him the drugs; sometimes she would stomp out and sleep in her car.

It was during this tumultuous time that Dr. Kenneth Stahl had entered her life.

She told the jury the story of how they'd met at the pain clinic when Ken had noticed her bruises and limping, how they'd confided their personal problems in each other, how the relationship had become a sexual one while her marriage to Vasco was becoming increasingly stormy. She spoke of a trip to Ken's Montana cabin and Ken's carping about his wife, whom he saw as a fat, chocolate-popping shrew he no longer found sexually attractive. She spoke of the hundreds of dollars in cash that Ken would leave behind after visiting her apartment—and how sometimes that made her feel cheap.

"Did you fall in love with Dr. Stahl?" Viefhaus asked her.

"Yes, I did," she said. "Very much."

"Do you think he was in love with you?"

"He showed me that he was. His actions said it. He wasn't a man of many words. When it came to love, he just showed you."

It was a love, she came to realize, that would never lead to marriage. It was clear that Ken would never divorce Carolyn, that divorce would just be another of the many things he would put off—like visiting his son, or spending more time in Montana, or starting up his own clinic, or getting plastic surgery on his eyelids.

"I was the one asking, like, 'Did you do this?' 'Did you do that?' " she said. His answer was a whiny "Well, no."

"It was 'Wah-wah-wah,' you know? Whenever he didn't want to talk about something, he would go, 'Wah-wah-wah,' " she said.

As much as she loved him, as kind and generous as he was, at times the sex would be uncomfortable, she said. In graphic testimony, she said that he would sometimes penetrate her digitally.

"That means that he would put his finger in your vagina, is that right?" asked Viefhaus.

"Yes."

"When he did this, would he have a glove on?"

"No."

"And sometimes he penetrated you with his finger anally, isn't that true?"

"Yes."

"And when he did that, did he do it with a glove on then?"

"No."

"When he would penetrate you like that, how long would he penetrate? Until what happened?"

"Until he would see blood on his fingers."

"And after he saw blood on his fingers, did you see any expression on his face?"

"Yeah."

"What would you see?"

"A smile."

When Adriana realized that Ken wasn't going to leave Carolyn, she told him that she didn't want to have sex anymore. "He said he understood," she recalled. "And he said, 'It doesn't matter who you're with. It doesn't matter if you get married. I'm going to be there. I'm going to be there for you.'"

After she'd stopped being intimate with Ken, she told the jury, she twice tried to commit suicide by swallowing pills, ultimately checking into a psychiatric facility where she was treated for depression. That's where she met the next man in her life, Greg Stewart. Their relationship produced a second child, her daughter, Ashley, but it was a relationship as bad as any in her life, filled with drug abuse—by both of them—noisy, violent arguments, visits by police and court appearances.

All the while, she said, her friendship with Ken continued—and so did the financial support. But now Ken was slipping money to Greg, with some of the cash going to drugs, and not expenses. Ken also bought her two cars, one for about $2,300, which Greg later wrecked, and another for about $4,500, which Ken put on his credit card.

By December 1998, she had had enough of Greg Stewart. She moved into the Avanti Apartments in Anaheim, whose proximity to the police department offered no relief from open drug abuse, gun brandishing and wanton partying.

Adriana said she stayed away from all that until a man calling himself Tony Satton entered her apartment. Tony was the maintenance man, and they met when she called to get her sink fixed. As with her other relationships, they were happy at first, but things took a dark turn as he started drinking more and using more drugs, including marijuana and speed. She would also get drunk and do drugs with him, she said.

It was during one of these drunken encounters with Tony, about three weeks after they met, that he told her about his criminal past. He said that back in North Carolina where he was from, he knew people who could "take care" of other people for money. Adriana then happened to mention that she had a doctor friend who wanted to take care of his wife.

Over the years Ken had spoken of "getting rid" of Carolyn. Adriana said she'd never taken it seriously. And even that time that Ken had called her and put Carolyn on the phone after a fight that had gotten violent, she always felt Ken was, in his heart, kind and would never really want to do away with his wife, no matter how mad or frustrated he was.

"And when you said that, what did Tony say?" asked Viefhaus.

"He didn't say anything at the moment. He walked out."

"He got up and walked out of your apartment?"

"No, he walked out of the room. He went in a room and he comes back inside and he says, 'Do it.'"

She thought that he was kidding. But he told her that people don't kid about something like that. Then he made threats against her and her children if she said anything about it, the first of many.

As time passed, Tony became increasingly paranoid. When he wasn't partying with the neighbors, Adriana said, he'd carry a shotgun around the apartment complex, or he would come into Adriana's apartment—using his passkey—and search the cupboard and shower, asking, "Woman, where did you go? Where have you been? Who has called you? Who has been here?"

Then one day, she said, he came into her apartment with the shotgun and said, "Woman, I need money. I need you to call your friend. And tell him I want to meet him."

She told him she had been kidding. "I was aware of the big mistake I made," she admitted to the jury. But Tony wouldn't listen. He needed the money, he said, and insisted she call the doctor friend. She complied. He pointed the gun at her as she dialed.

"I called him," Adriana said, "and I told him there was someone that wanted to meet him."

To her surprise, Ken said to have her friend meet him at the parking lot of the Circuit City store next to the Huntington Beach Mall, Adriana testified.

She recounted how they'd driven to the parking lot, how she'd gotten into Ken's van and "I told him that I had somebody in the car that was willing to do what Ken wanted."

"And what did Ken say?" asked Viefhaus.

Adriana's voice quavered as she answered.

"He . . . he . . . he seemed . . . he seemed glad that I told him that."

She didn't remember if they'd talked more in the parking lot; she was pretty sure they had already spoken by phone. But she did remember that Ken had given her an envelope.

"I didn't open it," she said. "Ken just told me what it was."

"What did he say it was?" asked her attorney.

"He told me there was money there. I didn't . . . I didn't ask how much or anything like that."

"Did he say it was money to give Tony?"

"Yes."

"And after he gave you the money, what did you do then?"

"I told him that . . . that he had . . . that he had threatened my kids and me and that I was scared that he was— that Tony was getting really scary, and to please don't go along with this."

"What did Ken say?"

"He asked . . . He asked me if he had hit me. And I said, no. And then he said, 'Well, at least he's nice to you, he's not hitting you.' "

"What did you say, if anything, to that?"

"I just said, 'Please don't.' "

"And what did Ken say?"

"Nothing."

She said she'd carried the envelope into the car where Tony was sitting with his shotgun, and gave him the money.

After that, Ken started calling her more frequently than before, sometimes asking for her, and sometimes just for Tony. She said that when she'd talked to Ken, she'd never discussed the deal with Tony. "I didn't want to know anything, I didn't want him to tell me anything, I just didn't want to," she said.

By November 1999, Adriana told jurors, she was no longer involved in a sexual relationship with Tony—that he had taken up with a teenaged runaway girl—but the plot between Tony and Ken was alive and well. Tony also continued to make unannounced visits with the passkey and threaten her and her children.

Then, on the day before the quinceanera party, she said, she'd been drawn back into their plot.

Tony "made me" call Ken and set up a second meeting in the Circuit City parking lot, she said. This time, Tony had carried a handgun with him as they drove there. At the parking lot, Tony walked to the van and talked to Ken. Tony returned and told her to talk to him.

Again speaking in a quiet voice, Adriana told jurors that Ken had spoken to her about Ortega Highway. He had remembered that she'd once driven there after a fight with Greg Stewart.

"He goes, 'Go drive over there, and I'll follow you.' "

"And then did you do that?" asked Viefhaus.

"Yes, I— Yes, I did."

"And once you got to Ortega Highway, where did you go?"

"I kept driving until Tony told me to stop. He told me to stop, to park on the side, and I did."

"And then what happened?" asked her lawyer.

"Then I saw Ken pull in behind me, and Tony walked out of the car and . . . he talked to Ken—Ken and him talked."

The doctor and the hitman, on Ortega Highway: Adriana insisted she didn't know what they'd said to each other.

Tony returned and told Adriana to talk to Ken, who was standing outside his car.

"And what did you two talk about?" asked the defense lawyer.

"I told him that this guy was very scary. I told him to please stop everything that he was thinking about doing. I told him, 'Please, Ken, you know, I'm scared of him. He keeps threatening me and my kids. Please, if you say you love me, please don't. Don't put me through this. Don't do this to me.' "

As they spoke, Adriana heard gunfire. Tony was shooting at a sign.

"And I told him [Ken], 'See, I told you. He just doesn't care,' " said Adriana.

Shortly thereafter, Tony summoned Adriana. "Come on, woman, let's go," he said.

"And I looked," she said, "before I got in my car, I looked behind, and I gave him a pleading look."

"To who?"

"To Ken," said Adriana. "And he just ignored it and went inside his car."

They drove back to the apartments, Tony and Adriana, and the next day, the day of the quinceanera, Tony came over in the late afternoon, entering her unit with his passkey. On the bed, she had placed two dresses she was thinking of wearing to the party.

"He told me, 'What are you doing? Where do you think you're going?' " she recalled. "And I told him, 'I'm going to the quinceanera with Raymond' "—the neighbor, Raymond Ruiz, who spoke to detectives later.

"And he says, 'No, you're not,' " continued Adriana. "And I said, 'But I want to go. I already told him I was going because I had been telling them for days that I was going.' And he said, 'You're not going there. You're not going anywhere. You're going with me.' "

She was instructed to give the excuse that she had a prior commitment with Tony.

As he instructed her, he pointed a handgun at her, saying, "Don't forget what I told you." The threat against her and her children.

"And then did you leave with Tony to go to San Juan Capistrano?" asked Viefhaus.

"He . . . he . . . he told me to get in the car, and that we were going to go up where we'd gone the day before," she said. "I told him I don't want to go with him. I told him I don't want anything to do with anything. I told him, 'I don't want to go with you, I don't want to do any of this. I don't want to be involved in any of this. Please.'

"I just wanted both of them to leave me alone," she continued. "I wanted both of them to just keep me out of it. I want to be left alone."

"When he told you that, did you believe that Ken would really be there?" asked her lawyer.

"No," she said. "I didn't even know if—I had no idea what was planned. I had no idea. He just told me to drive him, and he kept telling me, he kept telling me things, on the drive over there, and I didn't want to hear anything anymore."

She said they drove south on Interstate 5. That's all she remembered about the route.

"I was just driving," she said. "I was just driving and just didn't want to hear or do anything that Tony had to say. I just wanted to just not believe that anything bad was happening."

They exited in San Juan Capistrano and pulled into a gas station to wait for Ken. Fifteen or so minutes later, Ken drove up with Carolyn in the car. Tony held the gun in one hand and jabbed Adriana in the side with the other, and said, "Let's go." They followed Ken east on Ortega Highway. Tony didn't say much during the drive. Rap music by Tupac blared on the stereo. He seemed, Adriana said, "kind of hyper, pumped up, you know?"

She kept thinking, "This would be a good time for a cop to stop me."

Ken's car came to a halt. Tony told her to pass by and

make a U-turn. She did, and pulled up alongside Ken's car, in the middle of the street, hoping to block a car traveling down the highway, but none came.

"After you stopped, what happened?" asked Viefhaus.

"Tony got out of the car, jumped over my hood," said Adriana. "And I heard him say something to Ken about, 'Is everything OK?' And then I heard gunshots. And I heard Carolyn screaming. And I pushed— I wanted to go, and the car started rolling. I started pushing the gas, and I turned sideways and I saw Tony turned around and pointed the gun at me. And I just stopped. And he came. And he came."

Viefhaus asked if, when she'd heard Tony ask if everything was OK, if anybody in the car had responded. She said she hadn't heard anybody say anything.

"Did you look over at them in the car?"

"No, no, no."

"Did you then hear some shots?"

"Yes."

"And how many shots did you hear?"

"I don't know. There were several. I don't know."

"At some point the car started to roll forward?"

"Yes."

"Was that because you took your foot off the brake?"

"Yes."

"Were you going to leave?"

"Yes."

"Did you look over toward Tony?"

"I just kind of looked sideways."

"You glanced over to him?"

"Yes."

"Did you see him?"

"Yes," she said. "He turned around and faced me and pointed the gun at me. I just put the foot on the brake again.

I just stood there, and I just—and I was just looking right ahead. I wasn't doing anything. I was just—wasn't doing anything."

"At the time that you were there, were you frightened?"

"Yes."

"Were you afraid for yourself?"

"Yes."

"Were you afraid for your children?"

"Yes, especially if I was there and if something happened to me, what was going to happen to my kids? I couldn't be around to make sure they were OK."

"Do you remember Tony saying anything to Carolyn or hearing Carolyn at that time?"

"I just remember her screaming. I don't remember. It's hard to talk about her because it's so awful."

"Did he come back to the car to reload?"

"Yes, he did. He said, 'I want to know where you're going.' I said, 'Nowhere'. He said, 'Better not, because I was ready to pop you.' "

"And then what did he do? Did he go back to the car?"

"Yeah, he did."

"And what happened when he got back to the car?"

"He just came over and started firing again."

Adriana started crying on the stand. "I'm sorry. I'm sorry."

Her lawyer pressed on with the questions. No signal to the judge for a break. "Then did he come back again to the car?"

"He came back. He goes, 'Come on, let's go.' "

She drove back fast. She said she wanted to get pulled over: "To help me." Nobody did. All those speeding tickets, all those times she had been pulled over and didn't have money to get her car out of impound—this wasn't one of those times.

"When you got back to your apartment," Viefhaus asked, "did you go into the apartment?"

"Yeah," she said.

"And what did you do in there?"

"I just— I turned off all the lights. And I just sat in my room. And I just cried and cried and cried. And I could just . . . just . . . I just could hear everything over and over again."

"What did you keep hearing over and over again?"

"The shots. And Carolyn. And Carolyn saying, 'Help.' To help her."

Viefhaus asked Adriana if, the day she'd first talked to Ken in that Circuit City parking lot, if she wanted to see Carolyn dead.

"No," she said.

"When you drove down to Ortega Highway the day before this, did you know about what the plans were at that time?"

"No."

"At that time, did you intend that Carolyn die?"

"No."

"Did you want her to die?"

"I didn't want nobody to die."

"Did you ever want Kenneth Stahl dead?"

"No."

"Did you ever intend that he die?"

"No," she said, "I never wanted any of this to happen."

Viefhaus looked to the judge. "No further questions."

Only about one in five defendants ever testifies in his or her own defense. It's usually best that they keep quiet and leave the legal work to the professionals. But Adriana Vasco really had no choice. Had she not spoken to *The Orange County Register*, things may well have never gotten this far. It was her word against *her* word. The question was whether the jury believed that she had fallen under the psychological spell—and had so much fear—of Tony Satton, aka Dennis Godley, that she could be part of something as serious as a murder plot.

It was now up to Deputy District Attorney Dennis Conway to show that Adriana wasn't as helpless and clueless as she claimed. It was a rare opportunity for a prosecutor to confront any defendant—let alone a murder defendant—in court. Conway decided he would be aggressive, but not cruel. He had to shake Adriana's story, but he didn't want to beat up on her so much that the jury would begin to have sympathy—this was, after all, a woman who already claimed to have suffered the blows of more than a few men in her life. Conway didn't want the jury to think that he was another one.

There would be no greetings, no offers of water. He launched right into his questioning.

"Ma'am," he said, not even using her name, "you just finished your testimony on direct saying over and over again that you didn't know this was going to happen?"

"I didn't believe it was going to happen," Adriana said.

"So when you told Belen Lopez that you had another commitment with Tony, you didn't know what that commitment was involving? You just knew you had to go somewhere with him? Is that what you're telling us?"

"Yes."

"OK. And so when he said, 'You're going to drive us to Ortega Highway,' you're telling this jury that you had no idea what was going to happen there?"

"He told me when we were in the car. No."

His voice dripping with sarcasm, Conway asked, "So you thought maybe he was just going to go and shoot at the stop sign again like a couple days before?"

"I didn't think anything."

"You didn't think anything?"

"No."

"And you didn't bother to ask Tony because you were afraid to even ask him?"

"I didn't want to know anything."

"You didn't want to know?"

"I didn't want to know."

"OK, your mind, when you're out there, is a blank slate?" asked the prosecutor. "You're not even speculating or trying to figure out what they're up to?"

"No, because I didn't want to."

"So let me get this straight," Conway said. "This is after Ken—I'm sorry, after *Tony* has mentioned to you that he's a violent guy and he has friends that can kill people, right?"

"That was a while after, yes."

Taking Adriana through her relationship with Tony, he asked if, at the time he'd told her he had killer friends, she'd been sleeping with him. She said she had. In response to Conway's questions, she confirmed that she had been attracted to Tony at first, found him handsome, and wanted to sleep with him, and that she really didn't know "that he was violent at all."

"OK, but presumably when you had sex with him, you saw him naked, right?" asked Conway.

"Yeah."

"You saw those tattoos on him?"

"Yeah."

"And, by the way, at this time you're thirty-two years old, right?"

"Yeah."

"Yeah, you're not some sixteen-year-old teenager, are you?"

"Correct."

He led her through Godley's tattoos: the skulls with blood dripping off them and a demon on his arm.

"You're noticing these tattoos on him, aren't you?"

"But I also have noticed them on other people, a lot of people."

"OK, and other people like Boy Scouts or something?"

Viefhaus interrupted. "Objection, argumentative," he said.

"Sustained," said the judge.

Conway rankled the defense attorney again when he suggested that Adriana's testimony had been rehearsed.

"So that three-and-a-half-hour display we just saw with Mr. Viefhaus, that just happened? You didn't prepare for those questions at all?"

"Objection," Viefhaus said. "Improper, argumentative and not true."

The judge overruled the objection.

"That wasn't choreographed at all?" asked Conway.

"No."

"No?" asked Conway.

"No," said Adriana. "It was something that I have been having in me for a very long time."

But later, Conway narrowed in on one aspect of her testimony, suggesting it was in fact very well choreographed. "You spent an hour-and-a-half in the early part of your testimony talking about growing up and abuse and bad relationships. What's the reason you felt the need to share that with us?"

Viefhaus objected again. "Assumes a fact not in evidence: that she needed to share."

"Overruled," the judge said, then looked at Adriana. "And you may answer if able to."

"Just so they would know who I really, you know, what I was about and what I—who I was, who I am," she said.

"So it wasn't to tell them so maybe they'd feel sorry for you?" asked Conway.

"No."

"Or—you see that blonde woman in the suit, halfway back, that doctor?" He gestured to Dr. Kaser-Boyd, the expert hired by the defense to examine Adriana and testify about Battered Women's Syndrome. "She came and talked to you in the jail at some point?"

"Yes."

"Did you share all that, some of that information with her, too?"

"Yes."

"Is one of the reasons you're sharing that information with her so she can be called as a witness and tell this jury maybe you were battered or something? Is that why you shared that information with her?"

"Objection," said Viefhaus. But the judge again overruled him.

Adriana said that as far she knew the doctor had talked to her because "she wanted some tests about my personality," and Adriana had had no idea what the doctor's findings would be.

Conway turned to another line of testimony that he suggested was also choreographed—the testimony about being digitally penetrated by Ken. The prosecutor asked if she'd shared that disturbing information "so your expert back there can come in and say, 'Yeah, Ken was nice to her, but he's abusive, too, because he did sexual things to put her down'? That's not the reason you're telling the jury this?"

"No, I told my attorney many months ago," about this, she said.

"I notice," Conway continued, as much testifying as questioning her a classic cross-examination tactic, "when it comes to, you know, sex—because it makes everyone uncomfortable to just lay it out there and talk about it, that you're using the phrase 'being intimate.' And that's fine, you know, we're in a courtroom, and we all want to—We don't want to be crass or anything. But, Miss Vasco, I got to ask you, you're laying off this image like you're kind of, you know, traditional when it comes to sex. But you know what Scott and Jeffrey"—her Internet friends—"and these other people say about you when it comes to sex in the bedroom, don't you?"

"That, well, whatever we shared intimately has to do with two people. That's fine."

"And I don't mean to be distasteful, but he"—Scott—"says you were pretty freaky. And so does Jeffrey."

Viefhaus had heard enough. "Objection, calls for hearsay. Motion to strike."

But the judge overruled him again. Adriana said, no, the sex wasn't freaky, otherwise they wouldn't have kept calling her and dating her.

The prosecutor shifted gears, from questioning her about sex to grilling her on her feelings toward Carolyn—and whether Adriana felt that getting Ken's wife out of the picture would clear the way for her with Ken. The prosecutor elicited from Adriana that because of Carolyn's suspicions, Adriana and Ken always had to have sex at Adriana's house. But Adriana insisted that was fine with her. Conway also asked her about her testy phone conversations and near-meeting with Carolyn, her many pleas to Ken to just divorce his wife, and how this made Adriana feel.

"Didn't it come to a point that you shared his hatred toward his wife?"

"Never," said Adriana.

"Never?"

"Never did I hate her," she said. "I disliked what she

was doing. And maybe I didn't like her. But I never hated her."

Conway returned to the theme that Adriana wasn't as weak—mentally or physically—as she might want the jury to believe. The prosecutor noted that not all the violence in Adriana's relationships had been directed at her, that some fights had left Greg Stewart with scratches. Even the happy relationships, like the times she spent with Internet friend Jeffrey, had elements of violence.

"You know he told the police that sometimes you'd just start smacking him around?"

"He's lying," Adriana said. "I did bite him, but it was in a playful mood. We were in his room."

"Yeah," said Conway, "you're not the victim all the time. Sometimes you initiate the violence, don't you?"

"By verbally, maybe."

"And physically."

"No, I only strike back when they push me."

But was she pushed enough to strike out at Carolyn? The prosecutor returned to the day the plot had been hatched, pressing Adriana on just how it came to be that she mentioned to her tattooed lover Dennis Godley that she had a friend who wanted to get rid of his wife.

She said all this had happened as she'd started to lose control of her life; she was spending less time in church and more time doing drugs. She said Tony also started to change, issuing those threats to her and her children.

Yet, she acknowledged, threats or not, she still continued to be with him, helping him buy pot, allowing her children to be near him, sleeping with him.

"So the sex after the threats, was that forced sex?" asked Conway.

"One time I just kind of went along with it."

The sex—of any sort—only stopped when young Melissa, the teenage runaway who'd moved in with Godley, had entered the picture. But the murder plot had moved forward, with phone calls, meetings with Ken, money changing hands—all because Adriana had said something to Tony, she acknowledged.

"At that moment in time, when you put Tony in touch with Ken Stahl, the die was cast for Carolyn Stahl's death, and you knew it."

"No, I didn't," said Adriana. "I didn't know that. I didn't believe that."

"And you couldn't pick up a phone and dial 911 and tell the cops about what might happen?"

"No, I couldn't."

"You thought he was going to kill you and your kids? But you didn't think he'd kill Carolyn Stahl?"

"I didn't want to do anything that will upset Tony."

"You would rather Carolyn Stahl get killed?"

After an objection from Adriana's lawyer was overruled, she answered, "No. I didn't think Ken would go through with any of this, no."

But Ken did go through with it, and Conway brought Adriana back through that night on Ortega Highway. At each stage of the evening, she said, she knew what was happening as it happened, but couldn't stop it—this murder that took place out of cell phone range but right next to an emergency call box.

"It's dark out there," said Adriana, saying the first time she knew about the call box was when she read about it in the newspaper.

"There's nobody out there, huh?"

"That's when Tony told me then, 'I could just pop you, too, right now, throw you out of the car, because I don't have any witnesses.'"

It was not a good moment for the prosecution to stop, but it was evening, and the day had to end at some point.

"You want to take a break?" he asked Adriana.

"Yeah," she said.

The judge told the jury to come back at 9 a.m. the next day: Wednesday, November 20, 2002—the third anniversary of the murders.

The milestone didn't get a mention. Deputy District Attorney Dennis Conway resumed his cross-examination by wishing Adriana a good morning, something he hadn't done the day before.

That's as pleasant as it would get.

Adriana and other witnesses had repeatedly spoken about how much love there'd been between her and Ken, how Ken had supported her financially, how they'd been soul mates. Forgotten in all this love and tenderness, Conway suggested in pointed questions to Adriana, was Carolyn Stahl.

"Did you ever think about what Carolyn was going through? Did you ever think about that? When you're laying in bed with Ken and she's at home, knowing her husband's off sleeping with you, did you ever think of Carolyn?"

"She passed my mind a couple of times," said Adriana, "but I wouldn't really have a deep thought about it, no."

"Did you ever think of it from Carolyn's standpoint that there he is, not only off sleeping with you, but taking money from the household and giving it to you? Did you ever think of how Carolyn felt about that?"

"Well, no, because he—I mean, they both had their jobs, and I'm sure he had his own money. He told me he had his own money, his own account."

And as important as Ken was in her life, he wasn't the only man. Conway led her through all her relationships and romances, from Victor Vasco through the men she'd met on the Internet after the murders. And just as she wasn't the only one to become violent in some relationships, she wasn't the only one who was pursued.

"People don't march into your life and take control of you. You actually seek out relationships with men, don't you?"

"No."

"No? Even in custody, you got letters from men in other facilities."

"Yeah, because I'm isolated. I have no one to talk to."

Conway noted that some of her jailhouse letters "have explicitly sexual material that you're writing to guys you don't even know?" Freaky in bed, freaky by mail, the prosecutor was suggesting. Hardly a victim of men.

"Sometimes I do write to them," she said. "Respond to them. But it's not to the extent that they do, and it's not an everyday thing."

From here, Conway returned to the relationship with Tony, aka Dennis Godley, the one that Adriana claimed had made her do things beyond her control and understanding. She acknowledged that she did buy an assault rifle for Godley, but changed her mind.

"You sure that wasn't step one in the plan to do the murder where you do it from far away with a rifle?"

"No," she said, "because I didn't know anything about it."

Then he showed her pictures of her with Tony—pictures in which she appeared relaxed and happy, pictures from an outing to the swap meet, another with her embracing him.

"And this is when you're under his control and he's threatening you and making you do things and you can't remember anything, right? That's during that time period?"

He showed her another picture.

"That's you and Tony?"

"Yes."

"Looks like a happy couple, doesn't it?"

"I had to be happy around him."

"So he made you put that smile on your face?"

"I needed to be OK around him."

"And he made you take your arms and wrap them around him?"

"I needed to be OK around him."

"You have to be a pretty good actress to do that if you're in fear of your life and your children's life, wouldn't you say?"

"I was under the influence a lot of the time, so I can—I could cope with it."

"So you're some kind of zombie?"

"When you take speed you're not no zombie."

"We're hearing something different."

Viefhaus objected, and Conway withdrew the remark. He then asked, "Instead of the abuse causing you not to appreciate that you were setting up to kill Carolyn, are you now telling us it was because you were under the influence every day?"

Another objection, this one sustained.

"Are you telling us, ma'am, that you were under the influence of drugs or alcohol to the point that you couldn't appreciate what you were doing with him?"

"It could help me not to think about it. Just to disassociate with myself and be able to cope with his paranoia and all his questions and just to numb myself."

And yet, she said, she wasn't so drugged up—so numb and disassociated—that she couldn't get up and go to work or take care of her children. At the same time, she said, when she carried that envelope from Ken to Tony in the Circuit City parking lot, she didn't appreciate exactly what was happening.

"I didn't want to think about it," she said.

"And is that because you were afraid, you were under the influence, or some abuse in your past prevented you from knowing what was going on?" asked Conway.

"Pretty much fear—and denial."

"So fear and denial prevented you from processing information around you, right?"

"I was—I just wasn't thinking about it. I didn't talk about it."

"That's for the expert to take care of, right?"

Viefhaus lodged the inevitable objection, which was sustained.

After a lengthy two-day cross-examination, Conway lofted his last series of volleys at Adriana.

"Now, Miss Vasco," he began, "at some point, you knew that Ken wanted his wife dead?"

"Yes," she said.

"You knew that, because he had said it a number of times?"

"Yeah."

"And the only reason Tony found out that fact is because you told him, right?"

"Yes."

"And the only reason they got together, Tony and Ken, was because of you, right?"

"Yes."

"And if you didn't put Tony and Ken together, Ken and Carolyn would still be alive, right?"

Viefhaus objected, but the judge said, "I'll let the witness answer."

"Yeah," said Adriana, crying.

"That's a fact, isn't it, ma'am?"

"Now it is," she said.

"If you didn't do that, we wouldn't even be standing here having this conversation, would we?"

Conway didn't wait for her to answer.

"No more questions."

Before the redirect began, the jury was dismissed.

"If need be, we'll take a short break," Briseno told Adriana. "Is that what you'd like? Or do you want to continue?"

"I just want to finish this," she said.

The judge told her to "gather yourself," and sent her to the holding cell anyway, but first offered her some advice for the next round of re-direct questions by her attorney and re-cross by the prosecutor.

"Now," said the judge, "when the attorneys ask you a question, I need you to answer that as directly as you can. There might be an explanation for the answer, but unless the attorneys ask for that, please try not to do that."

"OK," she said.

"I think you'll find," the judge told her, "when you explain instead of answering the question, that only triggers off more questions. And it could prolong the amount of time that you're on the stand."

She was taken back to the cell, returning several minutes later more composed. There would be no reason to worry about her demeanor. After the dramatic initial testimony and emotional cross-examination, the remainder of her questioning was anti-climactic. Her attorney sought to clarify a number of issues, from the saucy jailhouse letters—she noted that other letters were to people in her jailhouse Bible ministry—to whether her testimony was orchestrated (she denied it, saying she'd spent all of forty-five minutes with her attorney going over it).

But as her lawyer tried to illustrate why she was so fearful of Tony Satton/Dennis Godley, Adriana did shed more light on the night of the murders—and what Godley had said after the shootings about why he'd killed Ken, too, showing how cold-blooded Godley really was.

"He told me because he couldn't see his hands on the steering wheel," said Adriana.

"Did he indicate that he'd instructed him [that] he wanted to have him keep his hands on the steering wheel?" asked Viefhaus.

"Yeah, he told me that, yes."

"He said that Ken didn't follow instructions, so he killed him?"

"Yes."

"What did he say about Carolyn Stahl?"

"He . . . he . . . he said that he told her before he started shooting her, he told her that her husband paid him to do this."

He asked Adriana why she never spoke much of Carolyn.

"It's hard to talk about her," said Adriana. "It's hard to talk about her. I don't like to talk about her. I don't want to think about her because—because I hurt her."

After two days of testimony, Adriana Vasco left the stand and sat at the counsel table next to her lawyer. The rest of the case would now be placed in the hands of an expert witness.

Chapter Thirty-One

Dr. Nancy Kaser-Boyd, a clinical psychologist and faculty member at UCLA Medical Center, had already been unceremoniously introduced to the jury by prosecutor Dennis Conway during Adriana's testimony. But when she got on the witness stand, as the defense's seventh and final witness, she gave her name for the record and ticked off her impressive credentials: doctorate in clinical psychology from the University of Montana, the teaching job at UCLA, author of articles and a book chapter, treatment of some six hundred patients and their family members over the last two decades.

Previously, outside the jury's presence, Kaser-Boyd was warned by the judge about the issues she couldn't discuss—most importantly, any testimony about what she felt was Adriana's intent before the murders. Even with these limitations, the defense hoped that she would provide much-needed psychological perspective, explaining Adriana's behavior in the months after she'd met Dennis Godley, leading up to the murders.

Kaser-Boyd began by giving the jury a mini-lecture on Battered Women's Syndrome. Explaining that it's a part of post-traumatic stress disorder, she said Battered Women's Syndrome starts with the trauma—both the physical variety, with hands and fists, and the less-appreciated psychological forms, such as manipulation through money or withholding love. Kaser-Boyd pointedly noted that a quarter of all battered women do fight back, "So that they may not look helpless to us on the outside, although they may feel helpless."

She then told the jury that she had given psychological tests to Adriana in jail. The first finding was that Adriana didn't appear to be trying to manipulate the test. On one of the tests, a standard psychological screening with 567 questions, Kaser-Boyd found that on a "clinical scale, she had one pronounced elevation.

"People who elevate there are impulsive," she explained, "they tend to be immature, they often come from abusive backgrounds, they have a history often of drug use, they have a history of very poor relationships. They may be angry people."

In talking to Adriana and going over her history, the psychologist said, "I saw somebody that has the pathology of relationships that we see in children that are abused, neglected or sexually abused. Her choice of partners has been problematic."

This pathologically bad taste in men, she explained, is common among people who grow up in abusive households. They come to believe that an abusive relationship is a normal relationship, developing feelings of helplessness and a sense that they are not good people. Denial, she said, is a coping mechanism. It blinds them in matters of the heart, so they don't see the bad in a battering partner until it's too late, and then fear takes control.

Unspoken but plain from her testimony was that this was Adriana.

As for the batterers, she said, they usually come from the home of a batterer, going on to live chaotic lives with fears of abandonment that show themselves by turning them into frustrated, controlling, jealous people. The implication was that Dennis Godley was the poster punk for this psychological profile.

If the woman is repeatedly battered by this man, a feeling of helplessness takes over, modified into what Kaser-Boyd called "learned helplessness."

"That person often takes a sort of frozen approach to the abuse itself, especially if it starts in childhood," she said. "We think of it as a situation of being entrapped and learning as a very young person that someone can take advantage of you and you can't do anything about it because you're a child or you don't know what to do about it." She said they also have feelings of worthlessness, particularly if there is sexual abuse and particularly if that occurs in "patriarchal cultures like the Mexican culture." She said these women are also needy, struggle with emotional control, find love in the wrong places, suffer depression and abuse drugs and alcohol, with everything blanketed in denial.

The bottom-line analysis of Adriana: "I think she has Battered Women's Syndrome."

Conway didn't even try to challenge these findings. Instead, he asked Kaser-Boyd how much she was being paid. She put the tab at $2,500 for the evaluation—that was $150 an hour—and another $1,900 for testifying, for a total of $4,400.

"OK, thank you ma'am," he said. "Nothing further."

The judge thanked the psychologist and looked to Viefhaus and Adriana.

"Any further witnesses on behalf of the defendant?" asked Briseno.

Viefhaus announced: "Defense rests, Your Honor."

But there would be no rest. Not for the next twenty-four hours. With Viefhaus conceding virtually every fact in the prosecution case, and Conway not challenging the psychologist's findings, everything hinged on the lawyers' powers of persuasion. Their summations the next day could well determine the outcome.

Chapter Thirty-Two

In trying to convince twelve people to unanimously convict Adriana Vasco of two murders with special circumstances, Deputy District Attorney Dennis Conway had a difficult challenge. Not only was there no physical evidence at the scene, or any eyewitnesses, but by his own theory of the case, Adriana didn't actually kill either Ken or Carolyn. Sitting in the car on Ortega Highway while Dennis Godley was doing the dirty work, Adriana may not even have seen the killings—only heard the gunshots and Carolyn's screams—meaning that Adriana, by all accounts, wasn't even an eyewitness to the very murders for which she was on trial.

All this meant was that, for the prosecution to be successful, it had to rely more than usual on what is normally the most boring part of any trial: the discussion of the laws as they apply to the case. There's an old saying among trial lawyers: If you don't have the law, argue the facts, and if you don't have the facts, argue the law.

Conway was going to argue the law.

More than many other cases, this one hinged on the jury's understanding and interpretation of not only the usual guilt-beyond-a-reasonable-doubt standard—which is often difficult enough for laypeople to grasp—but such legal concepts as aiding and abetting, intent, premeditation and deliberation, facilitating, withdrawal, express agreement and one that even lawyers sometimes struggle with: natural and probable consequence.

That's why Conway didn't begin his summation on Thursday, November 21, 2002, with an emotional appeal. Rather, he asked the jurors to put on their thinking caps. "You might want to take some notes," he said, "because I need to talk about the law first. And it gets a little complicated."

Using charts, Conway led the jury through the thicket of legal theories, seeking to show them that, while he couldn't put a gun in Adriana's hand, she was a double murderer nonetheless. Under his interpretation of the law, Conway contended that Adriana Vasco had been an aider and abettor to Dennis Godley, and to be convicted, she didn't even have to have had the intent to kill Carolyn Stahl. All that was required, he said, was "just knowing, in this case, that Godley is going to kill, help make that happen.

"Ask yourself: Does she know that?" said Conway. "Technically, if Ken Stahl was here, he would be responsible, too."

Adriana had clearly made murder happen, the prosecutor said, by putting Ken with Godley knowing that Ken wanted Carolyn dead—and also knowing that this Ken–Godley partnership would result in Carolyn's killing. "And you know what?" Conway said. "[Adriana] can be in a church, down on her knees praying, it doesn't matter. She's an aider and abettor. Getting the gun, giving it to him. Knowing their unlawful purpose. Aider and abettor.

Driving Godley out there that night knowing he's going to kill Carolyn Stahl. That's it."

As for Ken Stahl's death, that's a little more complicated, the prosecutor suggested. He said that under the law, a person can be held responsible even for a murder they don't want committed. It's possible, he said, under the legal concept of natural and probable consequences.

"Let's stop for a minute with Ken," said Conway. "You might think, 'What a despicable character. He got his comeuppance.' But you know, it's still an unlawful killing of another human being, and it's not in self-defense. Clearly, Godley's exterminating a witness. But under natural and probable, Adriana Vasco is also responsible even if she didn't want it to happen."

He said that this is how the law works: A regular person, looking at the situation objectively, should have known that a natural and probable consequence of hooking up a nefarious character like Dennis Godley with Ken Stahl in a late-night murder scheme could very well end with more than just the death of Carolyn Stahl—that it was natural and probable that Ken would get his, too. It doesn't even have to be a strong possibility that Godley would do in Ken—"just reasonably contemplated is enough," said Conway.

That ended the law lesson. From there, Conway went through the evidence, what little there was of it, and nearly all of it conceded by the defense, from Adriana's tortured personal history, through her relationship with Ken, to putting Ken with Godley and the night of the murders. Conway insisted Adriana had had "personal hate" toward Carolyn, that she'd been closely involved in the murder plot at every stage, that she'd known full well what was going to happen, and that, despite her tears on the witness stand, she had repeatedly lied to police and to the jury to save her skin by portraying herself as a victim. He ridiculed the defense—the Battered Women's Syndrome claim—as the legal equivalent of Ken Stahl's pressure-point injections.

"All these emotions, confusion, could keep you . . . from reaching the obvious decision and get you anesthetized—anesthetized to the fact that every word out of her mouth is a lie. And you get moved emotionally to the point that you're confused," said Conway. "It's a wonderful system. And now this part of it is the part where you take over and you make sure justice is done. Because the real victim in this courtroom is not Adriana Vasco. It's Carolyn Stahl."

Robert Viefhaus stood and took his turn—his one turn—to address the jury before deliberations. His adversary, Dennis Conway, would get another chance to rebut anything Viefhaus said. This was it for the defense, the moment made all the more important because Viefhaus had decided against giving an opening statement. This would be the one and only time that the defense attorney would speak directly to the entire jury.

"When we first talked about picking a jury," Viefhaus began, "the issue or question of sympathy came up, and I think I was talking to one of the jurors and said, 'We don't want any wimps on this jury.' " He told them not to be swayed by sympathy, not to be swayed by the fact that Adriana was a single mother with two children.

"It's not a matter of sympathy," he declared, "not about that at all. Might be a sympathetic situation, but sympathy is not what this case is about."

It is common for defense attorneys to say this, then lay on the sympathy thick in hopes of immersing jurors in emotion. And there would be plenty of time for Viefhaus to do just that. But like the prosecutor, Viefhaus had the facts against him. He had to appeal as much to the jurors' intellects as to their emotions, hoping their understanding and views on both legal and psychological concepts would result in reasonable doubt.

"When you talk about Adriana Vasco's position," the attorney said, "it's our contention that she's a battered woman, that she suffers from Battered Women's Syndrome and also post-traumatic stress disorder."

That, he argued, was critical in analyzing Adriana's role in Carolyn's murder. But first, he said, he had a word about Ken. Whether Adriana was a battered woman or not, Viefhaus urged jurors to reject the idea that Ken's death was a natural and probable consequence of everything that had led up to it.

"It seems to me one of the things you can't get over in this case is that Dennis Godley killed his boss," said Viefhaus. "How do you kill the guy that hired you? I mean, wow, this is really unusual. And that's why it's not a natural and probable consequence. That's what's bizarre about this case." He added, "I submit to you that's not reasonably foreseeable."

Not by Adriana. Not by anybody. "So whatever you think that Adriana did," said Viefhaus, "she's not guilty of the murder of Kenneth Stahl."

As for Carolyn's murder, he argued that the prosecutor had failed to show that Adriana had been involved in any conspiracy to kill her. He said that for a conspiracy to exist, she would have to have agreed with Godley and/or Ken with the "specific intent" to murder Carolyn. Adriana, he said, didn't want to have anything to do with it. "She never joined it if she doesn't have that specific intent," he said.

As for aiding and abetting, Battered Women's Syndrome takes center stage, he said, because it speaks to who she is and what she was thinking as these deadly developments unfolded. The defense attorney led the jury through Adriana's life history, the sexual abuse, the beatings, the emotional neglect and the violent relationships. Dr. Kaser-Boyd had looked at this history, he said, and found that Adriana fit a particular psychological profile: a profile of a woman who has a learned helplessness—who doesn't realize she can change her situation.

"The person always looks as if she is in control, and she never is," said Viefhaus. "And if you think about a woman in a battered relationship, the ignorant, the uninformed say, 'Why doesn't she leave?' But then you realize so many women do it and put up with it when they're being physically abused. Must be something more than that."

At each stage, the effects of Adriana's Battered Women's Syndrome came into play, the attorney said, from carrying the envelope of money from Ken to Godley in the parking lot to deciding to miss the quinceanera party and leave with the armed Godley for Ortega Highway.

"What's the most this foolish person can do with this attitude of learned helplessness?" asked Viefhaus. "It's passive things that they do to stop these things. She parked in the center of the road, hoping somebody would come by. Nobody does. But while she's sitting there terrified, holding on to the wheel, does she have an intent to kill Carolyn Stahl?" The attorney said that the psychologist had pointed out that one of the things battered women do is become frozen by fear. "They can't figure out . . . a solution, so they do nothing," he said. "They just sit there."

At the same time, Viefhaus said, other elements of Battered Women's Syndrome kicked in: denial and pathologically bad taste in men. "Adriana referred to this Ken as her guardian angel. She thought he was as pure as the driven snow and the most wonderful thing that God ever made," said the attorney. "Is she going to realize how serious it is?"

In short, she had tragically misjudged Ken. "He is a killer. She doesn't see it," said Viefhaus. "Is that because she's evil? Is that because she intended to kill Carolyn Stahl? Or is it because she is a battered woman?"

Adriana Vasco had fallen prey to two men who'd had control over her. "This young lady here, right here," said Viefhaus, pointing to Adriana in court, "met these two evil, domineering men and she didn't have a chance. She had no chance at all."

The attorney insisted that not only was the tattooed, drug-using, paranoid Dennis Godley a batterer, but so was respectable Dr. Kenneth Stahl, exerting his control over Adriana by pretending to love her. "Ken Stahl doesn't seem to be a person that knows how to love," said Viefhaus. "He doesn't go visit his son. He just sends him money. He doesn't relate to his wife. He just wants to kill her." As for Adriana, after the sex ended, he used money to control her. "He gave this woman, who hasn't got enough instinct to get out of the mess she's always in, he gave her crumbs so that she stayed in the mess," said Viefhaus.

As for a motive to kill Carolyn Stahl, the defense attorney asserted that Adriana didn't have one. She may have called Carolyn a witch or argued with her on the phone, but "you want to kill somebody for that?"

He answered his own question: No, not three years later, after she's stopped having sex with Ken. Plus, if Carolyn were out of the picture, she knew that Ken was never going to marry her and bring her into his doctor's society life. "Does that have a ring of truth to it? Do you think proper Ken Stahl, the anesthesiologist, is going to bring the young lady who's only trained to do office work, who doesn't have a college degree, doesn't have a medical degree, who doesn't understand the word *procrastinate*—are you going to bring her in?"

Ken, though, had plenty of motive, "because he's nuts," said Viefhaus. "All he cares about is money, and he doesn't want [Carolyn] to have even half of what he has. He's the manipulator. He's the one that has the plan. And she"—Adriana—"is the pawn.

"Does it make her stupid?" asked Viefhaus. "No. Does it make her unsophisticated? But as a battered woman, with all the things that Dr. Kaser-Boyd told us about her, it does explain why she's in the middle of this. And these two killers are utilizing her to kill this innocent woman."

When jurors looked at all the evidence, the lawyer said, they would *not* find beyond a reasonable doubt that Adriana had "had the intent to kill Carolyn Stahl when she drove down that road" or when she'd "sat there and arranged" for Ken and Godley to meet.

"She had no motive to do it, and the evidence just doesn't come up that high," he said. "So I would ask that after you review all the evidence, you find her not guilty of both counts."

Prosecutor Dennis Conway sneered. "I mean, 'Battered Women's Syndrome'?" he said sarcastically. "I mean, really. That's kind of a shameless use and application of Battered Women's Syndrome." He mocked Kaser-Boyd, saying that he suspected that at "some point in her life, in her career" that she'd "launched into this area with very noble thoughts and aspirations, to help truly battered women out. And it's resorted to this."

He said Adriana wasn't in any way a woman who "sees no way out.

"This is a woman that, let me get this straight, is with a

guy for two weeks, and that she is this emotional pinball that's bouncing around, just waiting to get plugged into some batterer that shows up, and assume the zombie role?" he said. "She knows where to get help and move on—not a symptom of a battered woman. She's done that twice. She can take care of herself."

He said the expert's $150-an-hour opinion was "reasonable doubt at a reasonable price."

"The reason that Adriana Vasco is still alive is the same reason that Carolyn Stahl is dead—because she's Dennis Godley's crime partner," said Conway. "This isn't about Adriana Vasco. This is about justice for Carolyn Stahl. The defense has attempted to bring Adriana's life in[to] the courtroom, tell you all these things to move you emotionally, and then say, 'Isn't that interesting?' Distract you from the evidence. I ask you to look at the evidence and take it all together."

After reading the laws to the jury and explaining to the panel how to fill out the verdict forms, the judge swore in the bailiff to take charge of the jury, then told them to go into the deliberation room and pick a foreman. "As soon as you do that, let us know, and we'll release you for the day," he said.

After the weekend, on Monday, November 25, 2002, the jury sent the judge a note with a question about the jury instructions. Clearly, the law was on their minds:

Clarify page 51 in general, especially: Does "consequences" apply to the action of the victim, or does consequences apply to the repercussions to the defendant's life after the murder.

It was a cryptic question about a word—"consequences"—that has different meanings in different legal contexts. The question appeared to speak to the legal concept of deliberation. That's the thinking process that a person—either the killer or, in Adriana's case, an alleged conspirator or aider and abettor—goes through before a murder.

Deliberation is a critical element to a murder charge. A person needs to "deliberate" about the consequences of the killing before acting to make it a murder. "Deliberation" can include years of planning and consideration of the consequences, or an incident that occurs in a matter of seconds—as when a driver deliberates over whether to run that yellow light, knowing that if it turns red, he can get a ticket. The issue was vital for Adriana because without the finding of deliberation—with no indication that she had thought about the consequences—the jury could find her not guilty of one or both murders.

The judge answered the question by reading a jury instruction required by the law; it was virtually indecipherable. He told the jury in a note that "consequences" are defined as those things "flowing from the act of killing" and may concern the consequences to both the killer and the victim. He noted that the jury can consider all the possible consequences, but need only determine that one of them existed to make the finding of "deliberation."

This was worded in the difficult language of the law. No Court TV legal pundit would be available to help sort it out. The jury was on its own for now, unless it sent out another note.

For those trying to guess what the jury was doing, the note seemed to offer good news to both sides. Clearly, the jury was not only wrestling with the nuances of the law, just as the prosecutor and the defense attorney had asked it to do, it was trying to get inside the mind of Adriana Vasco.

Chapter Thirty-Three

"I have been advised that the jury has reached a verdict or verdicts in this matter," said Judge Briseno.

"Yes, we have," said the foreman.

"Would you be kind enough to hand the verdict forms to the bailiff?" instructed the judge, and the foreman complied. The bailiff gave them to the judge. Briseno read over the forms without betraying any hint of what they said. In the tense courtroom sat Carolyn's sister, Linda Dubay, and two of Ken's cousins, Chuck and Jocelyn Downing. Near them was Adriana's sister, Norma Luna. Also on hand were Detectives Villalobos and Heaney.

Judge Briseno handed the forms to the court clerk who, in California, is the one who actually reads the verdict, not the judge or the foreman.

As Adriana gripped the hand of her lawyer, the clerk read the verdicts:

As to count one, the murder of Dr. Kenneth Stahl, the jury found Adriana Vasco guilty of second-degree murder.

As to count two, the murder of Carolyn Oppy-Stahl, the jury found Adriana guilty of first-degree murder.

With reddened eyes, Adriana turned and looked to her sister, Norma Luna, who was crying.

The judge polled the jurors.

Each said yes when asked if that was their verdict.

"It appears from the jurors' responses that the verdicts as read here in open court reflect the unanimous decision of the jury," said Briseno. "Therefore, I'm going to order the clerk to enter the verdicts into the record of the proceeding."

The verdict was severe. The two murder counts all but made automatic a life sentence without possibility of parole. The only nod to Adriana's defense was the second-degree conviction for Ken's murder rather than first. The distinction was academic. Pending appeal, Adriana would live the rest of her life in prison.

The judge then excused the jury, thanking panelists for their "patience and cooperation" and noting that, "We know that this is a difficult matter for all concerned." He also told them they were allowed now to talk about the case—several print and television reporters would be waiting outside the court building—and urged them to "make your best attempts to be truthful and accurate about what your statements are concerning your jury service on these matters."

Downstairs, outside the courthouse, only one juror spoke, the foreman. "I think a lot of her tears were for real," said Donald Tobias, a 65-year-old chiropractor from the upper–middle-class community of Placentia. "We felt that as long as she wasn't intoxicated or high, she had a pretty good idea this would happen." He didn't see Adriana as a Battered Women's Syndrome–suffering pawn of two abusive men: "We thought she was a pretty tough, street-smart person," he said.

Carolyn's family didn't speak to the media. But her sister, Linda Dubay, released a statement:

Now that the verdict is in, we can start to move forward—to remember Carolyn as the loving and wonderful person she was, and not how she died. Carolyn was truly an inspiration to her family, friends and many of her patients and co-workers. She will always be remembered by her sweet voice and loving . . . words. We have no ill will toward Adriana, but are happy to see justice served.

Adriana's sister, Norma Luna, said outside court that her sister is a "loving, warm person and mother" and that "we need to find a way to explain this to [her] children, that Mom's not coming home."

Chapter Thirty-Four

It's a routine motion and one just as routinely overruled, but defense attorney Robert Viefhaus was duty-bound to make it.

On Friday, January 24, 2003, two months after the verdict had been reached, he asked Superior Court Judge Francisco Briseno to second-guess the jury and grant a new trial for Adriana Vasco on the grounds that there had not been enough evidence to convict.

The jury, according to Viefhaus, had acted as if Dr. Nancy Kaser-Boyd never existed. The DA didn't cross-examine her in any meaningful way and didn't rebut any of the details of Adriana's background, and yet the jury "simply disregarded" Kaser-Boyd without any basis to do so. What's more, the jury didn't have enough evidence to support the natural-and-probable-consequence theory of Ken's murder.

"To think that he would go out and shoot his boss, that's what's so unusual about this case," said Viefhaus. "I bet I've mentioned this case to fifteen people, and every one of them, whether they read it in *Time* magazine or in the newspapers, makes the reference: 'This is the one where the guy shot the guy that hired him.' This scenario is so unusual, I don't think I would see it in a Hollywood movie. And they fictionalize things like this. They romanticize them."

The judge responded by saying that Viefhaus's motion for a new trial was "one of the best drafted legal briefs I've seen for some time." He acknowledged it was a close call, and one to which he had given a lot of thought. He also acknowledged that the appellate court would also want to review such issues as allowing Bill Rams's news story into the trial, perhaps the most damning evidence of all.

"But after careful consideration of the points raised by counsel," said Briseno, "I'm going to deny the motion for a new trial."

That cleared the way for Adriana's sentencing. The judge announced his preliminary sentence, one dictated by the law: life without the possibility of parole.

He gave Viefhaus an opportunity to respond to the tentative sentence. While the defense lawyer's motion for a new trial may have been sterling legal work, his arguments against the tentative sentence betrayed his defeated stance.

"Your Honor," he said, "I don't see where the court has any option in terms of the verdict. Of course I would ask the court to grant Miss Vasco probation, but I'm not sure the court can legally do that. I would also ask the court to reduce the findings of the jury to voluntary manslaughter. I'm not sure the court can do that. I would ask the court for any leniency the court can show Miss Vasco. Because of the way she was swept into this, and her background, I think she deserves any consideration the court can give her."

"Did you want your client to say anything?" the judge asked.

Adriana did.

She stood and started to cry.

"Just I want to say that I am very sorry for what happened," she began in tears. "I'm very sorry for the pain the families have to endure, especially the victim's family. I really didn't mean for any of this to happen. If there's something that I could do to lessen, anything I can say to them, to the victim's family, I would do it. And I just ask for forgiveness. Forgive me for all the pain that you've gone through. I know you have probably a lot of questions. I wish I had the chance to talk to you and ask you personally face-to-face for your forgiveness. I know there is not anything that I can do to bring them back, and I wish there was. Forgive me, please, forgive me."

She took her seat. The judge asked if anybody else wanted to speak. Viefhaus said there were two people. The first was Adriana's sister, Norma Luna.

"Good morning, Your Honor," she said. "I would like to speak on Adriana's behalf to let you know that I strongly feel Adriana was coerced into taking the action that she did out of fear for her and her family's life."

She called her sister's behavior "totally uncharacteristic of her." She said that while Adriana had long been "very stubborn about taking advice with her relationships with men in general," that Adriana's relationship with Dennis Godley was headed from the very beginning for "nothing but trouble for her."

Luna told the judge that Adriana's son, Mark, had come home from school one day, and had seen Dennis playing with a gun. "He told Mark if he ever mentioned the gun he [Mark] would be in big trouble," she said.

"I honestly feel that Adriana would never hurt or harm anyone under any circumstances, especially after this episode," said Norma. "Adriana Vasco has always been a devoted mother and would never jeopardize her children. So I beg the court to please take into consider[ation] in offering her the possibility of parole, her children, Mark and Ashley, who'd like to keep in mind that their mom will be coming home one day."

The judge's intended sentence, said Norma, "was too harsh, because her part in the crime seems to have been motivated out of fear rather than passion." Justice, said Norma, was not served.

Norma then directed her final words to her sister, who sat weeping at the defense table.

"Adriana," Luna said, "I just want to say that I love you. I will stand by you, and we'll keep on fighting this. So don't give up, sis. I love you."

The next and final person to speak on Adriana's behalf was a man whose testimony had helped convict her. James Stewart, grandfather of Adriana's daughter—and the man who'd testified about Adriana pointing out a handgun she had bought for Dennis Godley—stood before the judge, identified himself as the "common-law father-in-law of Adriana Vasco" and said he had a "short statement on her behalf " to read:

"In the more than seven years that I have known Adriana, she has shown herself to be a loving and caring mother to her two children and a thoughtful family member who's always willing to help others." he said.

"She had a pretty rough start in life in her childhood and even into her teen years. But despite that, she's never given herself over to pity or sorrow or petty meanness as some mean people do. She has always remained a positive person, trusting in the goodness of those around her. With very little help, she managed to get a good education, build a career for herself and decent life for her kids.

"She certainly isn't perfect, but who among us is? Even so, she has been a productive member of our community, with no previous transgressions other than a few traffic tickets. How are we to believe that she's magically turned into a calculating murderous criminal overnight?"

With that, Stewart blasted the jury that had apparently taken his own testimony to heart.

"I find it disappointing that the jury chose to believe her truthful testimony about those events she did participate in, but then chose to ignore her equally truthful account of the intimidation, coercion and threats to herself and her family that caused her to be involved," Stewart said. "I also find it disheartening to see that the jury could find no compassion whatsoever for this mother who has already spent over two years in jail without once being able to touch, hold or hug her children."

Stewart said he didn't believe the verdicts squared with Adriana's involvement "in these horrendous events" or with her motivation. Rather, he said, Adriana trusted the wrong people—"people she thought loved her, people she thought were her friends, people who, in the end, only wanted to use her." She also trusted the police and the jury—trust, he said, that was not rewarded.

"I believe she is not a danger to society," concluded Stewart. "I believe she can, again, become a productive member of our community. And I believe that she, her family and especially her children, have suffered enough."

James Stewart returned to his seat in the courtroom.

It was then time for members of the victims' families to speak. The first was Ken's cousin, Chuck Downing. He had asked that the press photographers in the courtroom not photograph him. He read a statement from Carolyn's sister, Linda Dubay, who was home in Michigan. It was the first time in the proceedings, going back through the pre-trial hearings, that anybody had said anything positive about Carolyn in court. The trial testimony had all been about Carolyn's suspicions, insecurities and shortcomings as a wife—and graphic details about the way she'd died.

"Carolyn Stahl was a very spiritual and loving person," he read. "She touched the lives of many, both as an optometrist and as a special friend and loved one. She believed that it was important to reach out to someone, even a stranger, every day and help brighten their day.

"She was very patient with the elderly," Dubay's statement continued. "She would always be the one at a gathering to go over and talk to the person alone in the corner. She truly had a gift of softening even the hardcore grumpy person."

Carolyn's sister then addressed Adriana's low opinions of Carolyn.

"We all, as members of the community, have a responsibility to protect the lives of others, including those that we dislike," the statement said. "Even those that we see as emotionally harmful to one are a vital part of someone else's life.

"While I wish Ken and Carolyn could have seen that and found a different way to move on, Adriana only saw Carolyn through Ken's eyes. She didn't see the way Carolyn affected so many others. Carolyn was a very important bond in our family, and a great sense of spiritual support for me."

As for her murder, "I will never be able to forget the intense pain of hearing of Carolyn's death or seeing my parents, who are in their eighties, be so destroyed by her death," the statement continued. "The hours that I've spent not understanding why Carolyn died, or who could have done such a thing to such a person as giving as Carolyn, will never go away. The hurt that my sister will never see my son, who was born shortly before her death, will stay with me forever. The fact that I cannot pick up the phone and call Carolyn when I am hurting and know she will be there is lost forever. The many months that I could not enjoy my three children because I was so distraught over losing Carolyn cannot be replaced."

And this, she said, was due to Adriana Vasco. "Adriana was there planning, following through on the plans, and initiated the meeting that set Carolyn's death in motion," Dubay's statement said. "Not only did she do nothing to stop the murders, she was there assisting. While I do feel Adriana is sincere that she is remorseful of her actions, we all need to take responsibility for what we have done. I don't believe that she was a helpless bystander in a horrible plot. I also can't help wonder: Would she really be remorseful if Ken hadn't died, too, or the police hadn't caught up with her?"

While Carolyn's sister felt sorry for Adriana and her children, Adriana still had to take responsibility for what she'd done. "Protecting your children's lives is never a justification for taking the life of an innocent person, especially when contacting the police would have been the salvation and protection for everyone," she wrote. "Adriana chose to participate or knowingly allow the death of Carolyn and should receive the full consequences that the court allows for murder."

Chuck Downing stepped aside to make way for his wife, Jocelyn, who described Carolyn as "not only a cherished member of our family, she was a dear friend." Jocelyn spoke of Colorado River rafting trips and Montana backpacking adventures with Carolyn, of new memories that would never be.

"We will never be given the joy to listen to the beautiful sound of her voice or see her beautiful smile. My family truly misses Carolyn. Her love was that of an angel sent from heaven above."

She said that Carolyn "only spoke kindly" of people and "always saw the good in each of us," making it difficult to understand "how anyone could take the life of a woman as precious and angelic as Carolyn. Carolyn's love and joy will always be a thread woven into the fabric of our family."

Jocelyn Downing stepped down, and the judge asked prosecutor Dennis Conway if he had any other family members wishing to speak.

"No, Your Honor," said Conway.

Nobody would say a word for Dr. Kenneth Stahl.

As he had earlier indicated, the judge rejected probation for Adriana, rejected dropping the first-degree conviction to second degree or the second-degree to manslaughter, and sentenced her to life without the possibility of parole for the murder of Carolyn, and 15 years to life for the murder of Ken.

The judge concluded the sentencing hearing with his last decision of the trial: "I'm going to order the sheriff to transport the defendant to state prison on a forthwith basis."

Chapter Thirty-Five

As any court watcher knows, a trial—particularly a murder trial—is good theater, the ultimate reality show. But so many of the machinations of the criminal justice system occur behind the curtain, in the offices of lawyers, in the hallways outside courtrooms. The case that goes to trial is the exception; the rule is the case that is decided outside of court in a plea bargain.

On Friday, May 21, 2004, it quickly became clear that even a high-profile death penalty case like the one against Dennis Earl Godley can have a very active life away from the public's eyes.

In a new hearing before a new judge, a stunning announcement was made.

"As I understand it," said Superior Court Judge William R. Froeberg, "the People are removing the death penalty from the case?"

Deputy District Attorney Dennis Conway answered simply, "Yes, Your Honor."

• • •

About ten days earlier, a panel of prosecutors had met to decide whether to proceed with seeking the death penalty, which in California means getting a lethal injection in a little room in the San Quentin State Prison. This was a gathering of the DA's so-called death committee. Prosecutors in conservative Orange County aren't shy about going for death, and if there were ever a case screaming out for it, this would be it.

Dennis Godley was accused of killing two people for no other reason than money—money that had gone to buy drugs. So cold-blooded, he allegedly had killed the man who'd hired him, Godley stood as somebody with no potential ever to give anything to society other than grief. Possessing a criminal record that stretched back to his teens, his life allegedly amounted to taking drugs, robbing a convenience store, beating up women and ultimately committing double murder. His lawyer seemingly had a difficult argument to spare his life.

The death meetings are closed to the press and public, but defense attorneys are welcome to make a contribution. Godley's attorney, Denise Gragg, accepted the invitation to make an early appeal for her client's life.

In California, juries—not judges—make death sentence recommendations after hearing often gut-wrenching appeals from friends and family of the victims and the accused. Naked emotion can—and often does—play as big a role in deciding the outcome as a sober consideration of the evidence and law.

Gragg pointed out to the death committee that, as awful a man as her client could be seen to be, the jury could also hear plenty of mitigating evidence, starting with details about Godley's difficult childhood—the father locked up for safecracking, Godley being raised by his grandmother, his grandfather's death denying him a father figure. Gragg also noted that Godley had two children, a boy and a girl, and that the boy happened to speak with a stutter.

While all of this was tangential to the question of whether Godley had killed the Stahls out on Ortega Highway, from the prosecution's standing, it was compelling evidence. The fact that Godley hardly spent any time with his children would be overshadowed by watching his boy take the stand and stammer out a plea to save his daddy's life. Should Gragg play the stutter card, a jury could easily see this as reason enough to spare Godley.

Between the potential for emotional penalty-phase evidence, and the fact that the prosecution's case against Godley was hardly rock solid, the death committee decided to seek the same sentence for Godley as it had for Adriana: life in prison without the possibility of parole.

In open court, Conway revealed none of this. He gave only the most cursory explanation of what had led to his office's decision to drop the death penalty. He told the judge the DA had had a death penalty committee meeting "which Miss Gragg was invited to, and presented a lot of compelling evidence that she had . . . that was not known to us." It was "information in regards to Mr. Godley's background."

Still, Conway had an important point to make for the benefit of the judge and the public.

"I just want the record to be clear," Conway stressed, "that the committee and the district attorney's office reevaluated the case with all this new information in mind and made the decision to not seek the death penalty based on that new information about his past. Just to be clear, it has nothing to do with the fact that now Mr. Godley is choosing to take responsibility by way of a plea."

That was the second surprise of the hearing.

Dennis Godley was entering a guilty plea.

The judge wanted to make sure that there was no quid pro quo.

"I guess what you're saying is that . . . the removal of the death penalty was not offered as an inducement for the plea?" asked Judge Froeberg.

"Yes, Your Honor," said Conway.

The judge turned to the public defender. "Is that your understanding, as well, Ms. Gragg?"

"That's my understanding," she said.

And with that, Froeberg addressed Godley directly.

"Mr. Godley," the judge said, "I have in front of me a two-page document titled 'Guilty Plea in the Superior Court.' Have you had an opportunity of going over that document with Ms. Gragg?"

"Yes, sir," said Godley.

"Is there anything you didn't understand or feel like you need to have explained further to you?"

"No, sir," he said. Godley also vouched for the fact that some initials placed on the left-hand column of each page were in fact his, and that he'd signed the document.

"Was it explained to you that you have a right to have a jury trial in this case?" the judge asked.

"Yes," Godley said.

"Do you know what a jury trial is?"

"Yes, I do."

"Are you willing to give up your right to have a jury trial?"

"Yes."

He also confirmed that he knew he had the right to confront and cross-examine witnesses, the right to remain silent and the right to testify in his own behalf. Dennis Godley said he was willing to give up those rights.

The judge officially told him that the counts against

him—first-degree murder, second-degree murder, and special circumstances of multiple murder and lying in wait—meant that the maximum penalty was life in prison without the possibility of parole.

"They [the DA's office] haven't offered you anything in order to get you to enter into this plea, is that correct?" the judge asked.

"That's correct," Godley said.

"Any promises, threats or inducements been made to you to get you to enter into these pleas?"

"No, sir."

And so, in open court, Dennis Godley admitted to what he had denied before: that on November 20, 1999, he and Adriana Vasco had murdered Kenneth and Carolyn Stahl.

"Is that true?" the judge asked.

"Yes, sir."

He also admitted to the two special circumstances.

"As to count one, then, violating penal code section 187, murder in the first degree, how do you plead: guilty or not guilty?"

"Guilty."

"As to count two, violating penal code section 187, murder in the second degree, how do you plead: guilty or not guilty?"

"Guilty."

The attorneys all agreed to accept those pleas.

"The court finds a knowing, free, voluntary, intelligent waiver of the defendant's constitutional rights, [and] further finds a factual basis for the plea," said Froeberg. "[I] will accept the plea."

Chapter Thirty-Six

"He knows what he did, and he wants to take responsibility for it."

Denise Gragg was making no attempt to sugarcoat things. Speaking to reporters outside of court after her client's surprise guilty plea, she noted that Godley would never be up for parole. Society was safe; he'd never walk out of prison again.

For a case that had taken four-and-a-half years to build, it was an abrupt end. Perhaps too abrupt. Nobody could quite understand why Godley had copped a plea.

For months afterwards prosecutor Dennis Conway insisted to anybody who would listen that his office hadn't dropped death in exchange for the guilty plea. The decisions were unrelated, he said, and the DA's office was ready to go to trial. So why didn't Godley duke it out in court? With death no longer hanging over him, he had nothing to lose. Gragg made only a few public statements on the matter, but in a probation report prepared for Godley's sentencing, she elaborated.

Gragg said that Godley had shown remorse for his role by pleading guilty rather than "putting the victims' families and the State through the trauma and trouble of trying him." As for Godley's former lover, Gragg told the probation officer that Adriana Vasco has "at least equal culpability" with Godley in the murders.

"Indeed," said Gragg in the report, "there is a good argument that Ms. Vasco and Mr. Stahl bore the primary blame for this tragedy."

The report by Deputy Probation Officer Louise D. Hoffman also offered, if not reasons, at least clues to how Godley could end up so incorrigible. Her report traced the sad, violent, drug-filled life of the now–34-year-old man. "The defendant seems to become involved in unlawful activity and gets arrested wherever he goes," wrote Hoffman. "It is obvious he is a danger to society and needs to be imprisoned."

The report also provided one of the only forums for somebody from Kenneth Stahl's family to be heard, including a heartbreaking note from Ken's mother, Bobbi Stahl:

The loss of my son, Kenneth Stahl, at the hands of Dennis Godley has been a tragic blow to me personally and to my family. Not a day passes that I do not grieve my loss. Whenever I hear a piece of music my son loved, or run into one of his patients, or hear from one of his friends, or when I glance over at his picture, or I use the walking stick he gave me, my heart again feels empty.

I could never imagine that I would have to plan my own son's memorial service, that I would have to write his obituary, or that I would have to explain to my great-grandchildren how their uncle faced such a tragic death at the hands of another. I never imagined that my son would not be around to take care of me. He was always available to me and always came to visit just to be sure that I was all right. He was my only son.

It is said that time heals all wounds. That is not true for me. The pain that pierced my chest the morning that I opened the door to the detectives to be informed that my son was murdered has never gone away. I was then and am now in mourning.

Dennis Godley is a cold-blooded murderer who should spend the rest of his life behind bars. It would be a crime against society to ever let him walk the streets a free man. He cannot be rehabilitated and would only commit brutal crimes again if he were ever set free.

The pain was echoed by Carolyn's mother, Ophia Sokolowski:

Carolyn was a loving and caring person. She is greatly missed by her loving family and friends. We were very close. We spoke by telephone at least twice a week. I miss hearing her soft voice and telling me about her life as an optometrist.

When I heard of her death and the brutal way that she died, I was in denial. I cried for two weeks and could not sleep, and was on sleeping pills for three months. I could not talk to my friends and did not want to see anyone.

We received so many letters and cards from Carolyn's friends, colleagues and patients, telling us how much they missed her and what a loving and patient person she was. It has been three years and the pain has not gone away.

On Friday, June 11, 2004, Dennis Godley walked into the Santa Ana courtroom wearing a mustard-colored jail jumpsuit and carrying a Louis L'Amour Western novel in his shackled hands. He appeared far removed from the drug-popping, paranoid killer described by Adriana Vasco. Rather, he seemed relaxed and often smiled.

In a ten-minute hearing, Judge William Froeberg announced that "the defendant has pled guilty to two counts of violating penal code section 187(a), murder in the first degree" and admitted to the special circumstances of lying in wait and multiple murder. The penalty is death or life imprisonment without parole.

"The People have elected not to seek the death penalty in this case," Froeberg said. "Therefore, the defendant is sentenced to life without possibility of parole."

Some distinctions were made: the life sentences would be consecutive, but running concurrent with the sentence from the Virginia case. It was academic. Godley would die in prison.

He was also ordered to pay $1,000 to the state as a restitution fine and ordered to provide bodily samples and fingerprints.

"It's my understanding the weapons were not recovered," the judge said.

"That's correct," said Conway.

"All right," the judge concluded, "defendant is remanded to the custody of the Orange County sheriff for delivery to the custody of the director of corrections at the state prison designated by the director as the place for the reception of persons convicted of felonies. Make that a forthwith order."

After the hearing, Gragg was asked about Godley's seemingly easygoing demeanor in the face of a life-without-parole sentence. "He was relieved," she told *The Orange County Register*. "He was glad to get this over with, glad his family didn't have to go through the ordeal of a trial and glad that the victims' families didn't have to go through a trial."

She added: "I was proud of Mr. Godley today."

Chaper Thirty-Seven

Jayson Blair of *The New York Times* never covered the Stahl murders. Nor did Stephen Glass of *The New Republic* or Jack Kelley from *USA Today*. But all three would find themselves brought into the Stahl case after Adriana Vasco's conviction. "There are indications of an epidemic of dishonest journalism in American media," according to legal papers filed in her appeal, which argued for a new trial on, among other grounds, the claim that the defense was wrongfully forbidden from challenging a reporter's credibility.

That reporter was of course Bill Rams of *The Orange County Register*, who was now being lumped in with this disgraced trio accused of journalistic fabrication. The appeal never said that Rams was a fabricator; rather, he argued that the jury would never know for sure how credible he really was, because Adriana's attorney couldn't cross-examine him.

When Adriana's appellate lawyer, Mark Alan Hart, presented this theory to a three-member panel of the 4th

District California Court of Appeal, the justices seemed as unimpressed as the pre-trial judge who'd originally rejected it. In an often-heated hearing in a Santa Ana court a few blocks from the building where Adriana had been convicted, the justices noted that Rams's credibility was bolstered by none other than appellant Adriana Vasco, whose testimony corroborated and expanded upon everything in the journalist's reports. Hart countered that it was unfair to look at the case that way, because her testimony had been necessitated by the original sin in the case: the judge allowing the reporter's shield to be pierced and Rams's unchallenged testimony to be heard. Had Rams been more vigorously challenged—or silenced—Adriana might never have testified at all, he argued.

Around it went, this legal chicken-and-egg debate, and eventually the justices tired of the discussion and asked Hart to move on.

Hart's second argument seemed to hold more sway with the panel: that the jury had wrongly applied a natural-and-probable-consequences theory in convicting Adriana of Ken's murder. It was always one of the weakest parts of the prosecution's case, this question of how Adriana could have dreamed that Dennis Godley, as twisted as he was, would kill his own boss. If anything, the justices noted, the evidence could be seen as supporting a competing theory: that Adriana had wanted—needed—Ken to live. Once her lover, he could have become something more to Adriana with Carolyn out of the way. Even if he didn't, Ken could always be counted on to provide some quick and easy cash for Adriana, and even for Godley. In fact, the trial record was unclear on whether Godley had ever been paid the entire amount for the hit. That Godley had killed Ken Stahl, the appeals court's reasoning went, could only be attributed to the random act of a disturbed mind: nothing natural and probable about it.

The panel retired without reaching a decision. The cruel irony, though, was that even if Adriana prevailed, the victory would be hollow. The best she could hope for is a new trial, and in the years since her first trial, the evidence against her has grown even stronger.

About nine months after her conviction, a DA investigator finally tracked down that teenage runaway who was living with Godley at the time of the killings. A minor player, mentioned only in passing during the original trial, at a second trial she could be one of the most important prosecution witnesses.

According to prosecutor Dennis Conway, the girl told the investigator that on the night of the murders, she had been in Godley's apartment when Dennis and Adriana came back in, late in the evening. "They were talking about 'whacking the bitch,'" said Conway. "Godley says, 'I've got blood on my shoes' and gives the shoes to Adriana to throw away." Even more incriminating, Adriana—according to the girl—then pulled a gun out of a jacket and said something to the effect of, "I'm glad the doctor got it, too."

But the new witness wouldn't be Adriana's only problem at a new trial. Dennis Godley had signaled that he would turn on Adriana as she did on him. Back when prosecutors were trying to decide whether to seek the death penalty against him, his defense attorney, Denise Gragg, made a provocative statement: If the case ever went to trial, she would contend it was Adriana who'd shot Carolyn Stahl first, not Godley. Ken was then gunned down by Godley, the lawyer would claim.

Godley had nothing to lose by telling the jury this or anything else; his plea deal spared him execution and he was never going to leave prison. Still, Godley's scenario would provide a tantalizing answer to those lingering questions about the bullet count: at least seven shots fired into the couple and their car from a model of gun that carried at most six. The gun had to have been reloaded, or there had to have been a second gun—or second shooter.

Could Adriana Vasco have hated Carolyn Stahl even more than she was admitting? And could she have been more calculating than even authorities had imagined?

Long after finishing work on the case, Detective Phil Villalobos still can't shake the idea of a two-gun, two-shooter scenario. He wonders if Adriana could have shot and wounded Carolyn while Dennis covered Ken with the gun, killed him and finished off the dying Carolyn. Or if Godley could have shot Carolyn first, while Adriana, sick and tired of Ken's ways, killed her former lover. Or if Godley shot both Ken and Carolyn, but Carolyn didn't die right away—and Godley ordered Adriana to finish her off. Or if Godley shot Carolyn, reloaded, and told Adriana to finish off the only witness: Ken.

Or maybe it just all went down the way Adriana said it did, with her sitting in the car wishing it were all just a bad dream. "It would be nice to talk to Dennis," said Villalobos. "Brian and I thought about that, you know, saying to him, 'Hey, it's all over. Off the record, just for us, what happened?' " So far, that conversation hasn't occurred, and probably never will. Villalobos knows that he may never get the whole truth—that some secrets remain on Ortega Highway.

In June 2005, the California Court of Appeal affirmed the conviction of Adriana Vasco. Her attorney, Mark Alan Hart, planned to take the case to the state Supreme Court.